Little Table Top

The Farm

Table Top

Rhododendron Spur

Battleship

Philip Parker is a writer, consultant and publisher specialising in
cartography as well as ancient and medieval history. He studied
history at Trinity Hall, Cambridge, and is the author of *History of
Britain in Maps* (2016), the *DK Eyewitness Companion Guide to
World History* (2010), *The Northmen's Fury* (2014) and *The A-Z
History of London* (2019).

He was the general editor of *Himalaya* (2013) and the award-winning
Great Trade Routes (2010). As a publisher Philip ran *The Times* Books
list, including works on ancient civilisations and *The Times History
of the World*. He lives in London with his partner and daughter.

The
Magnificent
Maps
Puzzle Book

RE·DE·TRIPOLI~

·SOL·DAN·DE·BABILLONIA·

The Magnificent
Maps
Puzzle Book

Philip Parker

BRITISH LIBRARY

First published in 2019 by
The British Library
96 Euston Road
London NW1 2DB
www.bl.uk

Catalogue-in-Publication Data
A catalogue record for this book is available
from the British Library.

ISBN: 978 0 7123 5299 4

Project Editor: Christopher Westhorp
Design: Blok Graphic, London
Picture Research: Sally Nicholls
Printed and bound in the Czech Republic by Finidr

"A map is the greatest of all epic poems.
Its lines and colors show the realization
of great dreams."

Gilbert H. Grosvenor, founding editor of
National Geographic

CONTENTS

INTRODUCTION

Maps are a unique window on the past, offering an insight into how our ancestors viewed the world around them, and how they wished others to do so. Humankind's transformation from hunter-gatherers to village agriculturalists and then to urban dwellers was accompanied by the accumulations of surpluses and the hardening of boundaries. It is no surprise, therefore, that among the very earliest of maps – dating from around 2300 BC – are clay tablets from Gasur, in what is today Iraq, which show field boundaries. Property after all, meant wealth, and wealth meant power.

Before long we have city maps and the very first world map (from Babylon, around 600 BC). From the Middle Ages the trickle of surviving maps becomes a steady stream, on parchment and on paper, and then in the great European Age of Exploration in the fifteenth and sixteenth centuries, a flood. European navigators such as Columbus, Cabot, da Gama and Magellan encountered new – at least for them – coastlines and the result was a plethora of charts, cartolans and atlases building up a picture of a world whose pieces were finally being knit together.

It is both instructive and an enormous pleasure to while away hours poring over these visual messages from history, to trace the first outposts of the British colony in seventeenth-century Virginia, the streets of Victorian London or the fumblings of nineteenth-century cartographers as they tried to fill in the blanks of the vastness of Canada's Artic north. *The Magnificent Maps Puzzle Book* gathers together a selection of 40 maps and charts from one of the world's great cartographic collections – that held by the British Library.

The collections of its current Map Room (which holds printed maps) and the Manuscripts Room (which looks after non-printed maps and charts) have their distant origins in the royal cartographic collections begun as early as the reign of Henry VIII, and continued under subsequent monarchs, some of whom, such as Charles II, were avid acquirers of maps. Much of this rich resource came into the possession of the British Museum in 1757 (at a time when the national museum and national library were situated together), and when that body's main reading room opened up in 1759, there was already a special six foot by eight foot (1.8 by 2.4 metre) table installed for readers who wanted to consult the map collection. Rather alarmingly, in 1763 a stove was installed in the 'Chart Room' to warm the icy fingers of readers, so putting the entire precious collection at risk of combustion.

In 1828 the map collection expanded still further with the acquisition of the complete Geographical and Topographical Collection of George III, including around 50,000 maps, charts and other cartographic items (the maritime charts were handed over to the Admiralty, because it was considered they still had some military use, and these only returned to the Map Room in 1952). Throughout the nineteenth century, the map collection burgeoned with the addition of new collections, including the Crace Collection of London Maps, further manuscripts from the Age of Exploration and military maps associated with Britain's growing imperial possessions and the accompanying conflicts, such as the Seven Years' War (1756–63).

By 1844 the map section was formed as a distinct unit of the British Museum, with its own Map Room established in 1914. The British Library became a separate entity in 1973 and in 1997 moved to its current site in St Pancras, where the modern Maps Reading Room and Manuscripts Reading Room are situated. There, the maps presented in this volume – and many other treasures, amounting to around 4.5 million cartographic items in total – can be consulted in their original form.

For many early cartographers, assembling their maps meant solving a series of puzzles: did the river on the west coast really meet the one that flowed from the east somewhere in the uncharted middle?; where exactly was the 'Land of the Great Khan'?; how to reconcile conflicting accounts by various explorers of the 'newfound lands'?; was there a great continent lying undiscovered in the southern ocean?; and were there really sea monsters lurking, ready to make a light supper of unsuspecting sailors? In the spirit of this search for answers, *The Magnificent Maps Puzzle Book* presents the maps with a series of quiz questions, each of which provides a clue to a place (or places) on the map they accompany. The place-names to be found are all on an enlarged section of a larger map and for those wanting to enjoy the visual splendour of the original, these are included before the quiz questions, together with a brief introduction to the map and the historical context in which it was drawn.

Some of the questions are less than straightforward – part of the fun, after all, is to pore over the maps and finding the answer instantly would mean ignoring all the other features, boundaries, towns, hills and rivers they contain. Overleaf, then, is a brief guide to the types of questions you might encounter – all the answers are contained on the 1787 map of Venice drawn by Lodovico Ughi.

The maps included cover a wide geographical span, from North America and the Caribbean to Europe, South Asia, Australia and New Zealand, and even the moon. They also encompass a wide chronological spread, over more than four centuries from 1561 to 1978. Many of the earlier maps have different place-name forms from today – such as Chesapeack Bay

This 1787 map of Venice by
Lodovico Ughi contains the
place-names from the six
example questions.

There are six main types of questions:

1 **Identifying the place-name which is the longest or shortest on the map or which has the greatest number of a particular letter.**

   For example: Which place-name has the largest number of the letter 'z'? *Answer*: Piazza di San Marco – two 'z's in Piazza; in fact, it is Venice's only piazza; the squares which are called that elsewhere in Italy are in Venice known as 'Campi'.

2 **Cryptic clues hidden in the place-name to be found.**

   For example: Pitch tent at the start of this? *Answer*: Campanile – 'camp' being a place you might put up your tent, and it forms the start of the place-name that is the answer.

3 **Questions which rely on general knowledge.**

   For example: You might find an Italian chicken here? *Answer*: San Pollo – *pollo* is the Italian for 'chicken'. The modern spelling is San Polo, both for the smallest of the six *sestieri*, or quarters, of Venice and for the fifteenth-century church of San Polo (or St Paul), which gives the district its name.

4 **Simple anagrams: these are generally signalled by a phrase such as 'confused' or 'mixed up' in the question. Simple anagrams are where the anagram is contained within the question.**

   For example: 'Robed carnival' in Venice. I'm a bit mixed up. *Answer*: Riva del Carbon, which is an anagram of 'robed carnival' (the Riva was the main coal docking station for Venice).

5 **More-complex anagrams, where you have first to work out an alternative means of expressing the clue, and this is the anagram which needs to be solved.**

   For example: Slaughter territory is all mixed up? *Answer*: Canal Grande, which is an anagram of 'carnage land', which is another way of saying 'slaughter territory'.

6 **Modifications of the letters in the place-name create a word with a different meaning.**

   For example: 'A' becomes 'e' to make a book. *Answer* S. Toma (or San Toma) – change the final 'a' to an 'e' to make 'tome'.

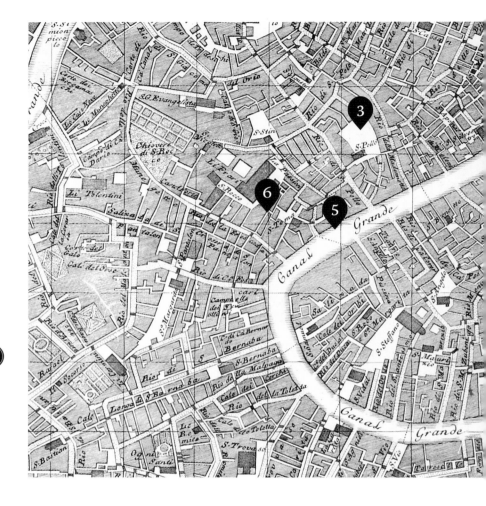

in Virginia – or which have since vanished from the map entirely; and some are in Latin, but the quiz clues will help guide you to the right spot. In a few cases, however, it is worth bearing in mind some older spelling conventions where 'v' is used in place of 'u' – hence 'Vrbino' instead of 'Urbino', and the old-fashioned letterform 'ſ' is often used in place of 's' until around 1800 (and so 'Tuniſia' instead of 'Tunisia'). There are a small number of anagrams where you might need to take abbreviations into account ('Ld' for Land, 'Is' for Island, 'C' for Cape, 'R' for River, 'B' for Bay), in which the fuller form has been generally used for the purpose of the anagram (even if abbreviated on the map).

Finally, the answer section includes a selection of what I found useful, interesting or simply downright odd information about the places

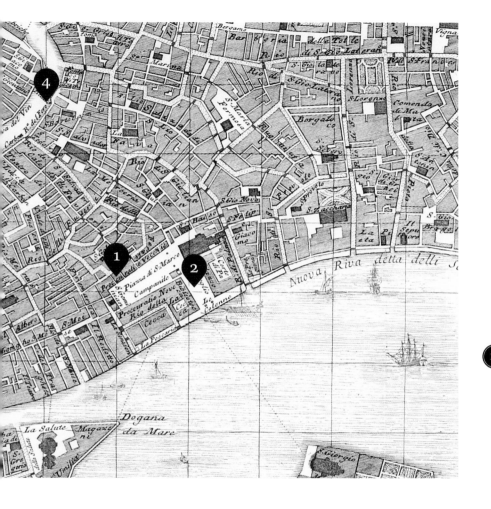

ANSWERS

1	Piazza di San Marco	4	Riva del Carbon
2	Campanile	5	Canal Grande
3	San Pollo	6	S. Toma (San Toma)

included. I hope that the process of working out the clues, finding the place-names and discovering the history behind them, as well as simply enjoying the beauty of the 40 very diverse maps, will encourage you to further cartographic exploration, in the British Library's collection and elsewhere.

8

5

5

5

4

5½

Brook

5

5

4

Southward

Boundaries

6

5

5

3

6

5

3

The Governours
or
Nutten Island.

Diftillery
Phil. Livingfton Efqr.
R.G.Livingfton

3

3

4

5

3

3

Red Hook

Mill Dam

Mill Dam

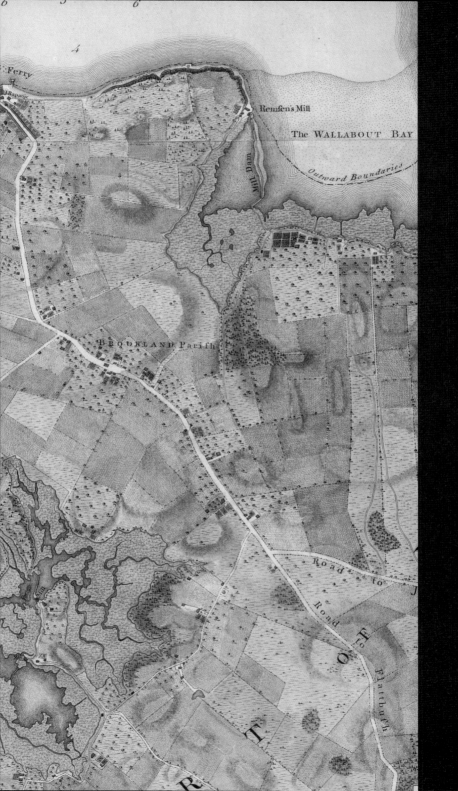

ANTEIQVAE VRBIS IMAGO ACCVRATISSIME EX VETV

ANCIENT ROME

1561

PIRRO LIGORIO

The ruins of ancient Rome – which even a thousand years after its fall remained an ever-present reminder of a glorious past – had long fascinated visitors, particularly after the Renaissance in the fifteenth century ignited interest in Roman scholarship and how its recovery might contribute to the advance of knowledge. Artists and architects came to wonder at the stone colossi of the old imperial capital, among them the Neapolitan antiquary and architect Pirro Ligorio, who designed the Casina Pio IV, an urban villa for the pope to whom he also dedicated his cartographic recreation of ancient Rome. Completed in 1561, this map was his third attempt at a visual resurrection of the city's past glory: it positively bursts with monuments, each lovingly and individually drawn, while even the *insulae,* the blocks in which most of the Roman poor lived, have a character of their own. In most case, Ligorio had little evidence to go on (save the Colosseum and the Pantheon, which were largely intact) and he built up the Mausoleum of Augustus to an extravagant six stories, creating a sense of what Rome might have been more than what it once was. Ironically, Ligorio drew his map, which he calls 'most accurately made', just before the time when a more-precise sense of the topography of the ancient city became possible, after the discovery in 1562 of the *Forma urbis* ('shape of the city'), the remains of a vast third-century Roman marble map of the city.

Questions

1 Here and in Washington, DC, it's the head of the nation.

2 You won't find lions here, but it may get a little racy.

3 Unsullied beekeeper?

4 Is the wolf here?

5 Devilish image rotates, everything is turned around.

6 You might make a speech from here.

7 Quite a beastly show gets put on here?

Answers are on pages 178–79 at the back of the book

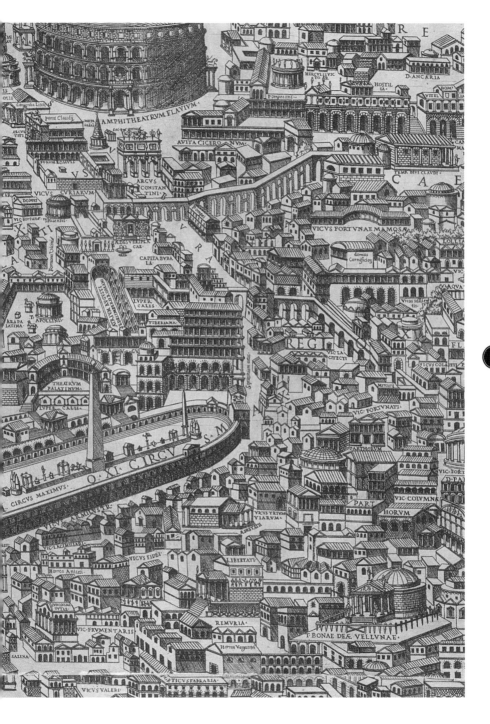

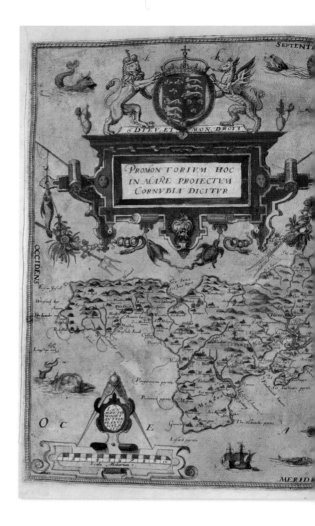

CORNWALL

1576

CHRISTOPHER
SAXTON

The mid-sixteenth century saw enormous advances in cartography in England. Among these was the publication of the first atlas of England and Wales, containing a series of county maps compiled by the Yorkshire surveyor Christopher Saxton (1542–1610/11). Assembled as part of a semi-official programme to map Britain at a time when there were very real fears of invasion by France or Spain, the project

was sponsored by Elizabeth I's Secretary of State and chief adviser William Cecil and Thomas Seckford, Master of the Court of Requests (which dealt with petitions), whose coat of arms appears at the bottom of the map. This map of Cornwall by Saxton was engraved in 1576, about two years after he began work, and received its own separate sheet (whereas some counties, such as Kent, Sussex, Surrey and Middlesex had to do with sharing a sheet, at a time when Saxton's funds were running out). Beautifully engraved and with an assortment of sea creatures and dedications filling the large area of sea necessitated by Cornwall's long, narrow shape, Saxton clearly hoped the queen would be duly appreciative, and in the dedication of the atlas she is shown surrounded by regal virtues such as peace and justice and allegorical representations of the geographical sciences.

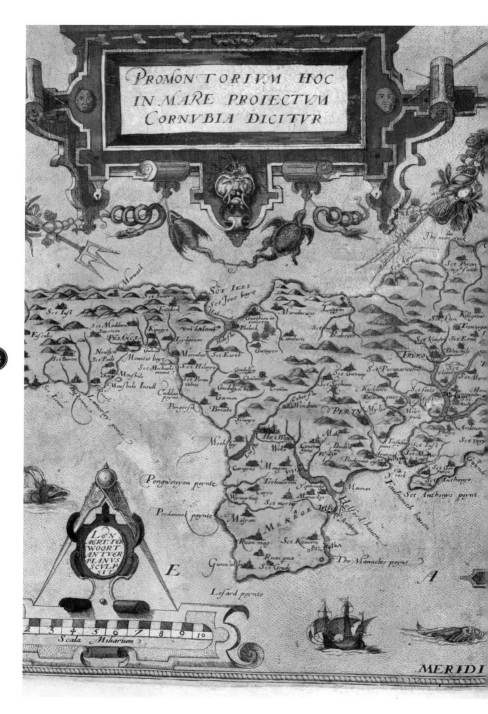

PROMONTORIVM HOC IN MARE PROIECTVM CORNVBIA DICITVR

The mars over

Sct Agnes

Sct Peran in ye sands

Morvah

Sct IEES

Sct Ieet baye

Sct Ives

Set Just

Trinideck

Hahonuth

Guethen in Coverin

Phelbis

Maradnewsay

Luggan

Killgreu

Trenrega

Escales

Sct Madderu Severote

PESANGE

Kengru

Vni Lalant

Lydgoun

Halfste

Camborn

Redrenth

Sct Ern

Sct Alen

Sct Buryan

Newfou Sct Paule

Guluill

Mounter boye

Mercalue

Sct Earth

Gwiwer

TRVRO

Sct Michaels mount

Sct Hilery

Gadalue

Sct Gwenne

Sct Peranarwethek

Sct elund

Sct Albert

Chron

Moushole

Sct Peran Velos

Clowance

Cremen

Crawis

Sct Sethiau

Kurklowe Restan aurea

Sct false

Mara

Moushole Insull

Cuddau poynte

Garmin

Goedalgh hill

Cohorfu

Wendron

PERYN Myler

Miler ponte

Pengerfik

Breate

Symes

HELISTON

Maker

Irfelony ponte

Sct Just

Methby

Wete

Caenon Syne

Buduk Wedin

Pendennis castell

Pengwetuyon poynte

Carayne

Mnagan

Uepte

Penarade

Mauan

Sct Gee gence

Sct Anthony

Predannos poynte

Trelowaren

Mauackey

Heyford haven

Sct Anthons poynt

Wenumiug

Sct meriny

Malvan

MENEGE

LEN AERTTER WOORT ANTVER PLANVS SCVLP SIT

E

Ruan mag

Sct Keuern

Ruan gua

Gunwalhe

Sct Grade

The Manacles poynt

A

Lefard poynte

Scala Miliarium
2 3 4 5 6 7 8 9 10

MERIDI

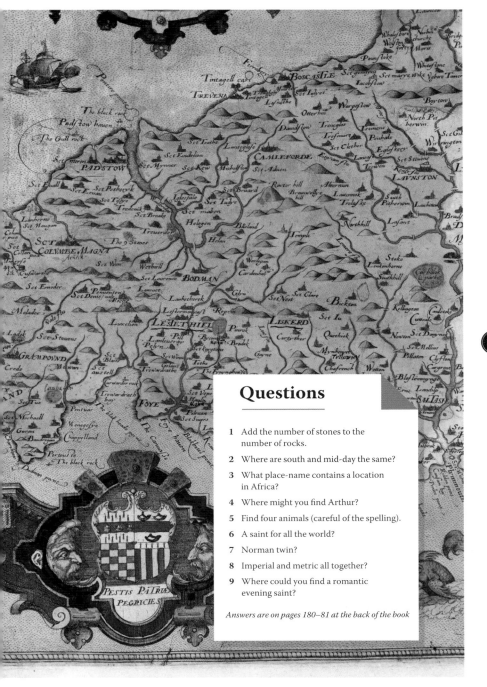

Questions

1 Add the number of stones to the number of rocks.

2 Where are south and mid-day the same?

3 What place-name contains a location in Africa?

4 Where might you find Arthur?

5 Find four animals (careful of the spelling).

6 A saint for all the world?

7 Norman twin?

8 Imperial and metric all together?

9 Where could you find a romantic evening saint?

Answers are on pages 180–81 at the back of the book

SCOTIÆ

SEPTENTRIO

NOR

PARS

GILSLAND

CVM

BRI

PARS

WESTMORLANDIÆ
et Cumberlandiæ Comit.
noua vera et Elaborata
descriptio. Añ. Dñi. 1576.

OCEA

NVS

BARONIA

DERWENT

COPELAND

EGREMOND

ALENDALE

COPELAND forest

OCCIDENS

CAS

ETRE

Scala Miliarium

AVGVSTINVS·RYTHER· ANGLVS·
SCVLPSIT· AÑ· DÑI· 1576

KIRKBY LONSDALE

PARS

MERIDIES

WESTMORLAND
AND CUMBRIA
1576

CHRISTOPHER SAXTON

T his map formed part of the very first atlas of England and Wales, published in 1579 and consisting of a series of county maps produced by Christopher Saxton (1542–1610/11), a surveyor and cartographer from Yorkshire. The project was underwritten by William Cecil, Lord Burghley, Elizabeth I's chief minister, and Thomas Seckford, the Master of the Court of Requests. It was a time when an invasion from Spain seemed imminent, with regular scares between the Dutch revolt against Spain in 1568 and the close shave of the Spanish Armada in 1588, when only the scattering of the Spanish fleet before Calais by Lord Howard and Sir Francis Drake would prevent an invasion force gathered on the Flemish coast under the Duke of Parma from making it across the Channel. The need for maps to aid in strategic planning of the country's defences against the Spanish should have meant that the south coast counties were best served. However, budgetary restraints, which were made more severe when the 1588 victory relieved the immediate threat of invasion, resulted in Kent, Sussex and Surrey having to make do with a single sheet. In the north, Westmorland and Cumbria, completed in 1576, received fuller treatment and the base map was still being used and updated two centuries after its compilation. The inclusion of the royal crest to the top right of the map identifies it as a royal and national project (and perhaps acts as a plea for more funds), while Saxton's patron, Seckford, has his own coat of arms included at the bottom right.

Newbye

Tornwat
Row
ast
Rou
Ca

Eden
flu:

Boulnesse

Beamont
Burgh Kirk anders
Grinsdal

Glason

Drumbugh
cast

Eustwath hill
Harin
N.

Cardronok

Kirk banton

Whitridge

Outerbye
Bainton pua

Orton Newb

le of the grune

Kirkbye

Fingland
The laithe
Wampull

Acton Croston

Bro

Thuresby

Skinburnenesse

Langnewton

Gamlesbye

Wampull flu

Ca

B

Owton

Silluthe

Raby cotes

Brounrigg

Lasen hall

West warde forst

Wulsty cast:
e Lies

Holme

Blencougey

The

Mawboro

Sowterfeld

Brumfeld

Warton

W. Ward

Newton in Ardale

Crockdale
Alhalowes

Warnell

Aspatre

Blynroset

Bolton

lonbye
Haton
cast:

Elne flu:

Harbybrow

The mynes

Cladbek

IERBYE

Ancautre

bye
Alwarbye

Owterside

Torpenny

Rowthwate

Sower

Plumland
Bodell

nbye
Gilcrosse

Wardall

Vldale

Mosedale

Mewtoobecon

erehm

Blencrake

Sunderland

Gry

ro Tallantire

Redman

Isle

Armanthwate

Cauda flu:

Wa

Bridekirke

Deuonbye

Huthwate

Setmurther

Basruthwate

Broughton

Skiddow hill

Lawrance

Bridgehm

COKERMOVTH
Widehop

Crosthwate

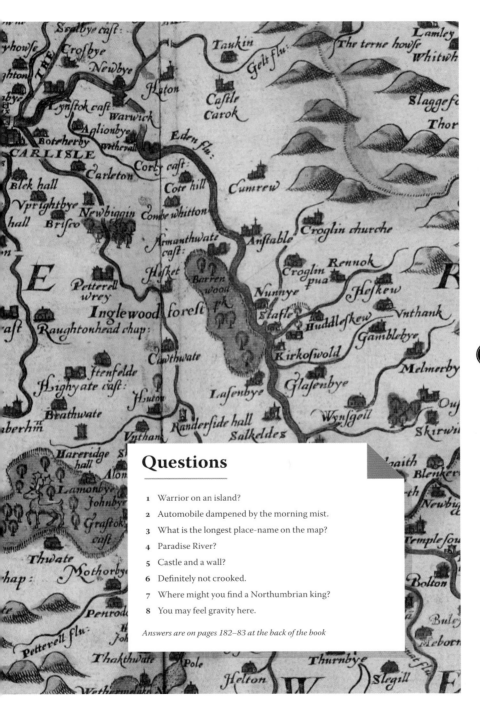

Questions

1 Warrior on an island?

2 Automobile dampened by the morning mist.

3 What is the longest place-name on the map?

4 Paradise River?

5 Castle and a wall?

6 Definitely not crooked.

7 Where might you find a Northumbrian king?

8 You may feel gravity here.

Answers are on pages 182–83 at the back of the book

IRELAND

1599

GIOVANNI BATTISTA BOAZIO

By the end of the sixteenth century, Ireland was in need of mapping, or at least such was the opinion of the English authorities whose grip on the island had tightened over the preceding decades. Ever since the Anglo-Norman invasion in 1169, English control had ebbed and flowed, and a semi-detached 'Old English' aristocracy had emerged, rooted in the soil of the land they now occupied. The Reformation, which pitted a now-Protestant England against its

resolutely Catholic Irish subjects, changed the power dynamic and in 1542 Henry VIII's proclamation as king of Ireland began a period of attempts at greater centralised control. A series of Irish revolts, led by Hugh O'Neill, Earl of Tyrone, and Hugh O'Donnell of Tyrconnell, culminated in the Nine Years' War (1595–1603). After a series of English defeats, Elizabeth I sent in Robert Devereux, 2nd Earl of Essex, in 1599 to try to bring matters under control. The map by the Italian Giovanni Battista Boazio was produced in this climate – Devereux needed to know the landscape in which he was to be operating. More detailed than any previous map of Ireland, it documents towns, small settlements, and even the Irish clan chiefs who held sway over swathes of territory. But anyone using it for practical military purposes needed to pay attention: to foil counterfeiters, the map includes several fictitious places, such as 'Elstrack's Isle', a phantom island named for the map's engraver, Renold Elstrack.

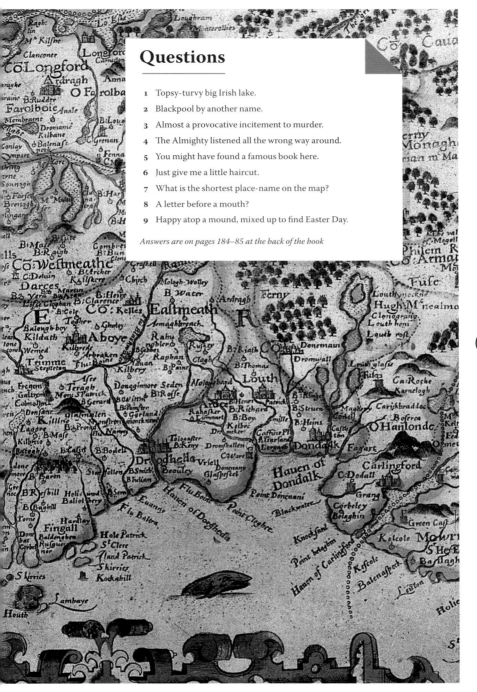

Questions

1 Topsy-turvy big Irish lake.

2 Blackpool by another name.

3 Almost a provocative incitement to murder.

4 The Almighty listened all the wrong way around.

5 You might have found a famous book here.

6 Just give me a little haircut.

7 What is the shortest place-name on the map?

8 A letter before a mouth?

9 Happy atop a mound, mixed up to find Easter Day.

Answers are on pages 184–85 at the back of the book

THE MEDITERRANEAN

1599

JOAN OLIVA

Joan Oliva, the prolific and meticulous Catalan cartographer who produced this map in 1599, lived in an age of flux, when the transition from the medieval world was almost complete and mapmaking was in ever-greater demand to chart the new discoveries of the past century. Oliva populates the edges of his chart with colourful figures of warriors and walled cities (and a rather unusual swordfish-like whale out in the Atlantic). The map is one of the late examples of the portolan tradition, which had grown up the trading cities of the Mediterranean in the fourteenth century, with networks of rhumb-lines crossing the ocean as navigational aids. Oliva's chart was needed more than ever because the Mediterranean continued to be a field of conflict between the expansive Ottoman Empire (which even occupied part of southern Italy in 1480) and a fragmentary alliance of western European Christian powers that only turned the tide after a naval victory at Lepanto in 1571 had confined the Ottomans to the eastern part of the sea.

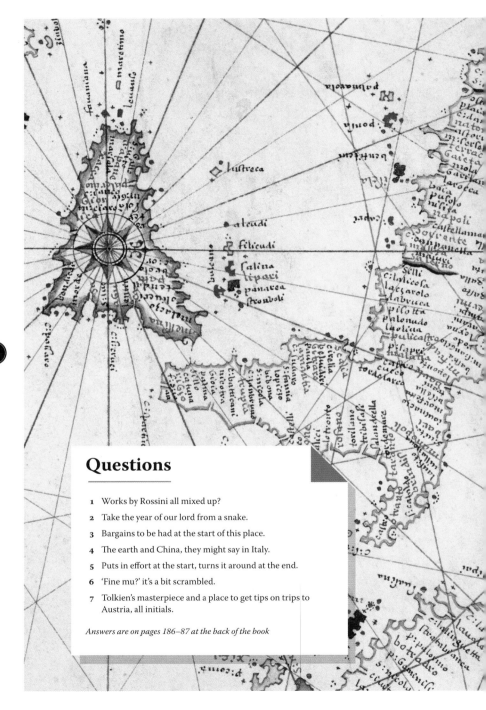

Questions

1 Works by Rossini all mixed up?

2 Take the year of our lord from a snake.

3 Bargains to be had at the start of this place.

4 The earth and China, they might say in Italy.

5 Puts in effort at the start, turns it around at the end.

6 'Fine mu?' it's a bit scrambled.

7 Tolkien's masterpiece and a place to get tips on trips to Austria, all initials.

Answers are on pages 186–87 at the back of the book

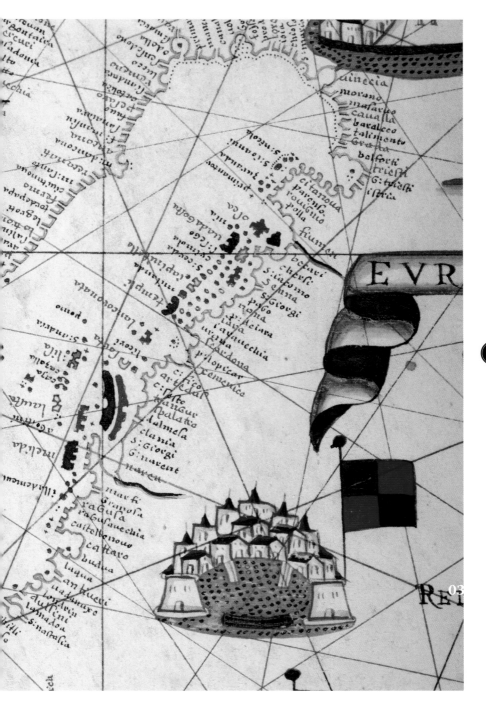

EVR

RE

03

VIRGIN

MONACANS

MANN AHOACKS

POWHATAN
Held this state & fashion when Capt. Smith
was deliuered to him prisoner

POWHATAN

MAR
GOAGS

CHI-
WONS

James Town

CHE SA PEAK BAY

KVSKARA WA
OOKS

TOCK
WOGHS

Cape Henry

Cape Charles

Smiths Iles

and halfe

Scale of Leagues

Leagues

THE
VIRGINIAN SEA

Discouered and Discribed by Captayn Iohn Smith
Grauen by William Hole

VIRGINIA

1612

JOHN SMITH

Jamestown, Virginia, was the first permanent English settlement in the Americas that survived (Walter Raleigh's ill-fated Roanoke, established in what is now North Carolina in 1585, was abandoned; its settlers were all gone when a delayed relief voyage reached the site in 1590, and their fate was never discovered). As part of the Jamestown colony's initial governing council, Captain John Smith was tasked with exploring the immediate area to survey the land, which England was now claiming. The map, drawn in 1612, is based on his travels (during which in 1607 he was captured by the local chief, Powhatan, and almost killed). It is oriented with west at the top and bears a portrait of Powhatan at the top left. The limit of the area Smith was able to view for himself is indicated by a series of Maltese crosses at the top (east) of the map, which begin roughly on a line with Powhatan's own village, beyond which Smith was not allowed to proceed.

Iames towne

Warraskoyack

Matho ma uk

Mattacock

Mokete

Kiskiack

Cantaunkack

andsamund

Mattanock

Ceader Ile

Capahowasick

Paranka-tank

arpes Ile

Poynt hope

Gosnolds bave

Tindals poyne

Mantoughquemea

Kecough tan

Wiffins poynt

Chesapeack

Poynt Warde

Mortons baye

Powhatan flu:

Poyne comfort

CHE

Cape Henry

Sanderis Poynt

Accohanock

Cape Charles

Accowmack

Cape harbour

Smyths Iles

THE

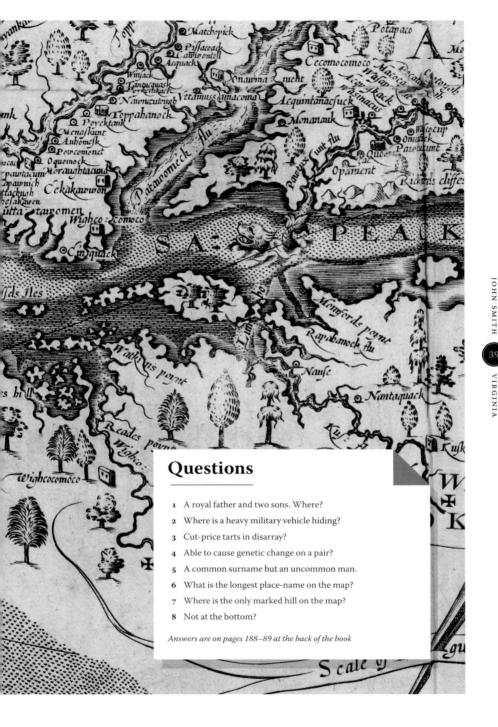

Questions

1 A royal father and two sons. Where?
2 Where is a heavy military vehicle hiding?
3 Cut-price tarts in disarray?
4 Able to cause genetic change on a pair?
5 A common surname but an uncommon man.
6 What is the longest place-name on the map?
7 Where is the only marked hill on the map?
8 Not at the bottom?

Answers are on pages 188–89 at the back of the book

VIL LECITTE

PARIS

1616

JAN ZIARNKO

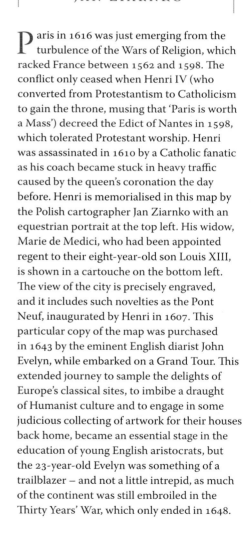

P aris in 1616 was just emerging from the turbulence of the Wars of Religion, which racked France between 1562 and 1598. The conflict only ceased when Henri IV (who converted from Protestantism to Catholicism to gain the throne, musing that 'Paris is worth a Mass') decreed the Edict of Nantes in 1598, which tolerated Protestant worship. Henri was assassinated in 1610 by a Catholic fanatic as his coach became stuck in heavy traffic caused by the queen's coronation the day before. Henri is memorialised in this map by the Polish cartographer Jan Ziarnko with an equestrian portrait at the top left. His widow, Marie de Medici, who had been appointed regent to their eight-year-old son Louis XIII, is shown in a cartouche on the bottom left. The view of the city is precisely engraved, and it includes such novelties as the Pont Neuf, inaugurated by Henri in 1607. This particular copy of the map was purchased in 1643 by the eminent English diarist John Evelyn, while embarked on a Grand Tour. This extended journey to sample the delights of Europe's classical sites, to imbibe a draught of Humanist culture and to engage in some judicious collecting of artwork for their houses back home, became an essential stage in the education of young English aristocrats, but the 23-year-old Evelyn was something of a trailblazer – and not a little intrepid, as much of the continent was still embroiled in the Thirty Years' War, which only ended in 1648.

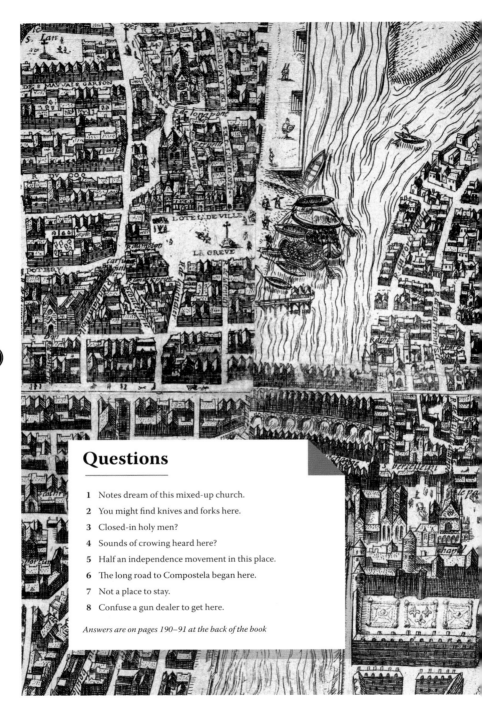

Questions

1 Notes dream of this mixed-up church.
2 You might find knives and forks here.
3 Closed-in holy men?
4 Sounds of crowing heard here?
5 Half an independence movement in this place.
6 The long road to Compostela began here.
7 Not a place to stay.
8 Confuse a gun dealer to get here.

Answers are on pages 190–91 at the back of the book

THE WORLD

1617

CLAES JANSZOON VISSCHER

T his very striking double-hemisphere map is typical of the products of Dutch mapmakers in the seventeenth century. Claes Janszoon Visscher, its compiler, was a talented artist as well as a cartographer, as evidenced by the vignettes of peoples and of important cities arrayed around his map. In the inner portion of the frame surrounding the map itself are placed biblical scenes, a fitting choice for a man who was a strict Calvinist, including the Fall of Man from the Garden of Eden and the Crucifixion. At the bottom right corner of the map, by 'TERRA AUSTRALIS' (the supposed, but as yet undiscovered, southern continent), Visscher tops the box containing his ascription as author with a picture of a man carrying two fishing nets – a pun on his own name, which means 'fisherman'.

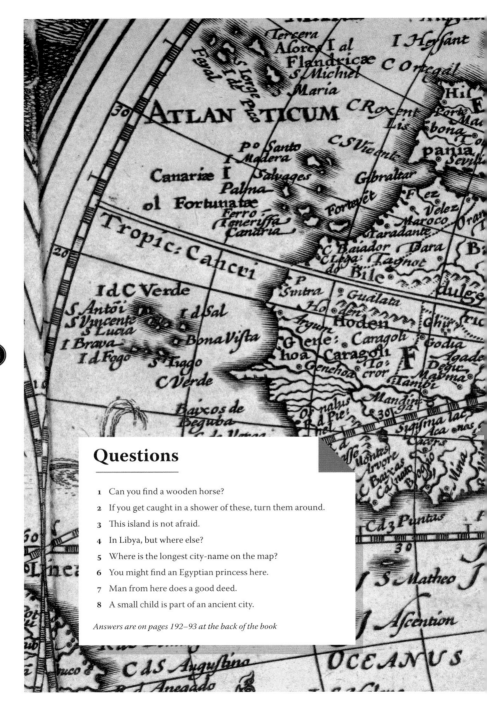

Questions

1. Can you find a wooden horse?
2. If you get caught in a shower of these, turn them around.
3. This island is not afraid.
4. In Libya, but where else?
5. Where is the longest city-name on the map?
6. You might find an Egyptian princess here.
7. Man from here does a good deed.
8. A small child is part of an ancient city.

Answers are on pages 192–93 at the back of the book

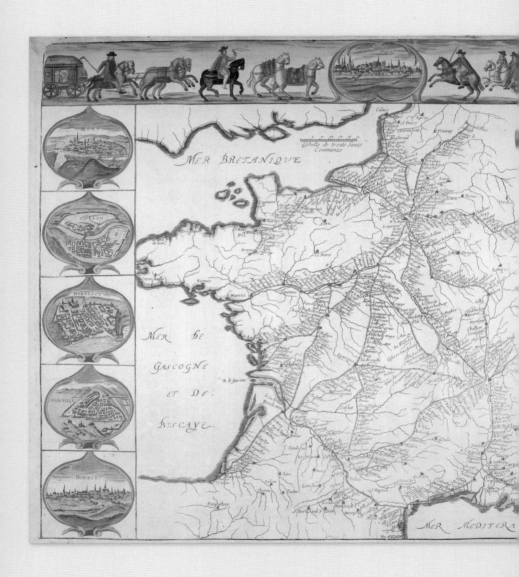

Echelle de trente lieues
Communes

MER BRETANIQVE

MER DE
GASCOGNE
ET DE
BISCAYE

MER MEDITERA

FRANCE'S
POST-ROADS

1636

NICOLAS BEREY

Although gorgeously decorated with scenes of travelling carriages and fine city-plans of ten French towns, this map has a very practical purpose. The French monarchy had been growing in strength and had emerged largely intact and unified from the Hundred Years' War (1337–1453) against the English and then a series of religious civil wars between Protestants and Catholics in the later sixteenth century. To govern such a large country, however, the French monarchs needed an effective road network along which royal orders could travel and trade be conducted. Maximilien de Béthune, the Duke of Sully, an exceptionally capable administrator who became director of the royal Council of Finance in 1596, secured the royal revenues and engaged on a programme of roadbuilding (and the start of a canal network). The map shows the system of post-roads which in part resulted, showing an arterial system of land communication that had begun to bind the kingdom more firmly together (although in places such as Brittany and inland Normandy it was only in its infancy). The map was produced by the engraver Nicolas Berey (1610–65), who founded a dynasty of engravers and cartographers still active in the mid-eighteenth century.

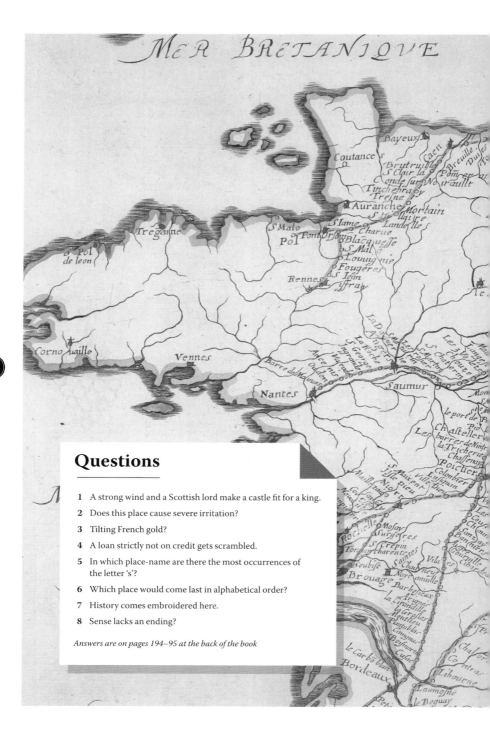

Questions

1 A strong wind and a Scottish lord make a castle fit for a king.

2 Does this place cause severe irritation?

3 Tilting French gold?

4 A loan strictly not on credit gets scrambled.

5 In which place-name are there the most occurrences of the letter 's'?

6 Which place would come last in alphabetical order?

7 History comes embroidered here.

8 Sense lacks an ending?

Answers are on pages 194–95 at the back of the book

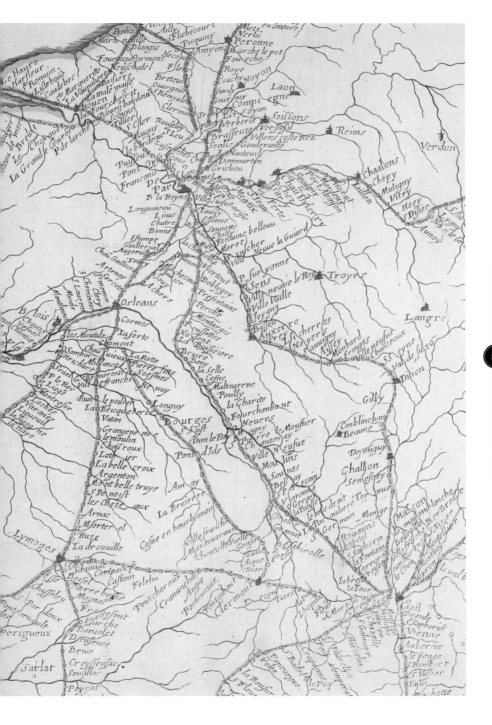

THE NORTH SEA

1646

ROBERT DUDLEY

The North Sea has long been one of Europe's principal avenues of power, carrying the ancestors of the Anglo-Saxons into Britain, the Vikings throughout northwestern Europe, and the Dutch and English across the globe. Such a strategic waterway and the coastlines which enclosed it badly needed to be mapped, particularly once the era of maritime empires got underway in the sixteenth century. This map of the North Sea coast, printed in around 1646, derives from plates included

in the *Dell' Arcano del Mare* ('Of the Secrets of the Sea'), the first maritime atlas of the world and the earliest one to use Mercator's new projection (useful for navigators because any straight line on the map represented a constant line of true bearing for sailing, but less so for geographical accuracy because it enhances the size of landmasses near the poles, such as Britain, while diminishing those nearer the Equator). It was produced by Robert Dudley, the illegitimate son of Elizabeth I's favourite, the Earl of Leicester, whose life was every bit as chequered as his father's. Dudley was the leader of a disastrous expedition to the New World in 1594–95 in which one vessel, the *Earwig*, sank and almost no treasure was seized from the Spanish. His main achievement was the discovery of an island in the Orinoco basin, which he called, modestly, Dudleiana. He fled England for Italy in 1609 with his cousin and lover Elizabeth Southwell, as a result of which he was declared an outlaw and had to scrape a living through various ventures, including cartography.

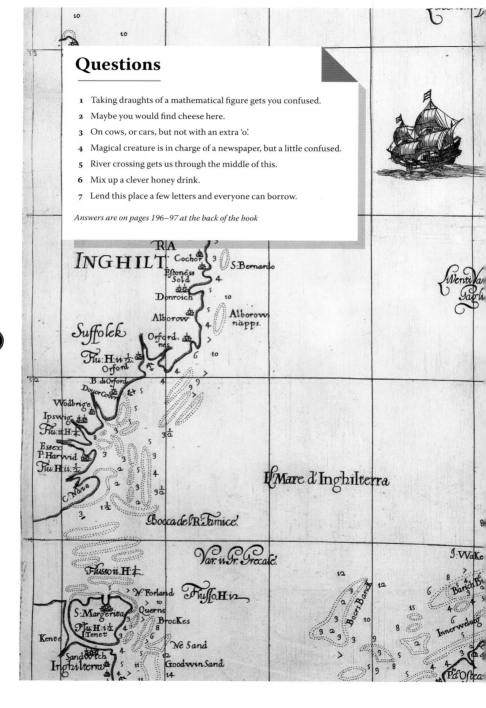

Questions

1 Taking draughts of a mathematical figure gets you confused.

2 Maybe you would find cheese here.

3 On cows, or cars, but not with an extra 'o'.

4 Magical creature is in charge of a newspaper, but a little confused.

5 River crossing gets us through the middle of this.

6 Mix up a clever honey drink.

7 Lend this place a few letters and everyone can borrow.

Answers are on pages 196–97 at the back of the book

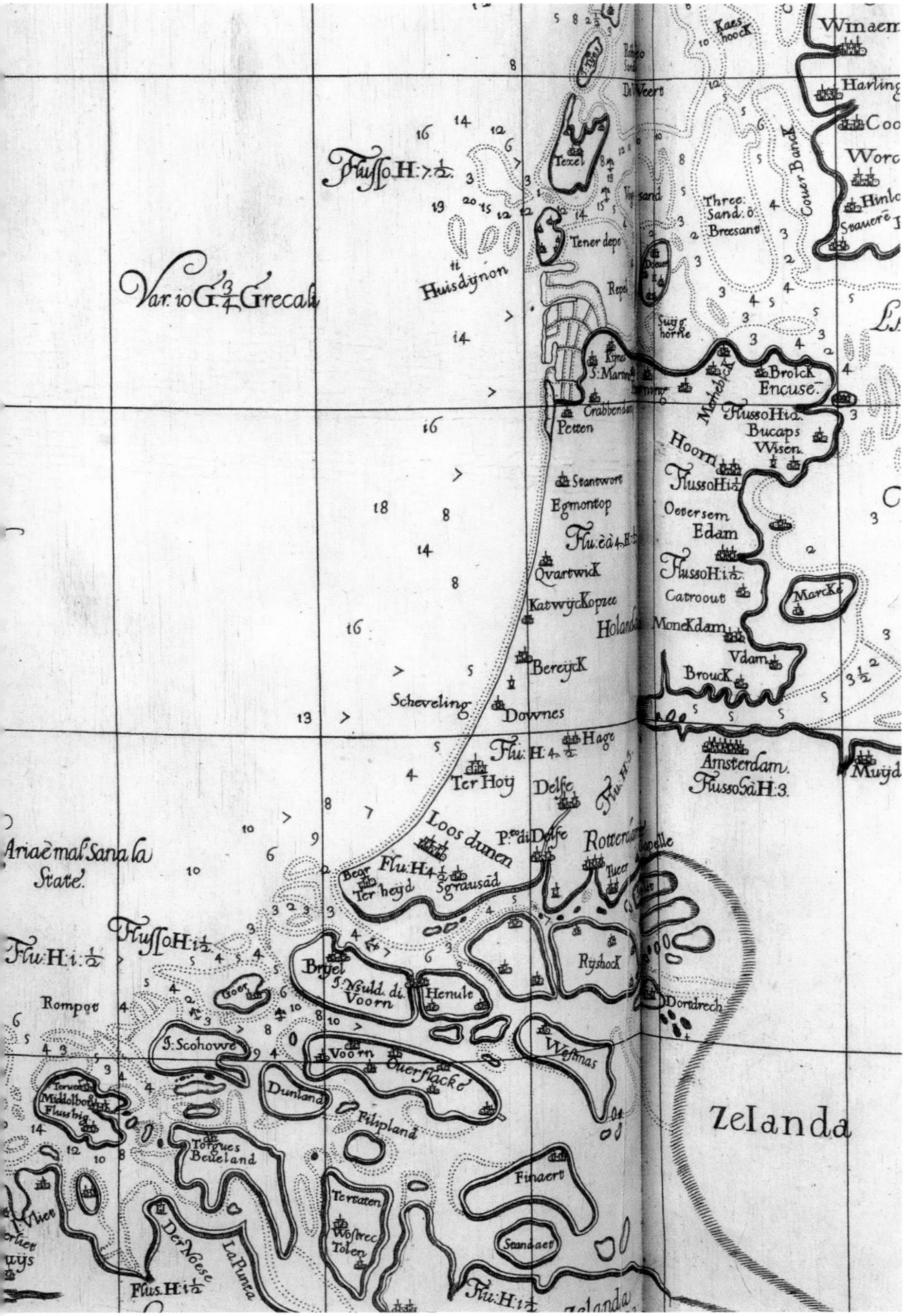
Winaem
Harling
Worc
Texel
Flusso H: 7 ½
Three: Sand: ö: Breesant
Couer Banck
Tener depe
Huisdynon
Var. 10 G. ¾ Grecali
Kaes hoock
Broick
Encuse
Flusso H: ½
Bucaps
Wisen
Hoorn
Petten
Crabbendam
Stanwort
Egmontop
Oeversem
Edam
Quartwick
Catroout
Marcke
Katwijckopzee
Holandia
Monekdam
Vdam
Bereijck
Brouck
Scheveling
Downes
Hage
Amsterdam
Flusso dà H: 3
Muijd
Ter Hoy
Delfe
Loos dunen
Rotterdam
Ariae mal Sana la State
Flu: H: 4 ½
Sgrausad
Ter heyd
Flusso H: i ½
Flu: H: i ½
Rompot
Briel
Goer
Voorn
Henult
Rijshock
Dondrech
I: Scohowe
Westmas
Dunland
Ouerflacke
Filipland
Torgues Beueland
Zelanda
Finaert
Tertaten
Wostrec
Tolen
Scandaet
Der Noese
La Punta
Flus. H: i ½
Flu: H: i ½

MOSCVA
al Archiepum Foederi Borisowiti

MOVRMANSKOY MORE

NOVA ZEMLA

obdora

Con dora

Permia

Wiatka

CAZAIN

MORDWA

ASTRACAN

CATANIA

SWEDEN

NOORDZEE

DANIA

MARE BALTICVM

POLONIA

PRVSSIA

LIT TAW

PODOLIA

MOLDAVIA

WALACHIA

BVLGARIA

ROMANIA

ARCHIPELAGO

NATOLIA

PONTVS EVXINVS ais ZORNO MORE

CRIMEA SEVTIA

PETIGORI

CABARDA

ARMENIA

MOSCOVIA

TABVLA RVSSIÆ
ex autographo, quod delineandum
curavit Fædor filius Boris Boris Aeruu-
tis, et ad Borea Borisam Duchuum, disque
loca, quantiu eo tabula evenire adeur Mos-
tu fieri potest, amplificata : et
Magno Domino, Tzaret Magno
Duci Michaeli Fæodrowitz omnium
Rusforum Autocratori Wolodimeriæ, Mof-
covite et Neupardiæ, Tzari Cazaniæ, Tzari
Abraxaniæ, Tzari Siberiæ, Domino Pleskoviæ
Magno Duci Smolenskiæ, Otwerfkiæ, Jugoriæ, Per-
miæ, Wiatkæ, Bulgariæ etc : Item Domino
et Magno Duci Novogardiæ Inferioris etc.
Domino regiomum hortus Kortkiræ,
et Græbiniæ Trans etc.
dedicata ab
Hessflo Gerrits
M. DC. XIII.

Amstelodami
Excusum Apud Guiljelmum Blaeu

1662

JOAN BLAEU

The Dutchman Joan Blaeu (1596–1673) was one of the most influential mapmakers of the mid-seventeenth century. He was part of a cartographic dynasty, succeeding his father Willem in 1633 as the official chartmaker for the Dutch East India Company, or Vereenigde Oostindische Compagnie (VOC). It was a vital position – since its establishment in 1602 the VOC's ships had made huge inroads into the Indian Ocean trade previously dominated by the Spanish and Portuguese, and accurate maps of the vast region made the task of its sea captains and offices much simpler. Blaeu's *Atlas Maior* (of 1662) was a massive enterprise. A true world atlas, it had 594 maps and 3,368 pages of accompanying text and was published in 11 volumes. It was a truly deluxe production and cost 450 Dutch guilders in its coloured form (roughly the amount a skilled craftsman would earn in a whole year). This map is from volume two, which covered Sweden, Poland and Russia, and shows an area in flux. In 1645 Sweden had occupied most of present-day Estonia and between 1654 and 1660 the Russians fought a border war with the Polish-Lithuanian Commonwealth, which began with the capture by Russia of the strategic city of Smolensk. In this part of the world, borders were certainly not a fixed thing.

SWE DEN.

Finlandt

Luxa

Vpsael

Stockholm

Hagelant.

Rewel

Narua

Wesenburg

Nie slos

Weysen stein

Haapsael

Pibus lacus

Plescow

Porchow

Derpt

Isbury

LIEFLANT.

Wolmer

Werder

Opaczko

Zawloc

ze

S. Maria

S. Nicol

Windaw

Culdinga

Nitaw

Adzul Krasnygrod

Riga

Rhuebury

Marienborg

Lasna

Iliua

Oskala

Klosian

Biell

Welikss

Libba

Midniki

Memel

Bausk

Baslaw

Sokol

Poniewies

Kievdany

Suras

Witepsk

Dantzik

Coningsbergz

Kowno

Troky Vilna

Dubinki

Miadzial

Orsza

Hoki

Smolen

Frawweburg

Elbig

Thorn

PRVSSIA

Augustow

Gredno

Borisow

Mohilou

Meisk

Radora

Kruyczo

Wlatislaw

Ploczk

Ciechanow

Wolkowiska

Slonim

Niesuves

Minsk

LIT TAW.

Nemen fl.

Propoisk

Cieciewsk

Pott

Warsaw

Liw

Bug fl.

Bresta

Pinsk

Slucz

Przipiecz fl.

Rzeczyca

Staradub

POLONIA.

Kazimirz

Sadomirz

Lubliu

Pole si a.

Horodac

Oucucze

Mozy

Rzeczyca

Homel

Novigrad

severski

Cracow

Chelm

Wlodzimirz

WO

Luzuc

Dubrowica

Czernilsel

Lubiecz

na

Czernih

Olyka

Ostrug

L Y.

Kiow

Nawoz

Moraviesk

Osurz

Przemissl

Krzemieniec

Saslaw

Bialacerkiew

Przeslaw

Dzies

Leopolis

Tarnopol

Krzemeneziz

Buczaczi

NIA.

Haliez

Suiatyn

Kamieniec

Braslaw

Czyrkash

Mandzaley

Dret

Colonia

PODO

Sa

Pyrobar

Cataraet.

MARE BALTICVM

Oelant

Godlant

JOAN BLAEU   RUSSIA

58

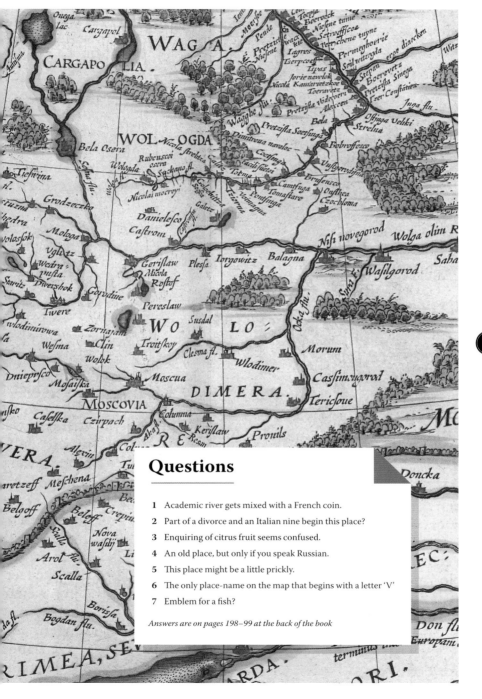

Questions

1 Academic river gets mixed with a French coin.

2 Part of a divorce and an Italian nine begin this place?

3 Enquiring of citrus fruit seems confused.

4 An old place, but only if you speak Russian.

5 This place might be a little prickly.

6 The only place-name on the map that begins with a letter 'V'

7 Emblem for a fish?

Answers are on pages 198–99 at the back of the book

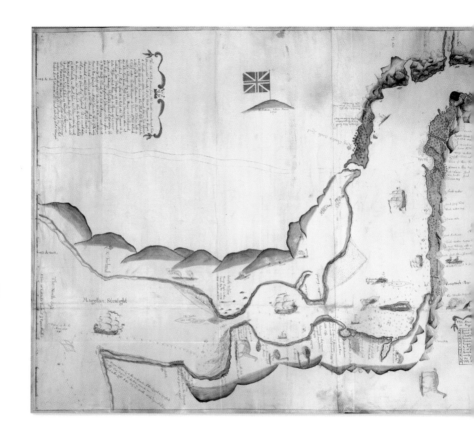

PATAGONIA

1671/72

SIR JOHN NARBROUGH

The Magellan Strait at the southern tip of South America was discovered by the Portuguese explorer Ferdinand Magellan in 1520 during the voyage that would ultimately result in the first circumnavigation of the globe. The British did not venture into the labyrinthine waters and treacherous currents of the Strait until the seventeenth century, as Spanish hegemony there waned. Sir John Narbrough, a veteran of the Second Anglo-Dutch War, was despatched in 1669

on an expedition to pioneer new trading links in the Americas and beyond into the Pacific. Aboard the *Sweepstakes*, a 36-gun ship built at Yarmouth, Narbrough was ordered 'not to meddle with the Coast of America nor Send on Shore, unless in the Case of great necessity'. Short of supplies, he finally landed close to the Spanish fort at Valdivia, hoping to buy provisions, but the Spanish detained four of his men. He was unable to make any trade agreement or to find any route through which to promote trade further west, nor was he able to make any effective communication with the natives of Patagonia. Despite the relatively disappointing results of his voyage, Narbrough did commission a glorious map of it, with pen images of the Patagonians, vignettes of local fauna and detailed annotations of places where water and a sheltered harbour might be had. Narbrough claimed the land he passed through for Britain, but to no avail because it remained in Spain's possession until 1818, when the Chileans declared their independence.

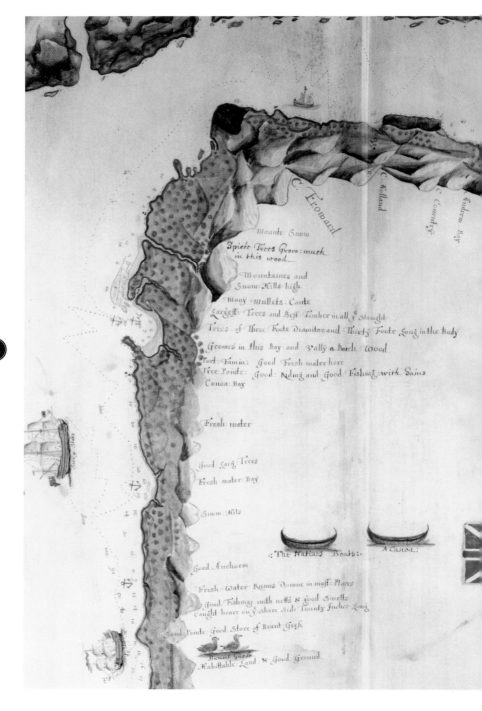

C: Froward

C: Holland

C: Coventry

Fulcon Bay

Mounte: Snow

Spiere Trees Grow: much in this wood

Mountaines and Snow: Hills high

Many Mullets: Caute

Largest Trees and Best Timber in all y Straight Trees: of Three Foote Diamitor and Thirty Foote Long in the body

Growes in this bay: and Vally a Birch Wood

Port: Famin: Good Fresh water here

Tree Pointe: Good: Riding and Good Fishing: with Sains

Conoa: Bay

Fresh: water

Good Larg Trees

Fresh water Bay

Snow: Hils

The Natives Boats:

A Canoa:

Good Anchorm

Fresh Water Runns Downe in most Places

Good: Fishing with nets & good Smelts Caught heare on y shore Side Twenty Inches Long

Sand Pointe Good Store of Brant Geese

Brant Geese

Habittable Land & Good Ground

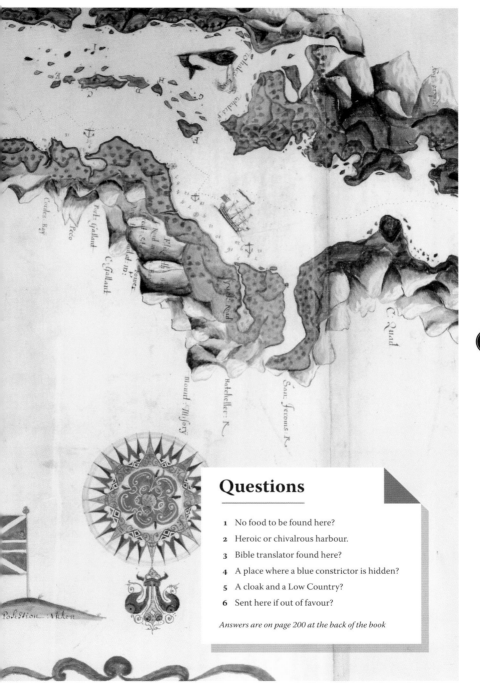

Questions

1 No food to be found here?

2 Heroic or chivalrous harbour.

3 Bible translator found here?

4 A place where a blue constrictor is hidden?

5 A cloak and a Low Country?

6 Sent here if out of favour?

Answers are on page 200 at the back of the book

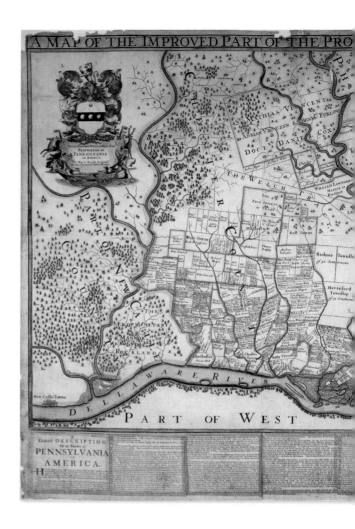

PENNSYLVANIA

1687

THOMAS HOLME

The foundation of the Colony of Pennsylvania in 1682 by the Quaker William Penn was supposed to mark a godly moment, when religious freedom could be established far from the persecution blighting the lives of non-conformists back in England. Penn divided the land up into parcels for his 250 main backers, the 'first purchasers', and then set about the surveying and subdividing of the land. He tasked his chief surveyor Thomas

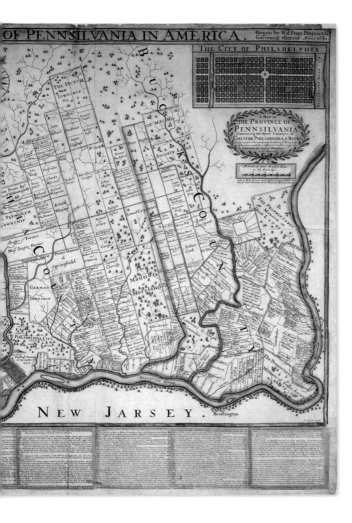

Holme first to produce a map of Philadelphia, all pleasing grids and rectangles, and then in 1683 the far more arduous, yet vital, task of creating a map of the entire colony to entice would-be settlers. The process was prolonged, embittered by arguments between claimants to various areas and it took four years to complete. The final result took enormous care over who owned which tracts of land, with the names of each clearly marked (and large areas apportioned to particular national groups, such as the Welsh and Dutch). It did neither Holme, nor Penn, much good because immediately the map was printed it ignited a renewed round of boundary disputes, with litigants claiming they had been allocated less than their rightful shares.

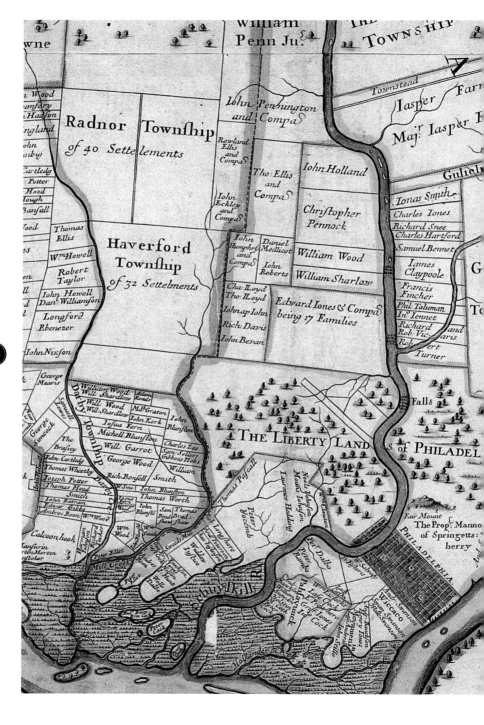

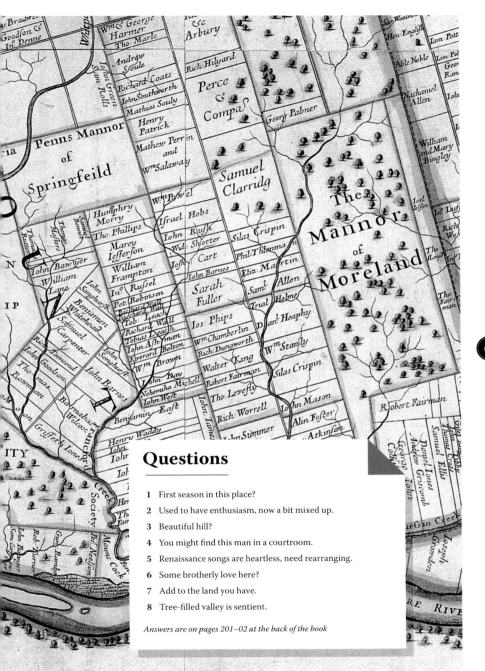

Questions

1 First season in this place?

2 Used to have enthusiasm, now a bit mixed up.

3 Beautiful hill?

4 You might find this man in a courtroom.

5 Renaissance songs are heartless, need rearranging.

6 Some brotherly love here?

7 Add to the land you have.

8 Tree-filled valley is sentient.

Answers are on pages 201–02 at the back of the book

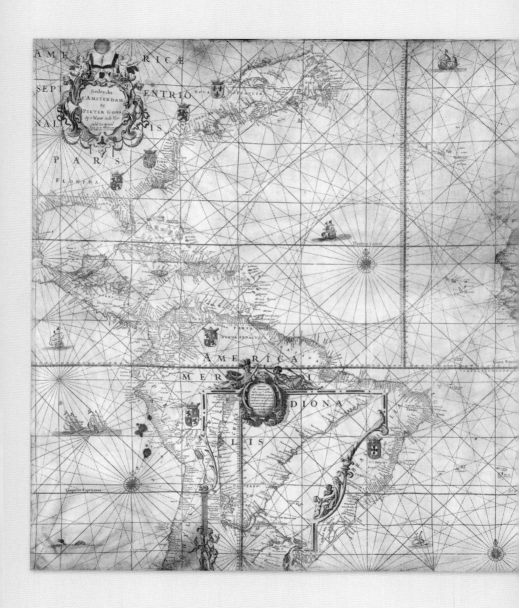

THE ATLANTIC
c.1690

PIETER GOOS

Pieter Goos, the Dutch cartographer who produced this map in c.1690, was one of the finest mapmakers in the golden age of Dutch mapmaking. It formed part of his *Zee-atlas,* whose charts were adorned with sumptuous illustrations, some of them picked out in gold leaf. The atlas appeared just at the end of a particularly expansive phase in Dutch colonial history: the Netherlands had just lost New Amsterdam to the British in 1664 (which was soon after renamed New York), and its grasp had slipped from possessions in northern Brazil, which Portugal reconquered in 1654. This chart of the Atlantic Ocean was one of three larger-format maps included in the Atlas (together with maps of Europe and the Indian Ocean) which could be mounted separately as wall-maps.

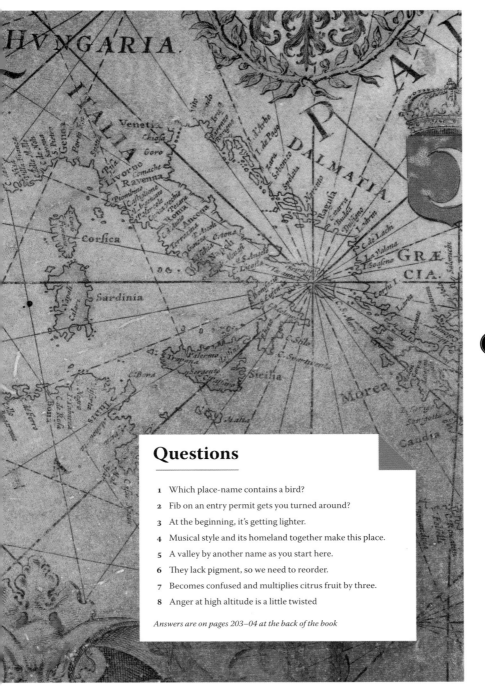

Questions

1   Which place-name contains a bird?

2   Fib on an entry permit gets you turned around?

3   At the beginning, it's getting lighter.

4   Musical style and its homeland together make this place.

5   A valley by another name as you start here.

6   They lack pigment, so we need to reorder.

7   Becomes confused and multiplies citrus fruit by three.

8   Anger at high altitude is a little twisted

Answers are on pages 203–04 at the back of the book

THE PHILIPPINES

1734

PEDRO MURILLO VELARDE

The Spanish first arrived in the Philippines in 1521, when Ferdinand Magellan landed in southern Leyte during the pioneering circumnavigation of the globe that would cost him his life a few weeks later during a dispute with the inhabitants of Mactan Island. The Spanish occupation of the islands got underway in 1565, and by 1734 – when this map was produced – the Philippines were firmly embedded within an imperial system that spanned the world from the Americas to Asia. The map was engraved by the Jesuit priest Pedro Murillo Velarde. A former rector of the great pilgrimage church at Antipolo near Manila, he was also an able cartographer. Producing this, the first full map of the Philippines, Murillo Velarde adorned it with sketches of the ethnic groups to be found in the islands and several city plans, including of Manila and Zamboanga. He also wrote a definitive history of the Philippines, in which this map appeared.

Castagan.
Banganalala.
Playa honda ó Pay-nauen.
Banganbucao.
Cabangoan.
Capones.
Subic.
Frayle.

PAMP.
Porac
Liban
Mexico.
Bacolod
Betis
Guagua
Sismua.
Minalin.
Apalit.
Macabebe.
Hago noy.
Paom bom.
Carban.a
Samal.
Abucay.
Oriong.
Bataan.
Cabcaben.
Mariueles.
Morong
Bagac.
Puercas.

BVLAC
Quinua
Guiguinto.
Bigaa.
Bucaui
Malolos
Bulacan.
Polo.
May
Marili
Tambobo
Tondo
Sta Cru
quina
Minondo
Manila.
Mala te
Poluoorij
Parañ
Piñas.
Nasr
Indang.
Tanavan

Orane
Pajac
Bodabod
Binangbang
Cruz
Siguin
Dapdap
Cavite
S.ty
Ygsey
Policuaullo
Frayle
Cavite
Uyuinay
Bacor
Cavite
Marigondon.

Monja.
P.ta Fuego
Fortun
Calumpan
Limbones
Loot
Nasu bug.
Lian.
Calatagan
S.n Pedriño.

Laguna
de Taal
Taal.
Balayan
Cafayay
Bauang

P.ta de Asufre
P.ta de Palapa
P.ta de S.n Tiago
Maricaban.

I.a de Cabras.
Tili Pan.
Ambil.
Luban.
Golo.
Iamilo.
P.ta del Elcarbe

P.ta de Galeras.
Calauite.
S.to Thomas.
Ilo.
Manolo.
Camoran.
Baradero.
Balaigu

P.ta de Calavite.
Paluan.
Tubile.
mburao.
MIN

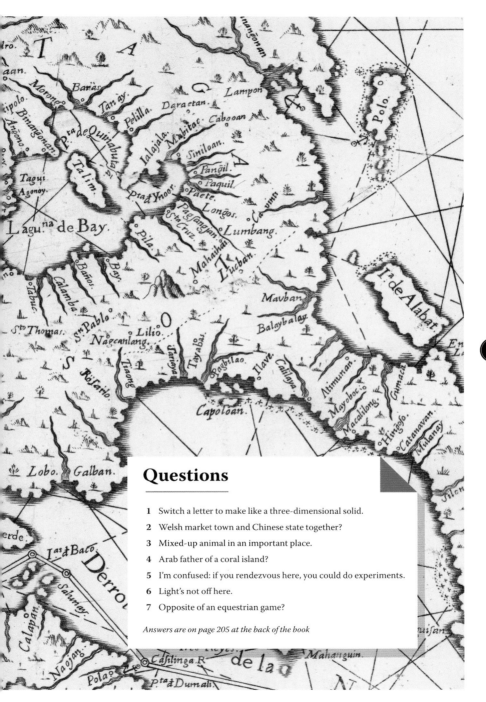

Questions

1   Switch a letter to make like a three-dimensional solid.

2   Welsh market town and Chinese state together?

3   Mixed-up animal in an important place.

4   Arab father of a coral island?

5   I'm confused: if you rendezvous here, you could do experiments.

6   Light's not off here.

7   Opposite of an equestrian game?

Answers are on page 205 at the back of the book

LONDON

1746

JOHN ROCQUE

John Rocque came from a French Protestant family, which had fled persecution in France in the late seventeenth century. He first achieved fame as a garden designer, conducting surveys (and making drawings) of gardens including Richmond House, Chiswick House and Hampton Court. In 1739 he began work on a much grander project, a survey of London, whose vast growth in the preceding 50 years had rendered

previous maps redundant. It took him seven years to complete the work and have it engraved before the final 24-sheet map of the capital was published in 1746. The project had been too much for one man to finance on his own and as a result its publication was supported by 246 subscribers, each of whom agreed to buy a copy of the map, and among their number was Frederick, the Prince of Wales. Although more comprehensive than any previous map of the whole of London,

amounting to over 5,000 street names and including many small alleys and yards which previous cartographers had not covered (Rocque even depicted 'Tiburn' near Hyde Park, the gibbet popularly known as the 'Tyburn Tree' that was used for public executions), its fine detail still had surprising omissions: including missing out the name of Hyde Park Road, the very street on which Rocque had his drawing office.

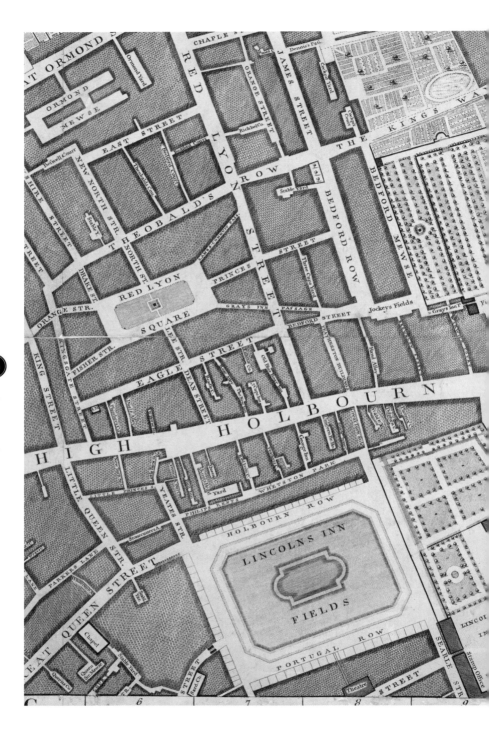

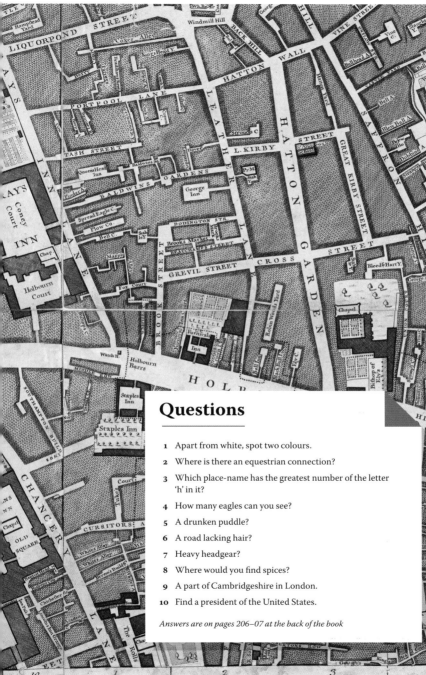

Questions

1 Apart from white, spot two colours.

2 Where is there an equestrian connection?

3 Which place-name has the greatest number of the letter 'h' in it?

4 How many eagles can you see?

5 A drunken puddle?

6 A road lacking hair?

7 Heavy headgear?

8 Where would you find spices?

9 A part of Cambridgeshire in London.

10 Find a president of the United States.

Answers are on pages 206–07 at the back of the book

THE ARCTIC

1753

PHILIPPE BUACHE

The French mapmaker Philippe Buache, appointed Royal Geographer to the king of France in 1729, had a particular fascination for the new discoveries being made in the Arctic regions of northeast Asia and North America. The Bering Strait had been found by the Danish explorer Vitus Bering in 1728 and further Russian expeditions pressing east into Siberia, and American and British expeditions pushing west (such as that of the Scottish explorer Alexander Mackenzie, who reached the

Canadian Pacific coast overland in 1793), were beginning to fill in the gaps in maps of the region, which had hitherto been largely blank. Buache was an exponent of a school of speculative geography, quite prepared to construct maps of less well-documented regions through a mixture of interpretation of explorers' accounts and informed guesswork. On this map of the Arctic, many of his guesses were unfounded and many of the features he mapped (such as the large 'Mer de l'Ouest' and the alleged Chinese settlement of Fou-Sang)

proved fictitious. Yet Buache was certainly prepared to admit that much of his mapping of this little-known region was unconfirmed. He draws a sweeping peninsula cutting down from Alaska and almost touching Kamchatka, which he only 'supposes' to be there and admits that, regarding connections between the Pacific and the 'Grande Eau' (itself fictitious), that *'on soupçonne'* ('one suspects') that these exist.

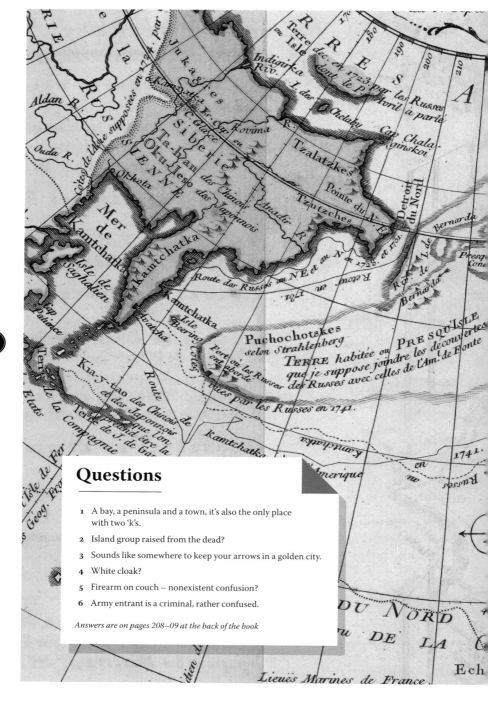

Questions

1 A bay, a peninsula and a town, it's also the only place with two 'k's.

2 Island group raised from the dead?

3 Sounds like somewhere to keep your arrows in a golden city.

4 White cloak?

5 Firearm on couch – nonexistent confusion?

6 Army entrant is a criminal, rather confused.

Answers are on pages 208–09 at the back of the book

CTIQUE

Monts

270

260

250

240

Lac de Valasco

Lac de Fonte

Lac Ronquillo

B.ᵉ de Repulse

C. Smith

Det. d'Hudson

Marble

Natuanam

Baye Sir Tho. Nest

Savage

Eau de Wager

Chesterfield

Polaire

Eau de la Grande Eau

Cercle Parmentier

Rive. de Parmentier

Baye

Lac Belle

Conasset Ville

Rio los Reyes

Minhausset

Port de l'Trena

Haro Riv.

Whale cove

Welcome

Charkill

R. Nelson

d'Hudson

Lac des 2. déscharges

Grande Eau

On soupconne qu'il y a en cet endroit quelques communications de la Mer à la Grande Eau

R. Bourbon

L. des Forts

NOUV.

L. des Bois ou la Pl.

L. Anisquagha gamou

Terres reconnues par les Russes

Fou-sang des Chinois

Mer

DE

L'OUEST

L. Bourbon

R. de Poscoyac

L. Ouiriagon

L. des Prairies

L. des Bois

SIOUX

Moin

R. du

Archipel de St. Lazare

Ouachipouanes

Côte Merid.ᵗᵉ indiquée par Guill. Delisle

Quivira

Teguaio

Panis

Entrée de Fuca

Entrée d'Aguilar

Cap Blanc

Cap Mendocin

B. de Pinos

R. Colorado

Nouveau Méxique

Rio del Coral

LA MER DU SUD

P.ᵗᵉ de Monterey

California

Mer

NDE MER

Canal S.ᵗᵉ Barbe

L.ᵉ S.ᵗ Clement

C. d'Engaino

Lieues Communes de France

Vermei

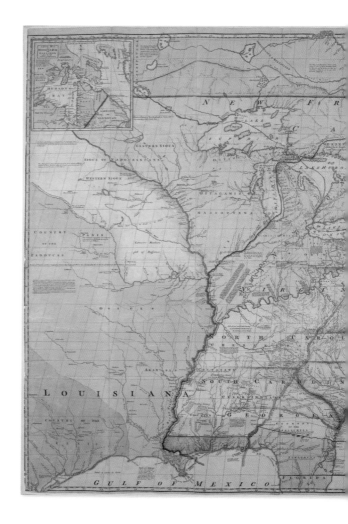

NORTH AMERICA

1755

JOHN MITCHELL

M aps are often a by-product of territorial disputes and that between the French and British in the mid-eighteenth century over North America was particularly lively, erupting into outright warfare in 1754 in a conflict known as the French and Indian War (which before long became just another theatre in the global Seven Years' War between the two countries). Virginia-born John Mitchell was commissioned in the

early 1750s by the Earl of Halifax, President of the Board of Trade, to compile a map to support British claims in the Ohio Valley. Mitchell's resulting map was large (over six feet/1.8 metres wide) and detailed, outlining the geography and settlements of North America in a way never-before attempted. He marked the western boundary of the British claims with a bold red line (and the borders of the individual colonies with a variety of coloured lines – red for the Carolinas, greyish-

blue for Georgia). The French claims were delineated by a solid yellow line, clearly demonstrating the irreconcilability of the two nations' positions (which was resolved by the war largely in favour of the British). The red line later formed the basis of the future United States' claim to a boundary far to the west of the original 13 Colonies, a territorial expansion they successfully achieved in the 1783 Treaty of Paris, which ended the Revolutionary War with Britain.

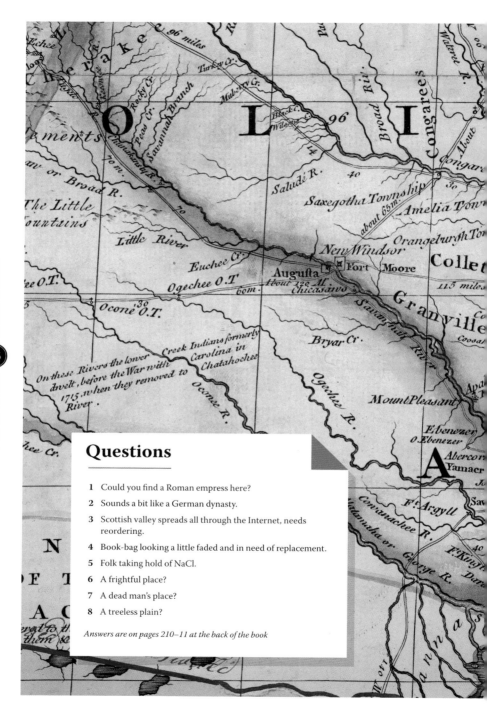

Questions

1 Could you find a Roman empress here?

2 Sounds a bit like a German dynasty.

3 Scottish valley spreads all through the Internet, needs reordering.

4 Book-bag looking a little faded and in need of replacement.

5 Folk taking hold of NaCl.

6 A frightful place?

7 A dead man's place?

8 A treeless plain?

Answers are on pages 210–11 at the back of the book

THE TROSSACHS

1755

WILLIAM ROY

T he folded-over mountains and lake-studded
countryside of the Trossachs in the region of Loch
Lomond create a dramatic landscape – and one ideal for
those on the run from the authorities. They proved their
worth as a refuge after the defeat of the Jacobite uprising
led by Charles James Stuart ('Bonnie Prince Charlie') at
Culloden Moor in April 1746, and their intractability
presented the English with something of a problem in
hunting down the last remaining rebels. The solution
was to map them. In 1747 William Watson, the Deputy
Quartermaster of the Board of Ordnance, was ordered
by the Duke of Cumberland, in charge of the pacification
of the Highlands, to produce a military survey. This task
Watson entrusted to his deputy, William Roy, who for
seven long years travelled the length and breadth of the
country, accompanied by six surveying parties. The work
on the Highlands was complete by 1752 and, as well
as a map of hitherto unparalleled accuracy in charting
the difficult terrain, it is a piece of art in itself. Washed
with a tint to bring out the features of the landscape, it
evokes, far more than mere contour lines ever could, the
forbidding grandeur of the Trossachs.

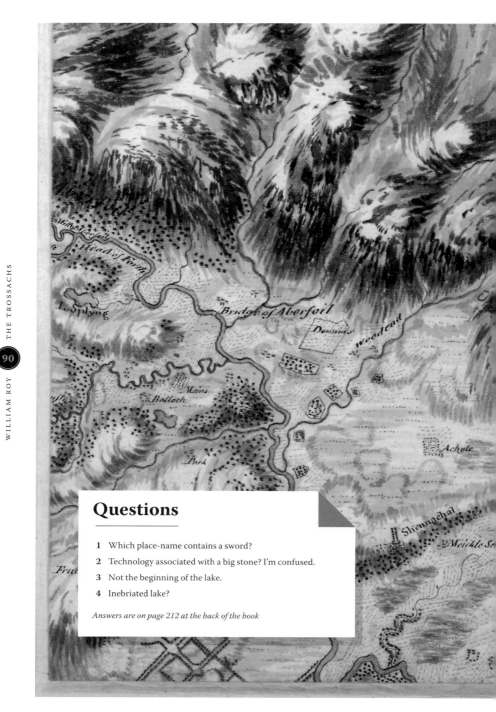

Questions

1   Which place-name contains a sword?
2   Technology associated with a big stone? I'm confused.
3   Not the beginning of the lake.
4   Inebriated lake?

Answers are on page 212 at the back of the book

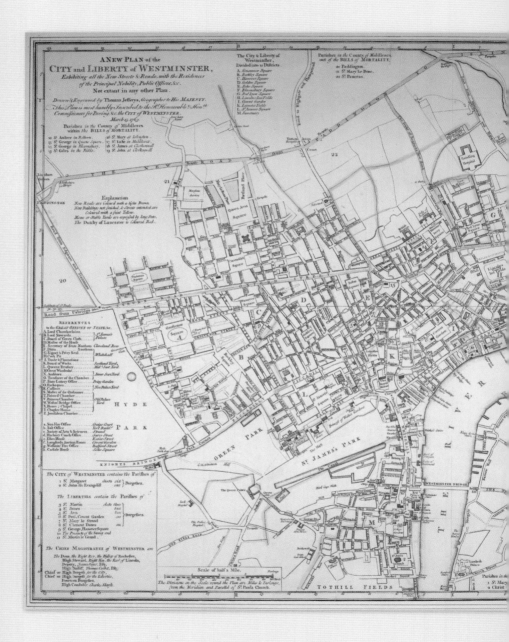

A NEW PLAN of the
CITY and LIBERTY of WESTMINSTER,
Exhibiting all the New Streets & Roads, with the Residences
of the Principal Nobility, Public Offices &c.
Not extant in any other Plan.

Drawn & Engraved by Thomas Jefferys, Geographer to His Majesty.
This Plan is most humbly Inscribed to the Rt Honourable the Hon.ble
Commissioners for Paving &c. the CITY of WESTMINSTER.
March 15, 1766.

Parishes in the County of Middlesex
within the BILLS of MORTALITY.

Scale of half a Mile.

TOTHILL FIELDS

WESTMINSTER

1765

THOMAS JEFFERYS

London in the 1760s was in urgent need of mapping. Over the preceding half-century, it had expanded westwards at an alarming rate as noble estates such as the Grosvenor and Portman were divided up into plots and laid out as elegant squares and connecting streets. It is to this period that such set pieces as Cavendish Square and Hanover Square owe their existence (the latter named in homage to George I, who had been the Elector of Hanover before his accession to the British throne in 1714). A road was even constructed to bypass the growing urban sprawl: the 'New Road', now known as the Euston Road, was opened in 1756 and it marked the northern boundary of the city (which would before long itself be leapfrogged as new suburbs opened to the north). Thomas Jefferys engraved all this with loving precision, his clear lines boldly showing urban features 'not extant on any other plan' (as they had only just been built). The official cartographer to George III, he also produced fine maps of North America and the Caribbean (see pages 112–13).

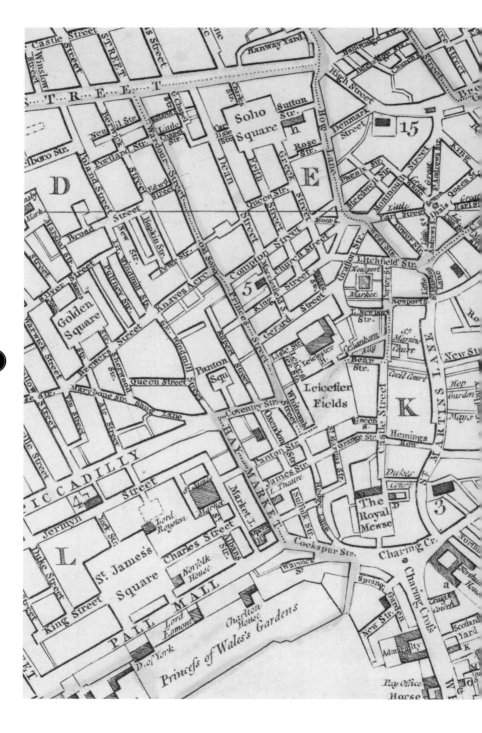

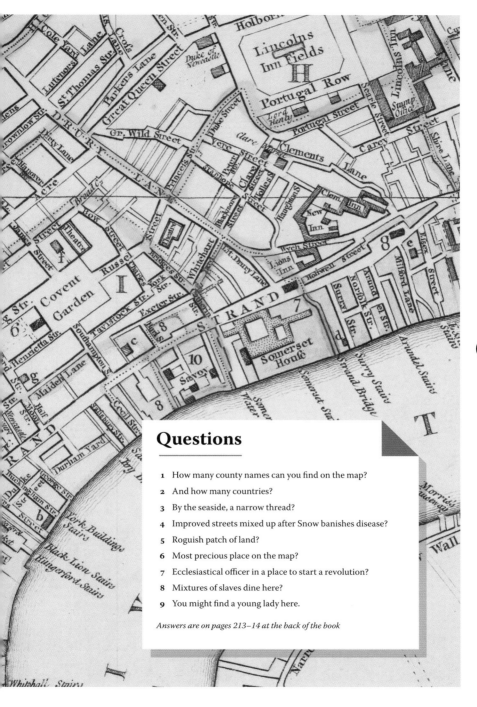

Questions

1   How many county names can you find on the map?

2   And how many countries?

3   By the seaside, a narrow thread?

4   Improved streets mixed up after Snow banishes disease?

5   Roguish patch of land?

6   Most precious place on the map?

7   Ecclesiastical officer in a place to start a revolution?

8   Mixtures of slaves dine here?

9   You might find a young lady here.

Answers are on pages 213–14 at the back of the book

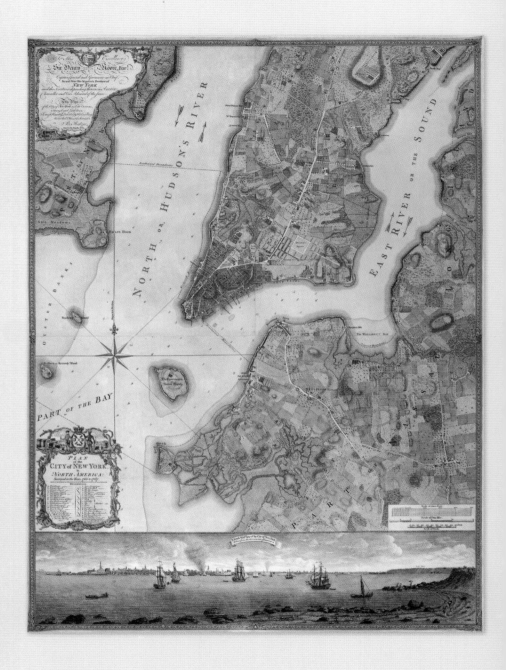

PLAN of the
CITY of NEW YORK
in
NORTH AMERICA:
Surveyed in the Years 1766 & 1767

NORTH or HUDSON'S RIVER

EAST RIVER or the SOUND

PART of the BAY

NEW YORK

c.1770

BERNARD RATZER

The growing level of dissent in Britain's 13 Colonies in the Americas after the introduction of oppressive legislation such as the Stamp Act in 1765 (which levied a duty on all printed papers) left the authorities at a disadvantage. They simply did not know the territory as well as the growing band of dissenters and revolutionaries, and in New York officials had to rely on a map made by Thomas Bradford in 1730 (with some additional material added in 1755), which covered only the southern part of the city and was well out of date. The British commander, General Gage, ordered a new survey, which was carried out by Lieutenant Bernard Ratzer. The officer paced New York's streets for over six months from October 1767, a potentially hazardous occupation

at a time when the British were becoming increasingly unpopular, and the final result was the most detailed map of the city yet produced, detailing all the street names and the expanding boundaries of the growing city. One copy of the original printing made its way to Britain, where it entered the collection of George III (although its surveyor may have been disappointed that, owing to an engraving error, his name was misprinted as Ratzen). The map marks a moment frozen in time – less than a decade later, in 1776, the American Revolutionary War broke out; shortly after the British reoccupied the city in September that year, a fire broke out on the West Side, destroying around 500 buildings and leaving one-quarter of New York in ruins.

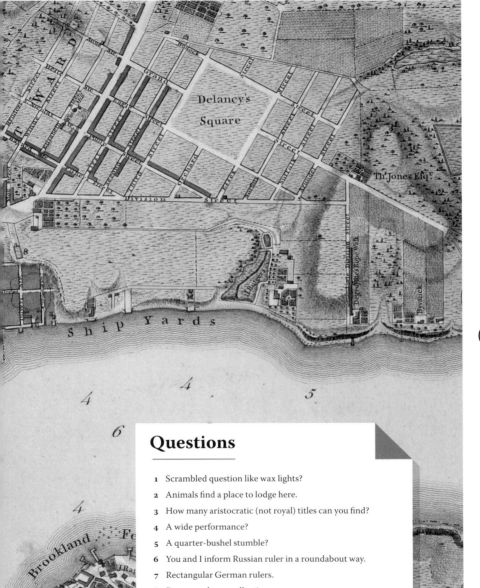

Questions

1 Scrambled question like wax lights?

2 Animals find a place to lodge here.

3 How many aristocratic (not royal) titles can you find?

4 A wide performance?

5 A quarter-bushel stumble?

6 You and I inform Russian ruler in a roundabout way.

7 Rectangular German rulers.

8 Power-pack gun collection.

Answers are on pages 215–16 at the back of the book

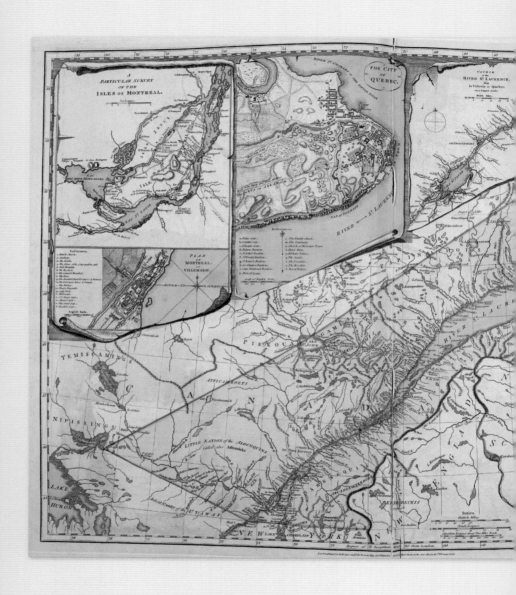

CANADA

1776

FRENCH SURVEYORS/ JONATHAN CARVER

The map shows the French province of Quebec, just after it had fallen into British hands between 1758 and 1760, a conquest ratified by the Treaty of Paris in 1763. It was based in large part on the work of French surveyors (the French had been in possession of the land for over 150 years), as the title scroll of the map acknowledges, but it was supplemented by the work of Captain Jonathan Carver, a British military surveyor. Later hired to conduct a survey of the Upper Mississippi, Carver's book *Travels Through the Interior Parts of North America*, which recounted his adventures, was an instant best-seller back in London. A copy of the book reached Benjamin Franklin, then American ambassador in Paris, and it helped to shape the negotiations in 1782 for an agreed boundary between British Canada and the United States, particularly in the region of the Great Lakes.

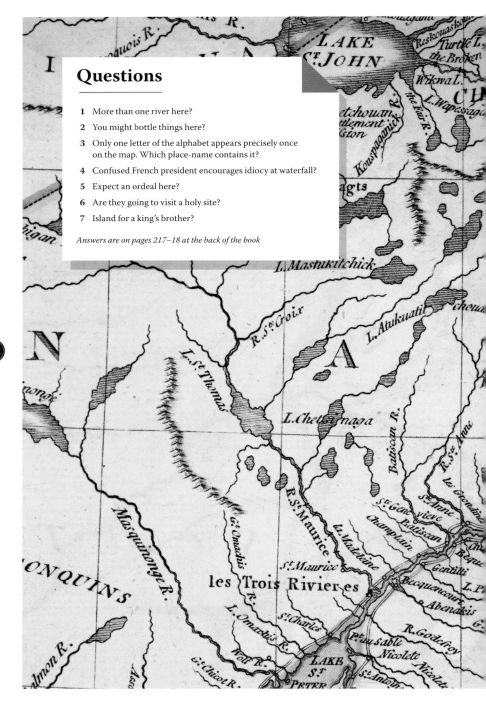

Questions

1   More than one river here?

2   You might bottle things here?

3   Only one letter of the alphabet appears precisely once
    on the map. Which place-name contains it?

4   Confused French president encourages idiocy at waterfall?

5   Expect an ordeal here?

6   Are they going to visit a holy site?

7   Island for a king's brother?

Answers are on pages 217–18 at the back of the book

A PLAN of BOSTON in NEW ENGLAND with its ENVIRONS.
including MILTON, DORCHESTER, ROXBURY, BROOKLIN, CAMBRIDGE, MEDFORD, CHARLESTOWN, Parts of MALDEN and CHELSEA.
With the MILITARY WORKS Constructed on those Places in the Years 1775, and 1776.

BOSTON

1777

HENRY PELHAM

The map of Boston freezes a moment in time. It was surveyed in 1775 by Henry Pelham, a Boston resident (but a British loyalist), to document both the extent of the city and the fortifications, which the American revolutionaries had built to choke the life out of the British garrison. An advanced line seals off the neck of the Shawmut peninsula, which formed the heart of old Boston before the town expanded by the filling in of wharves and stretches of river to leave formerly waterbound areas today well away from the river's edge. At the top of the map is a facsimile of the 'passport' issued by James Urquhart, the town major, to allow Pelham free passage (the surveying of land at such a time of tension might otherwise have got him arrested as a spy). The quality of the engraving is fine, as befits work associated with the half-brother of the great Bostonian portraitist John Singleton Copley. In letters to his half-brother, Pelham documented Boston's agony as it endured a long siege by the revolutionaries: 'Fences pulled down, houses removed. Woods grubbed up. Fields cut into trenches … a great number of Wooden House, perhaps 150, have been pulled down to serve for fuel.' It was all in vain, though, for by the time the map was published in 1777 it had become redundant, because in March the previous year the British had evacuated the city, never to return.

Questions

1 A mental vote churned around to make flour?

2 Loading for a signature?

3 What links a housekeeper, an explorer and a car manufacturer to make a point?

4 A painter's mound?

5 This water's name is also mysterious.

6 Use your brain to find this place.

7 This place sounds like a flower.

8 Shelter here from the battle?

Answers are on pages 219–20 at the back of the book

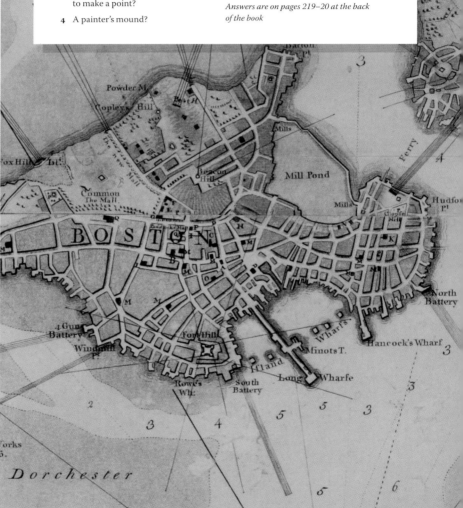

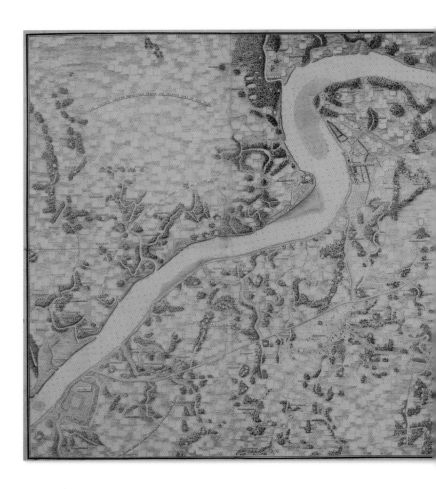

EAST BANK OF
THE HUGHLY

1785

MARK WOOD

I n the 1780s the British East India
Company was still coming to terms
with the vast expansion of the territories
it controlled in North India following the
victory of its army led by Robert Clive at
Plassey in 1757. By the mid-1760s, most
of Bengal and parts of Bihar had been
annexed, followed by a push westward
towards Varanasi and the lands of the
Nawab of Ghazipur. At the heart of this
newly expanded domain was Fort William,

the East India Company's chief stronghold in India, first built in 1696, and the scene of the infamous 'Black Hole of Calcutta' incident in June 1756, when over 140 British prisoners, imprisoned in an airless dungeon at the fort after its fall to the Nawab of Bengal, suffocated to death. It was this atrocity that prompted Clive's intervention, the defeat of the nawab and the British annexation of Bengal. Mark Wood, a captain in the service of the East India Company's army, was tasked in 1780

with producing a map of the area around Fort William (which later grew into the enormous metropolis of Kolkata). It took him four years to produce this meticulously draughted map, with features such as woods, fields and waterways lovingly engraved. The section shown is part of the 24 Parghanas district, just to the west of Fort William.

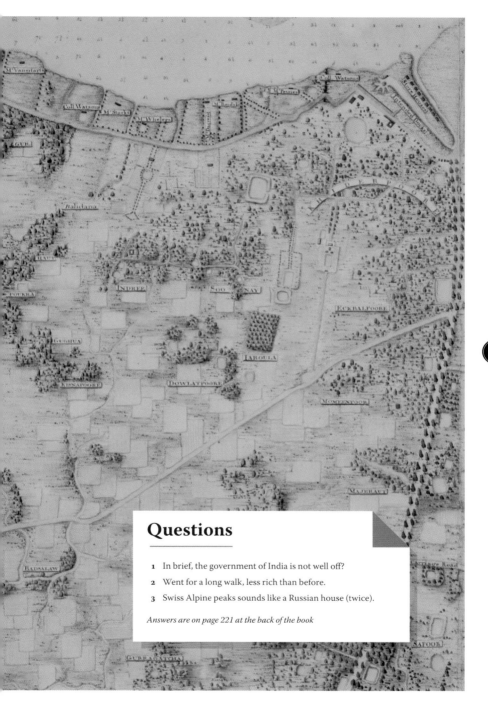

Questions

1   In brief, the government of India is not well off?

2   Went for a long walk, less rich than before.

3   Swiss Alpine peaks sounds like a Russian house (twice).

Answers are on page 221 at the back of the book

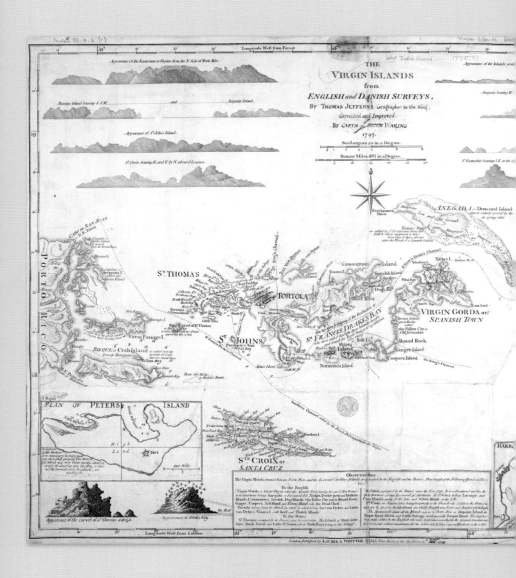

THE
VIRGIN ISLANDS
from
ENGLISH and DANISH SURVEYS,
By THOMAS JEFFERYS Geographer to the King,
Corrected and Improved
By CAPTN WARING
1797

THE VIRGIN ISLANDS

1797

THOMAS JEFFERYS

B ritain's possessions in the Caribbean had grown steadily since the acquisition of Jamaica in 1655, and the addition of a part of the Virgin Islands to the east of Puerto Rico underlined the need for better maps to show the new colonies. Thomas Jefferys, whose career began as cartographer to George III when he was still Prince of Wales and continued in an official capacity once his patron became king in 1760, was a prolific mapmaker (see pages 92–5). His publications included a map of North America surveyed for him by one John Green, a shadowy figure who originally went by the name of Bradock Meade, but who had changed identity after he became caught up in a scandal involving the kidnapping of a 12-year-old Irish heiress as a means of extorting money. Meade's accomplice was hanged; he spent time in jail, and afterwards, understandably shy of publicity, went under a variety of aliases, including Green and Rogers. Jefferys himself gained more fame than wealth from his work and he died, impoverished, in 1771. His papers were gathered together and part-published as a *West India Atlas*, of which this plate formed a part. The map is replete with topographical views and annotations of interesting features of the islands, including two insets giving details of the major harbours.

Green Island

Mitre Rock

Little Tobago

Great Tobago

King's Channel

Jost van Dykes

Little van Dykes

Fisherman's Head

Cammanoes

Guana I.

Green Island

Brewers Bay

Point

Cooks Pt.

East End Bay

East Pt.

Red Hook Pt.

C

LEYANGO

Little James

TORTOLA

Beef Island

Garden Bay

Fat Hog Bay

Tower Fort

Harbour

Christian's Fort

Rose Bay

Salt's Pt.

Sunken Rock

Jansens Pt.

Buck Id.

Thatch Islands

Cam. Islands

Frenchman's Key

Dutch Head

Sea Cows Bay

Salt Id.

the Virgins Gangway of the Freebooters

St. James's Passage

St. JOHNS

SR. FRANCIS DRAKES

who first sailed through these Islands in

and found the Depth from 10 to 25

very rocky

Frenchman's Rock

or Birds Key

Castle

North Fort

English Keys

Peters Island

Drake's Channel

Witch I.

Ducks I.

South Pte.

Crawl Bay

Wells

the Dead Che

Ram's Head

Normands Island

South W. Pt.

n Bluff

d Bay

Wills Bay

Cane Bay

Little Cane Bay

River Bay

Southern Channel calle

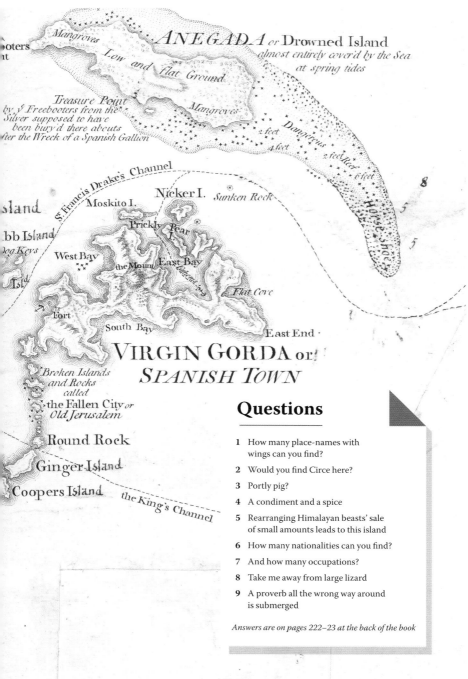

MANGROVES
oters
it

ANEGADA or Drowned Island
almost entirely cover'd by the Sea
at spring tides

Low and *Flat Ground*

Mangroves

Treasure Point
by y.ᵉ Freebooters from th.
Silver supposed to have
been bury'd there abouts
ter the Wreck of a Spanish Galleon

2 feet
Dangerous
4 feet
2 feet *Reef* 6 feet
Horse Shoe

St. Francis Drake's Channel

island
bb Island
eg Keys
Isl.

Moskito I.

Nicker I.

Sunken Rock

Prickly Pear J.

West Bay
the Moun.
East Bay
Gorboma ?

Flat Cove

Fort

South Bay

East End ·

VIRGIN GORDA or
SPANISH TOWN

Broken Islands
and Rocks
called
the Fallen City *or*
Old Jerusalem

Round Rock

Ginger Island

Coopers Island

the King's Channel

Questions

1 How many place-names with wings can you find?

2 Would you find Circe here?

3 Portly pig?

4 A condiment and a spice

5 Rearranging Himalayan beasts' sale of small amounts leads to this island

6 How many nationalities can you find?

7 And how many occupations?

8 Take me away from large lizard

9 A proverb all the wrong way around is submerged

Answers are on pages 222–23 at the back of the book

CAERNARFONSHIRE

1816

ROBERT DAWSON

Official support for mapping in Britain, as elsewhere in Europe, was often prompted by concerns about possible foreign invaders. Without knowing the terrain, it could not be defended. The Ordnance Survey (OS), founded in 1791, was a 'child' born out of paranoia about the intentions of the French Revolutionary government. (Not without some justification – an invasion force gathered in 1798 and then

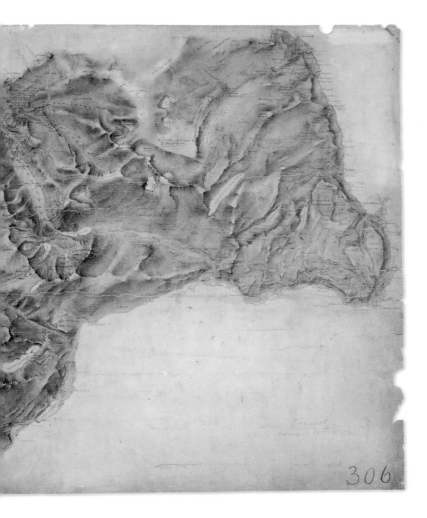

306

another in 1803, when around 200,000 men of the Armée de l'Angleterre camped around Boulogne waiting for the order to cross the Channel, and in 1797 the French really did land in Wales, albeit with a small force that was soon dealt with when it became drunk after raiding a wine store.) Even after the immediate threat had passed following the British naval victory at Trafalgar in 1805, the OS continued its work, gradually assembling a map of England and Wales. The compilation of this map of Caernarfonshire must have been gruelling, involving a team of geodetic surveyors working on the ground, first to establish 'triangles' based on landmarks, and then painstakingly recording geographical features. The Caernarfonshire map was surveyed by one of the OS's most talented operators, its senior surveying teacher Robert Dawson, whose finely sketched contouring brings a vivid sense of immediacy to the landscape.

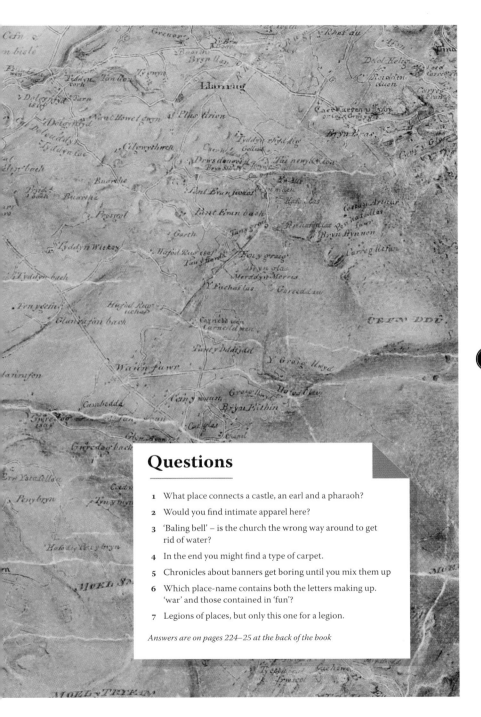

Questions

1 What place connects a castle, an earl and a pharaoh?

2 Would you find intimate apparel here?

3 'Baling bell' – is the church the wrong way around to get rid of water?

4 In the end you might find a type of carpet.

5 Chronicles about banners get boring until you mix them up

6 Which place-name contains both the letters making up. 'war' and those contained in 'fun'?

7 Legions of places, but only this one for a legion.

Answers are on pages 224–25 at the back of the book

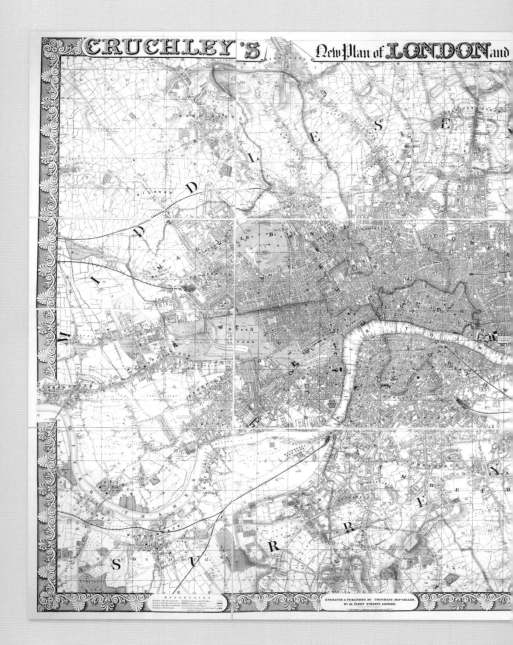

CRUCHLEY'S New Plan of LONDON and

ENGRAVED & PUBLISHED BY CRUCHLEY, MAP-SELLER,
No 81 FLEET STREET, LONDON.

LONDON

1847

GEORGE CRUCHLEY

B y the late eighteenth century, the River Thames was appallingly congested, with thousands of small boats clogging up the waterway and inadequate provision to dock and unload cargo (which had instead to be done by a fleet of lighters, or small boats, whose boatmen took a hefty cut and were not averse to pilfering). A Parliamentary Commission in 1796 proposed the building of a series of new docks to improve the situation, beginning north of the river with West India Docks, which were opened in 1802. The excavation of the new facilities transformed the area in the map, with the Surrey Commercial Docks bringing new life south of the river, as dock workers, industries and new housing all swarmed in. George Frederick Cruchley, who compiled this map, saw the need to document a rapidly changing London, and his 'New Plan' went through at least 11 editions between 1827 and 1857. The area around the docklands, in particular, is a testament to the rapid rate of change, with traditional features such as the watermen's steps (some picturesquely named, like the Shepherd and Dog Stairs and Pageant Stairs) juxtaposed with the massive basins of the new dock system.

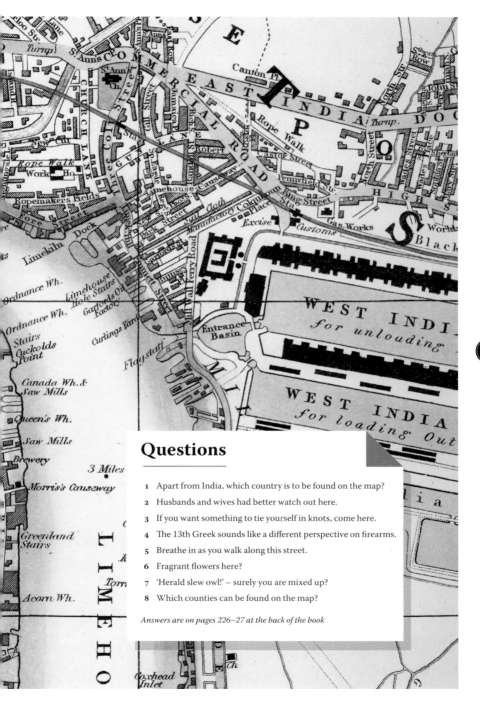

Questions

1. Apart from India, which country is to be found on the map?
2. Husbands and wives had better watch out here.
3. If you want something to tie yourself in knots, come here.
4. The 13th Greek sounds like a different perspective on firearms.
5. Breathe in as you walk along this street.
6. Fragrant flowers here?
7. 'Herald slew owl!' – surely you are mixed up?
8. Which counties can be found on the map?

Answers are on pages 226–27 at the back of the book

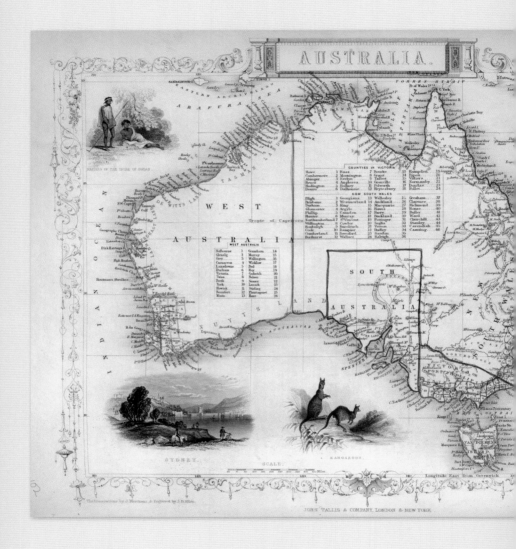

AUSTRALIA

1851

JOHN TALLIS

John Tallis's *Illustrated Atlas of the World*, which includes this map of Australia, was issued in 1851 to accompany the Great Exhibition held in London that year. Beautifully engraved, it shows a country where there were still plenty of blanks. The coastal areas, heavily settled since the arrival of the First Fleet in 1788, are densely scattered with towns and other settlements, while the inhospitable deserts of the interior are only lightly populated with a sprinkling of place-names and a dose of speculation. Lake Torrens in South Australia is optimistically shown as a long horseshoe-shaped waterway sweeping into the interior and the whole of inland Western Australia and the Northern Territories is a blank. The first successful south to north crossing of the continent did not take place until John McDouall Stuart reached the north coast on 24 July 1862 (and arrived safely back in Adelaide five months later).

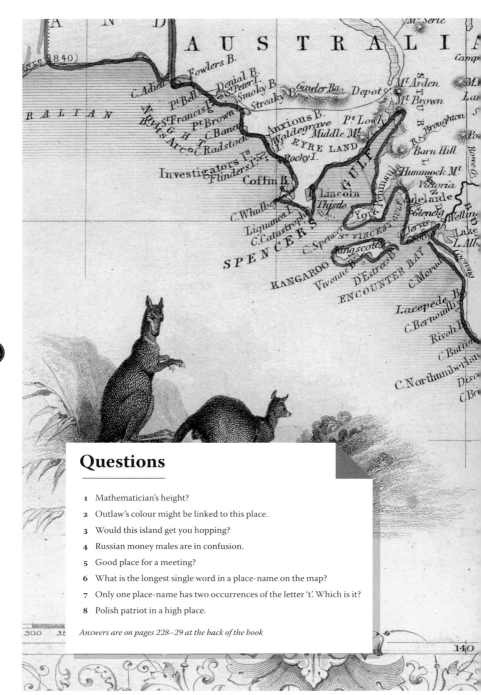

Questions

1 Mathematician's height?

2 Outlaw's colour might be linked to this place.

3 Would this island get you hopping?

4 Russian money males are in confusion.

5 Good place for a meeting?

6 What is the longest single word in a place-name on the map?

7 Only one place-name has two occurrences of the letter 't'. Which is it?

8 Polish patriot in a high place.

Answers are on pages 228–29 at the back of the book

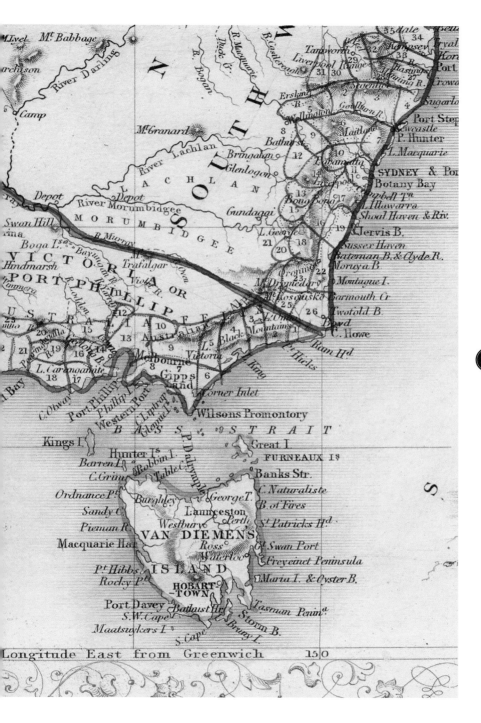

Mt Livel   Mt Babbage
Murchison   River Darling   R. Bogan   R. Castlereagh
                                                    R. Macquarie
Camp   B. of N. W.

N

Mt Granard   Erslang R.   Tamworth
                                                    Liverpool Range   2   Hastings
                                    River Lachlan   Bringalow   Wellington   31 30   Suventa   Manning R.   Crowa
                        Glenlogon   Bathurst   R.   Goulburn R.   8   9   Maitland   Newcastle   Port Step
LACHLAN   Gundagai   12   Parramatta   Newcastle   P. Hunter
                                            10   11   Liverpool   L. Macquarie
MORUMBIDGEE   River Morumbidgee   13   Bong Bong   15   Campbell Tn   SYDNEY & Po
                        Depot   Depot   14   Liverpool   Botany Bay
Swan Hill   R. Murray   L. George   21   20   18   22   Illawarra   Shoal Haven & Riv.
Boga Is?.   23   Mt Dromedary   Jervis B.
VICTORIA   Bayouri R.   Trafalgar   Ovens   25   26   Montague I.   Sussex Haven
Hindmarsh   PORT PHILLIP   Viola   Mt Kosciusko   Twofold B.   Bateman B. & Clyde R.
                        Loddon R.   Mt Cole   Bald   Boyd   Moruya B.
                    20   15   10   Ausn   13   1   C. Howe
21   R. 19   Victoria   14   9   Victoria   King   Bass Hd.
L. Caranoamite   8   Gipps   6   Pt Hicks
18   17   Melbourne   Land
                    Port Phillip   Corner Inlet
            Western Port   Wilsons Promontory
                Alberton   B A S S   S T R A I T
Kings I.   Hunter Is   Great I.
        Barren I.   Robbin I.   FURNEAUX Is
        C. Grim   Tablet   Banks Str.
Ordnance Pt   Burghley   George T.   C. Naturaliste
        Sandy C   Westbury   Launceston   B. of Fires
        Pieman R.   Perth   St Patricks Hd
            VAN DIEMENS   Gt Swan Port
Macquarie Har   Ross   Freycinet Peninsula
            Waterloo
Pt Hibbs   I S L A N D   Maria I. & Oyster B.
        Rocky Pt   HOBART
                -TOWN
    Port Davey   Bathust Hr   Tasman Penina
        S.W. Cape   Storm B.
    Maatsuylers I.   S. Cape   Bruny I.

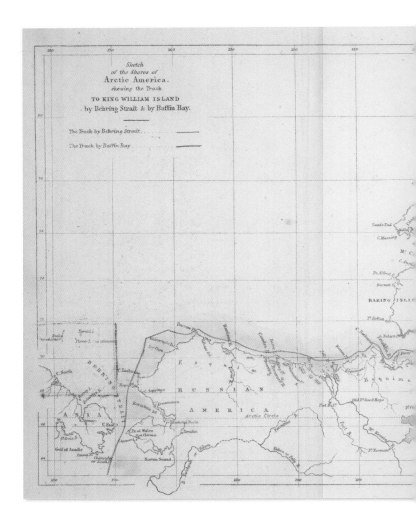

THE FRANKLIN
SEARCH

1857

LADY JANE FRANKLIN

Lady Jane Franklin was a remarkably determined woman. Her husband set out in May 1845 in command of an expedition to chart the Northwest Passage, a sea route to the Pacific believed to exist to the north of Canada. After a stop on Orkney he vanished, and neither Sir John Franklin nor his crew were ever seen alive again. Lady Franklin began a vigorous lobbying campaign to get the British government to send out a search expedition. She published this map

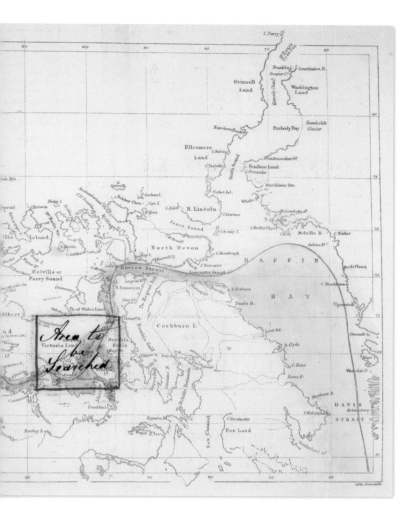

in 1857 in a pamphlet entitled *A Letter to Viscount Palmerston* (then the prime minister), indicating with a bold pen annotation where she considered the search should best be concentrated. Expeditions were soon combing the Canadian Arctic, beginning with an overland mission led by John Rae in 1848, and at the effort's peak in 1850 over a dozen ships were involved. On a further expedition in 1854, Rae uncovered evidence that some of Franklin's crew had turned to cannibalism in an attempt to survive the harsh conditions. In 1859 Francis

Leopold McClintock found a message left in a cairn on King William Island, which showed that the crew had tried to trek inland. After an expedition in 1984 exhumed some of the graves it was determined the crew had suffered lead poisoning, possibly from tins of food improperly soldered with lead, and cut-marks were found on the bones, which supported earlier reports of cannibalism. The wrecks of Franklin's two ships the *Erebus* and *Terror* were located off King William Island in 2014 and 2016.

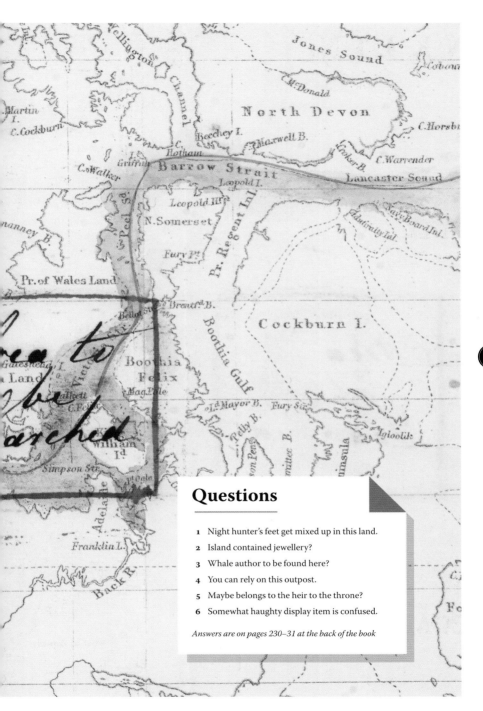

Questions

1 Night hunter's feet get mixed up in this land.
2 Island contained jewellery?
3 Whale author to be found here?
4 You can rely on this outpost.
5 Maybe belongs to the heir to the throne?
6 Somewhat haughty display item is confused.

Answers are on pages 230–31 at the back of the book

STANNARD & SON'S PERSPECTIVE VIEW OF AFG.

WITH ALL THE PASSES LEADING TO THE CITY OF CABUL, TOGETHER WITH OUR INDIAN BOUNDARIES TO QUETTAH, & THE RUSSIAN TO KHIVA & THE RIVER OXUS, COMPILED FROM THE LATEST RELIABLE SOURCES.

PRINTED & PUBLISHED AS THE ACT DIRECTS, OCTr 12th 1878, BY STANNARD & SON'S, POLAND ST OXFORD ST LONDON W.

AFGHANISTAN

1878

ALFRED CONCANEN

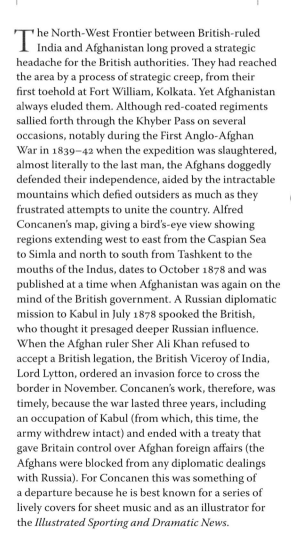

T he North-West Frontier between British-ruled India and Afghanistan long proved a strategic headache for the British authorities. They had reached the area by a process of strategic creep, from their first toehold at Fort William, Kolkata. Yet Afghanistan always eluded them. Although red-coated regiments sallied forth through the Khyber Pass on several occasions, notably during the First Anglo-Afghan War in 1839–42 when the expedition was slaughtered, almost literally to the last man, the Afghans doggedly defended their independence, aided by the intractable mountains which defied outsiders as much as they frustrated attempts to unite the country. Alfred Concanen's map, giving a bird's-eye view showing regions extending west to east from the Caspian Sea to Simla and north to south from Tashkent to the mouths of the Indus, dates to October 1878 and was published at a time when Afghanistan was again on the mind of the British government. A Russian diplomatic mission to Kabul in July 1878 spooked the British, who thought it presaged deeper Russian influence. When the Afghan ruler Sher Ali Khan refused to accept a British legation, the British Viceroy of India, Lord Lytton, ordered an invasion force to cross the border in November. Concanen's work, therefore, was timely, because the war lasted three years, including an occupation of Kabul (from which, this time, the army withdrew intact) and ended with a treaty that gave Britain control over Afghan foreign affairs (the Afghans were blocked from any diplomatic dealings with Russia). For Concanen this was something of a departure because he is best known for a series of lively covers for sheet music and as an illustrator for the *Illustrated Sporting and Dramatic News*.

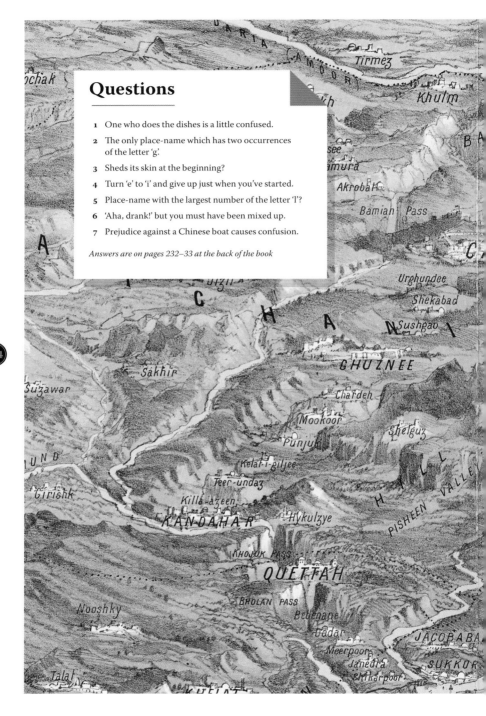

Questions

1 One who does the dishes is a little confused.

2 The only place-name which has two occurrences of the letter 'g'.

3 Sheds its skin at the beginning?

4 Turn 'e' to 'i' and give up just when you've started.

5 Place-name with the largest number of the letter 'l'?

6 'Aha, drank!' but you must have been mixed up.

7 Prejudice against a Chinese boat causes confusion.

Answers are on pages 232–33 at the back of the book

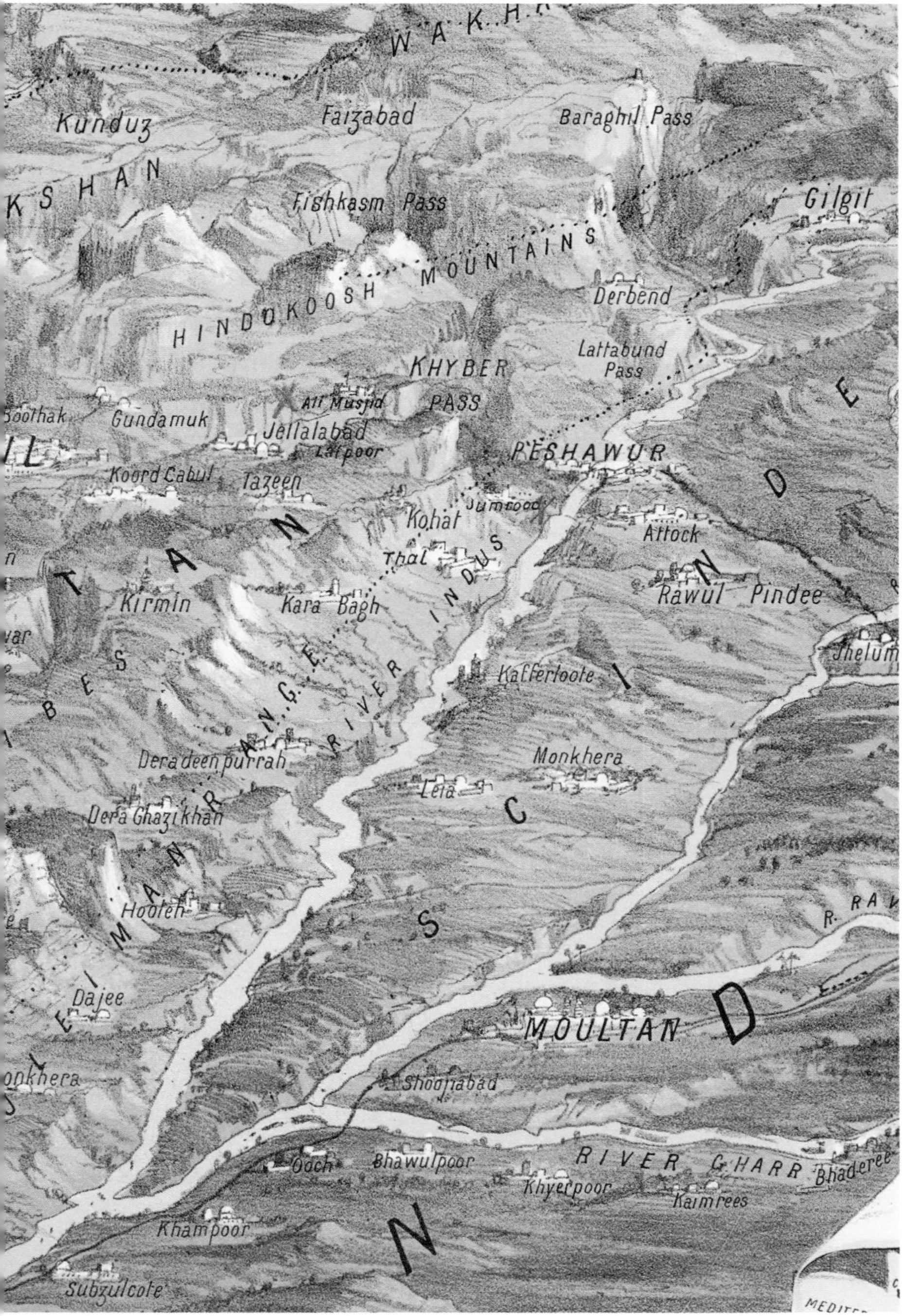

WAKHA

Kunduz

Faizabad

Baraghil Pass

KSHAN

Tishkasm Pass

Gilgit

HINDOKOOSH MOUNTAINS

Derbend

Lattabund Pass

KHYBER PASS

Soothak   Gundamuk   Ali Musjid   Jellalabad   Latpoor

Koord Cabul   Tazeen

PESHAWUR

IL

TAN

Kohat   Jumrood

Thal   Attock

Kirmin   Kara Bagh   Rawul Pindee

RIVER INDUS

Jhelum

BES

RANGE

Katterloote

Deradeenpurrah   Monkhera

Dera Ghazikhan   Leia   C

MAN

Hooleh   S

Dajee

RAV

onkhera   MOULTAN   D

Shoolabad

Odch   Bhawulpoor   RIVER GHARR   Bhaderee

Khyerpoor   Kaimrees

Khampoor   N

Subzulcote

MEDITER

POVERTY IN
LONDON'S EAST END
1902

CHARLES BOOTH

Although born into a wealthy shipping family, Victorian social reformer Charles Booth made the less fortunate his life's work. Specifically, mapping the poor. His great work of social geography, *Life and Labour of the People in London*, published between 1889 and 1902, was compiled from huge numbers of interviews conducted by a panel, which included his cousin, the Fabian Beatrice Webb, and the statistician George Arkell. Booth's publication attempted to create a survey of the relative levels of poverty and deprivation in London's boroughs and was accompanied by a series of detailed maps colour-coded according to the predominant social class living in an area, street by street. The coding ranged from yellow, the highest, representing 'Upper-middle and Upper classes. Wealthy' through a gradation of decreasing affluence, down to dark blue for 'Very poor, casual. Chronic want' and black, the very lowest, which Booth labelled as 'Lowest class. Vicious, semi-criminal'. The East End, depicted in this map from the 1902 edition of Booth's book, shows a surprising level of red hues, indicating relatively well-to-do families, although there are significant patches in the north and in courts and alleys off the main road, which were afflicted with almost chronic poverty.

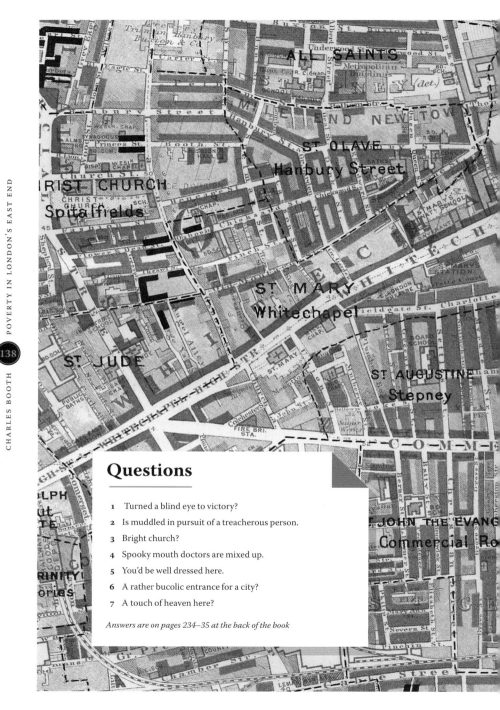

Questions

1 Turned a blind eye to victory?

2 Is muddled in pursuit of a treacherous person.

3 Bright church?

4 Spooky mouth doctors are mixed up.

5 You'd be well dressed here.

6 A rather bucolic entrance for a city?

7 A touch of heaven here?

Answers are on pages 234–35 at the back of the book

UNDERGROUND ELECTRIC RAILWAY

THE TUBE

1907

LONDON UNDERGROUND
RAILWAYS

M id-Victorian London faced a transport crisis.
Although horse-drawn buses had begun to
provide some level of public transportation, their
capacity was limited. The railways did facilitate
long-distance travel, but were not practical for those
living in the suburbs. It was obviously not possible to
demolish great swathes of the capital to make way for
new stations and so a new solution had to be devised.
The first underground railway, the Metropolitan, from
Baker Street to Farringdon, was opened in 1863 and
gradually extended east and west, joined in 1864 by a
rival District railway to provide a circular route around
the centre. By the 1880s, though, even this system was
proving inadequate and new deep-level tunnels were
cut through, with trains run by electricity, rather than
diesel (which caused choking fumes underground).
The City and South London Railway was begun in 1886
to run south, ultimately to Stockwell. The Charing
Cross, Euston and Hampstead Railway opened up
in 1907, providing a route to the north of the centre,
and the Great Northern, Piccadilly and Brompton
Railway began operations in 1906, running through
from Finsbury Park in the north to Hammersmith in
the west. By 1907 the system was more complex than
ever and tube maps such as this began to appear to help
confused travellers navigate. Unlike today's versions,
which are based on a revolutionary design introduced
by Harry Beck in 1931, the tube lines are superimposed
on a map of the street grid above ground, making them
a challenge to read and a torment to plan a route with.

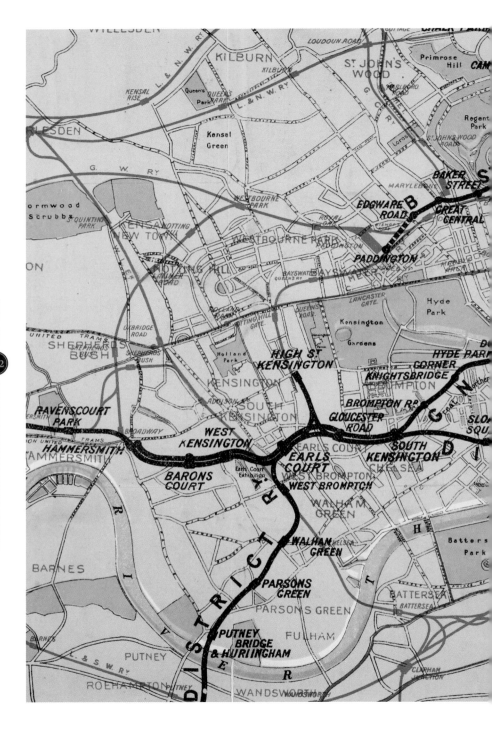

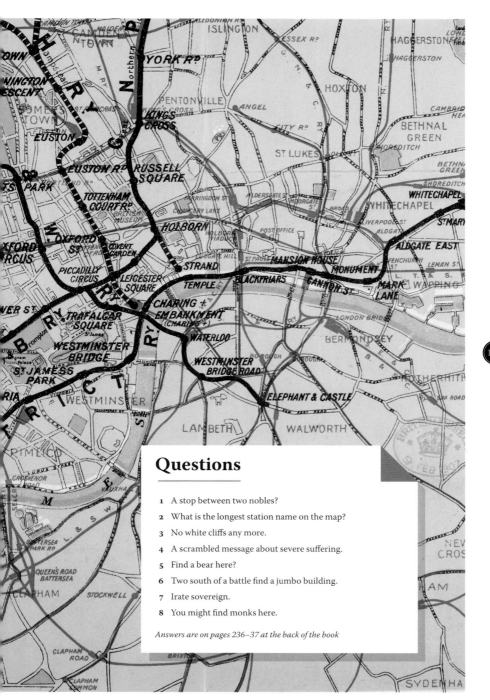

Questions

1 A stop between two nobles?

2 What is the longest station name on the map?

3 No white cliffs any more.

4 A scrambled message about severe suffering.

5 Find a bear here?

6 Two south of a battle find a jumbo building.

7 Irate sovereign.

8 You might find monks here.

Answers are on pages 236–37 at the back of the book

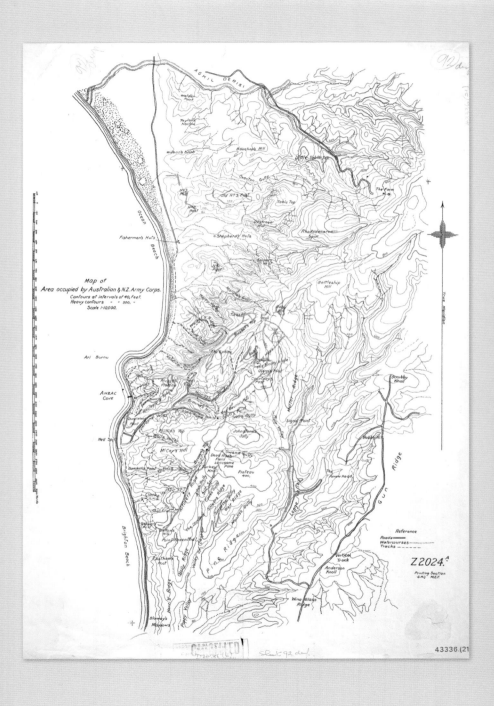

Map of
Area occupied by Australian & N.Z. Army Corps.
Contours at intervals of 40 Feet.
Heavy contours   -   - 200. -
Scale 1:10,000.

AGHIL DERISI

Walden Road

Taylors Hollow

Wilson's Knob

Baucheps Hill

Little Table Top

Overton Gully

The Farm

Old N? 3 Post

Table Top

Destroyer Hill

Rhododendron Spur

Fishermen's Huts

Shepherdy Huts

Ocean Beach

Battleship Hill

Ari Burnu

ANZAC COVE

Hell Spit

Plugge's Top

MacLaurin's Hill

Johnstone's Jolly

Scrubby Knoll

Hobby's Hill

Signal Point

The Temple Head

Steele's Post

Dead Man's Field
Lonesome Pine

Plateau
400.

Brighton Beach

Slacks

Turkey Knoll

Cheshire Ridge

Holly Ridge

War Ridge

Holly Ridge

Vertical Track

Anderson Knoll

P I O N R i d g e

GUN Ridge

Wine Glass Ridge

Reference
Roads
Watercourses
Tracks

Z 2024.ª

Printing Section
G.H.Q. M.E.F.

Blamey's Meadows

Brighton Beach

Rhatham's Post

True Meridian

True Meridian

43336.(21

GALLIPOLI

1915

GENERAL HEADQUARTERS, MIDDLE EAST FORCES

The Gallipoli Campaign of 1915 was supposed to knock Ottoman Turkey out of World War One with an Allied thrust north from the Gallipoli peninsula towards Istanbul, which would force the Turkish government to sue for peace. Instead, the Allied forces that landed on 25 April 1915 at Cape Helles and Anzac Cove soon lost their impetus as Turkish resistance stiffened, becoming bogged down in the maze of ridges, gulleys and high points which dotted the peninsula. The invasion force consisted of large contingents of French and British troops, and the men of the Australian and New Zealand Army Corps (ANZACs) who for the next eight months endured terrible conditions as successive attempts to break out failed (including the establishment of a new bridgehead at Suvla, a little to

the north). The map shows the position in June, when the lines had become largely stagnant: the green of the Turkish positions opposed to the truncated red bulge of the Allied holdings, while the close-packed contouring vividly suggests the bewildering complexity of the terrain. Most of the features of the landscape have been given new names by the Allies (with Ari Burnu, north of Anzac Cove, one of the few to retain its original Turkish form). Some were named for commanders, such as Monash Gully, others like Bloody Angle or Dead Man's Hill are in bitter homage to the huge losses the ANZACs suffered during the campaign before their final withdrawal from Anzac Cove and Suvla on 20 December 1915, and from Cape Helles on 7 January 1916.

ustralian & N.Z. Army Corps.

at intervals of 40, Feet.
tours   ”   ”   200, ”
ale 1·10,000,

Happy Valley

Walker's Ridge

Mule Gully

The Sphi

Burnu

Reserve Gully

Plugges
Plateau

Maclagan's Ridge

Reserve

Monash   Gully

Braund's Hill

Bridges Road

ANZAC
COVE

Mac
Sco

Queensland
Point

Shrapnel Valley

Phillip's Top

White Valley

Hell Spit

McCay's Hill

Brown's Dip

Dead Man
Field
Loneso
Pi

Dawkins Point   Victoria   Gully

Turkey
Knoll

Road   Gully   Spur

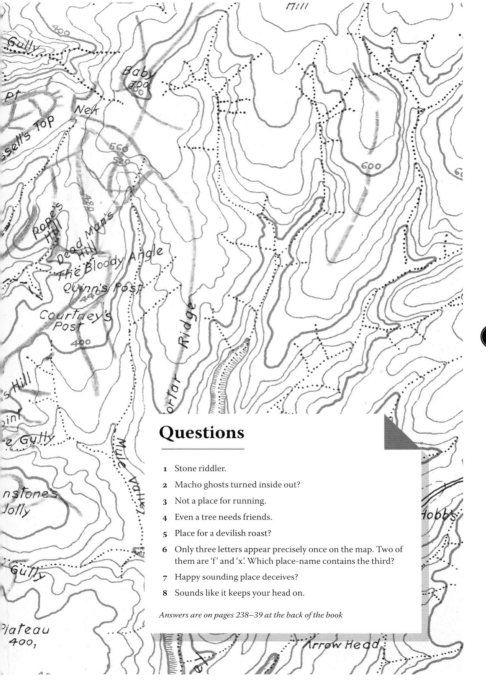

Questions

1 Stone riddler.

2 Macho ghosts turned inside out?

3 Not a place for running.

4 Even a tree needs friends.

5 Place for a devilish roast?

6 Only three letters appear precisely once on the map. Two of them are 'f' and 'x'. Which place-name contains the third?

7 Happy sounding place deceives?

8 Sounds like it keeps your head on.

Answers are on pages 238–39 at the back of the book

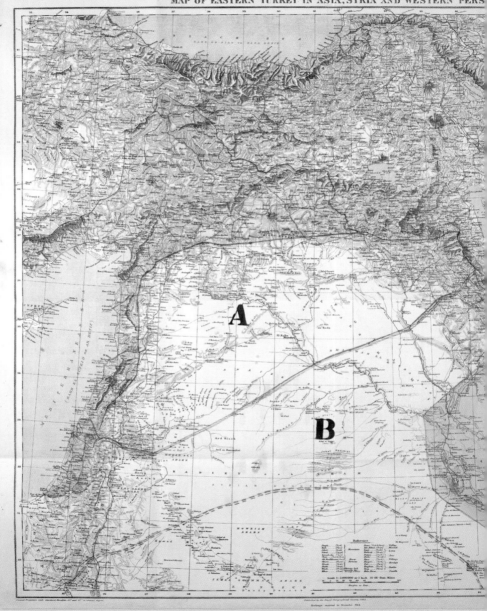

THE SYKES-PICOT
AGREEMENT

1916

MARK SYKES AND
FRANÇOIS-GEORGES PICOT

To the western European powers which carved up the globe in the nineteenth century, cartography was power. Maps were used by imperialist policymakers to make lines in the jungle, steppe and sand which native peoples were forced to accept. When the Ottoman Empire began its terminal decay in the 1870s, France and Britain sought to benefit in its southern provinces by means of a mixture of promises to local Arab leaders and diplomatic sleight of hand. The Sykes-Picot Agreement, a secret convention negotiated in 1915–16 between the British diplomat Mark Sykes and his French counterpart François-Georges Picot, created two areas in Syria, Iraq, Jordan and Palestine. In Area A the French would hold sway (with an area marked out in the west representing direct rule, and the rest supposedly enjoying a semi-independent status under Arab rulers). Area B to the south was to be the British sphere of influence, with Iraq – more heavily shaded in pink – and northern Israel under their direct control, while what is now southern Israel was to come under international control. The plan never came fully to pass, because the British complicated matters when Prime Minister Arthur Balfour signed a declaration in November 1917 promising to support Jewish immigration into a homeland in Palestine. Then, the plan, which had promised territory on Turkey's northern border to Russia, was leaked by the Bolsheviks who had come to power after the Russian Revolution and rejected it as an imperialist project. Once it became public knowledge, the Sykes-Picot plan was disowned, leaving the map as a monument to imperialist designs.

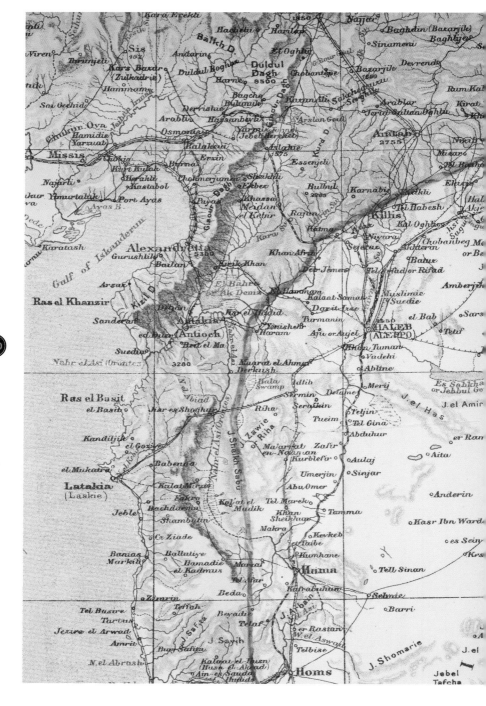

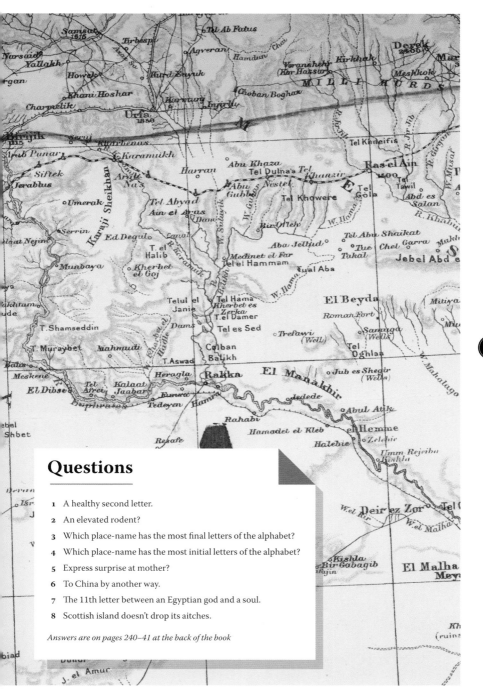

Questions

1 A healthy second letter.

2 An elevated rodent?

3 Which place-name has the most final letters of the alphabet?

4 Which place-name has the most initial letters of the alphabet?

5 Express surprise at mother?

6 To China by another way.

7 The 11th letter between an Egyptian god and a soul.

8 Scottish island doesn't drop its aitches.

Answers are on pages 240–41 at the back of the book

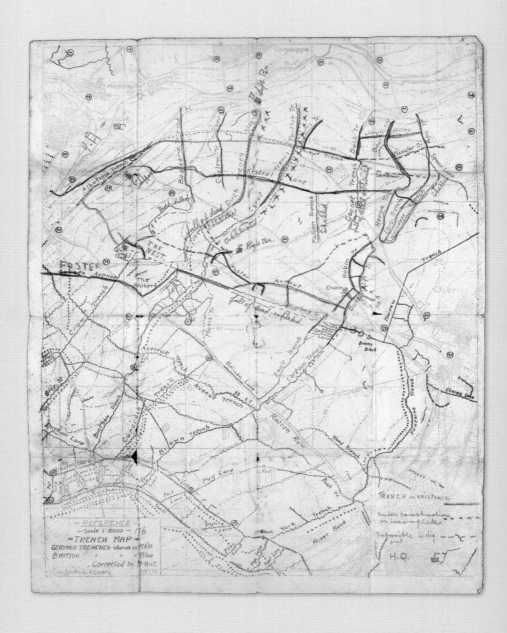

TRENCH MAP
Scale 1:10000 — 176
GERMAN TRENCHES shown in RED
BRITISH · Blue
Corrected to 11·8·17.

TRENCH in existence.
Under construction
or incomplete
impossible to dig
out

H.Q.

THE TRENCHES
NEAR ARRAS
1918
BRITISH MILITARY
INTELLIGENCE

The trench warfare into which World War One degenerated from September 1914 called for a different type of mapping. Very accurate surveying was needed to allow for artillery assault without preliminary ranging shots, which gave away the element of surprise, and to delineate the enemy's trench lines in order to establish objectives for localised offensives. When the British Expeditionary Force arrived in France in 1914, it had just a single officer responsible for mapping, but four year later there were 5,000 men involved in the British Army's cartographic effort, producing millions of map sheets between them. Aerial photography, a new innovation, meant overlapping images could be produced and sent to cartographers to produce a flat-sheet map. Trench lines were added on top of the base printed map, with British trenches generally outlined in blue and the German lines in red. Although there were long periods of relative immobility, small adjustments still had to be made – and this map is shown as corrected to show the position on 7 August 1918. The sector southeast of Arras and south of Guémappe saw two significant periods of fighting: in April 1917 during the Second Battle of Arras, when the Allies made significant advances in the area, including around Guémappe, and during the Hundred Days' Offensive from August 1918, when Allied forces rolled back a German offensive that had begun in the spring and advanced rapidly forwards, making the kind of territorial gains in days and weeks that had previously taken months and years and cost hundreds of thousands of lives.

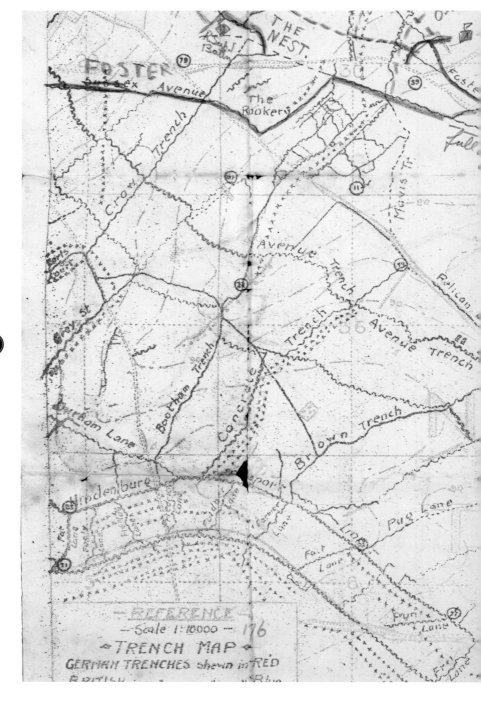

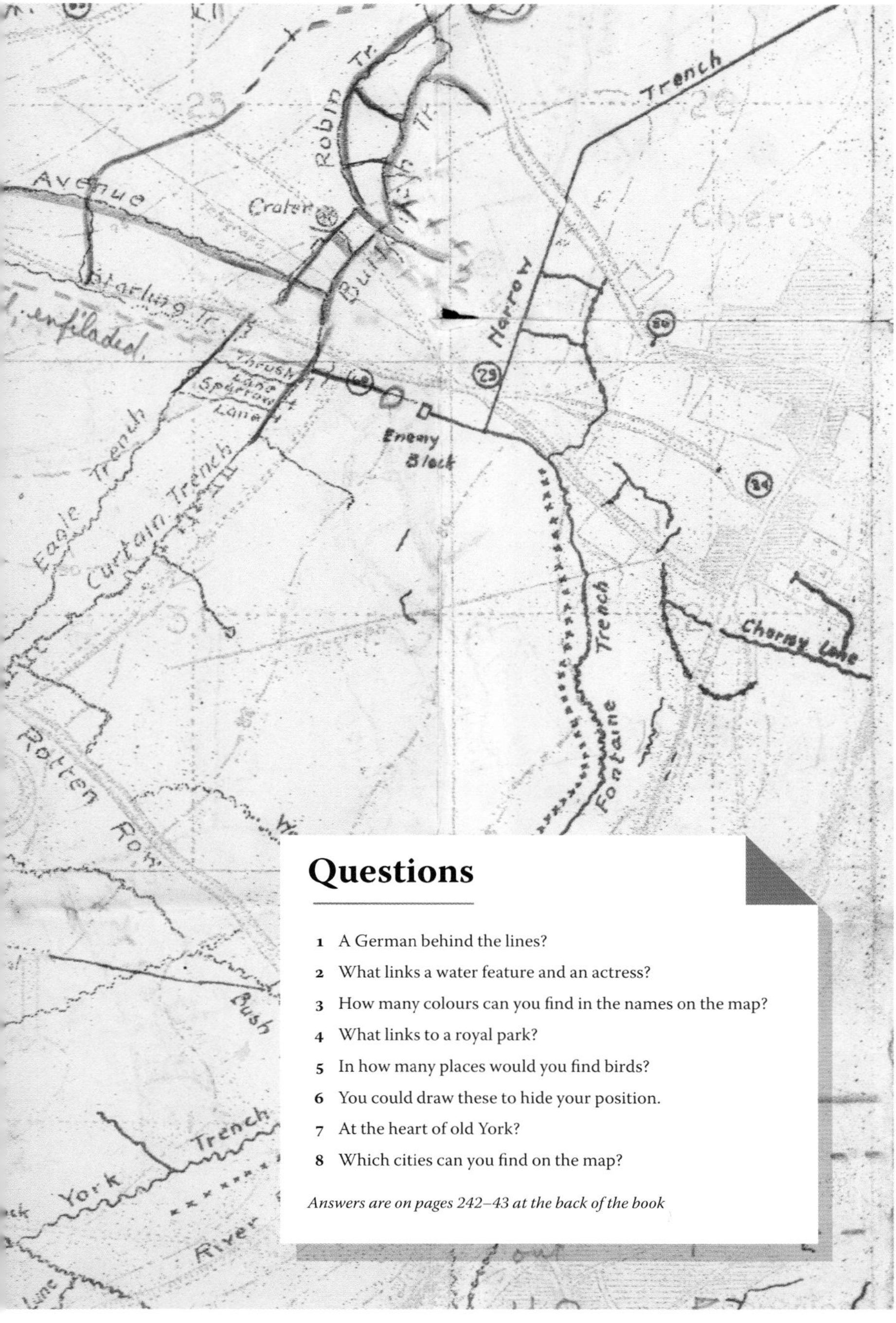

Robin Tr.

Trench

Avenue

Crater

Cherisy

Bullring Tr.

Harrow

Enfiladed.

Starling Tr.

Thrush Lane

Sparrow Lane

Enemy Block

Eagle Trench

Curtain Trench

Fontaine Trench

Chorny Lane

Rotten Row

York Trench

York River

Bush

Questions

1 A German behind the lines?

2 What links a water feature and an actress?

3 How many colours can you find in the names on the map?

4 What links to a royal park?

5 In how many places would you find birds?

6 You could draw these to hide your position.

7 At the heart of old York?

8 Which cities can you find on the map?

Answers are on pages 242–43 at the back of the book

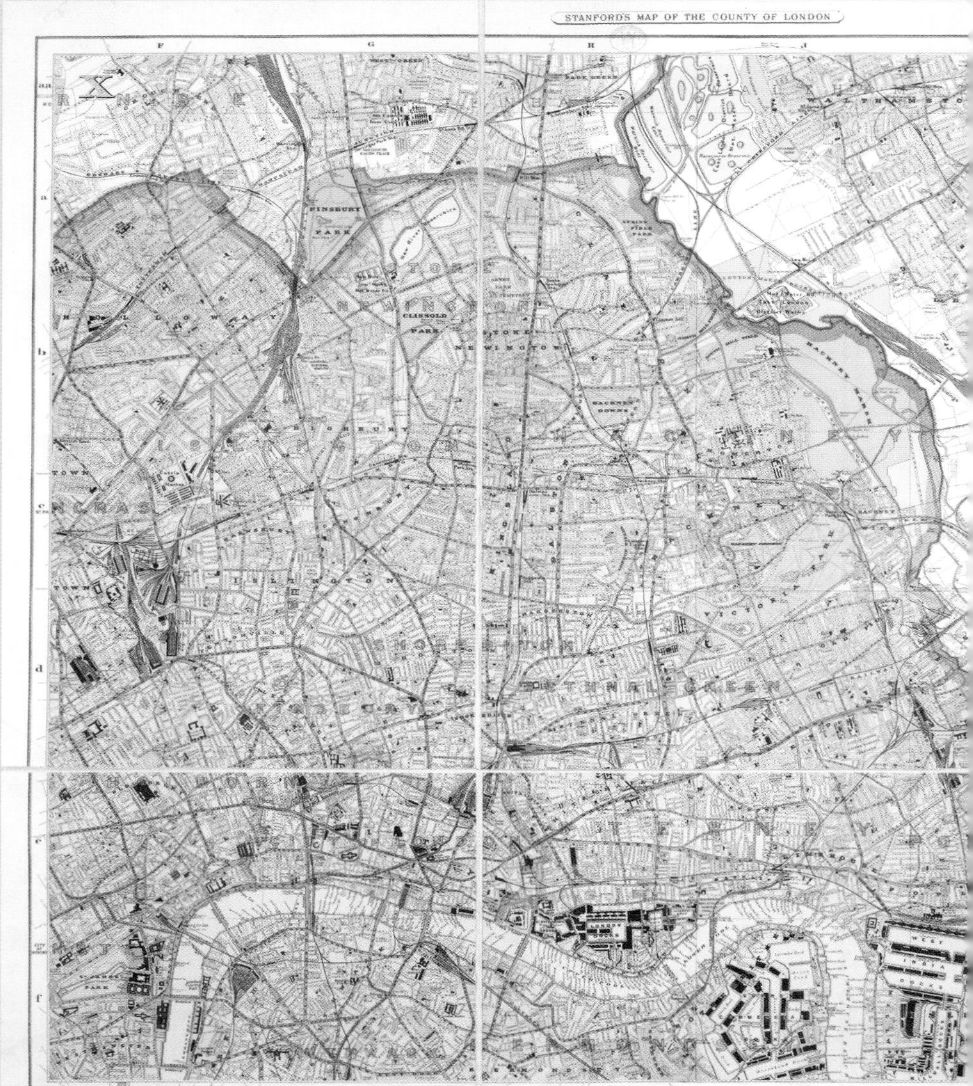

STANFORD'S MAP OF THE COUNTY OF LONDON
F
G
H
J
FINSBURY PARK
CLISSOLD PARK
STOKE NEWINGTON
HACKNEY DOWNS
HACKNEY MARSH
VICTORIA PARK
ISLINGTON
HIGHBURY
SHOREDITCH
BETHNAL GREEN
WALTHAMSTOW
WEST INDIA DOCKS
PRINTED IN GT BRITAIN

LONDON

1928

STANFORD'S LIMITED

As London grew during the reign of Queen Victoria from a relatively modest 1.8 million inhabitants to a giant of 6.5 million people by her death in 1901, so it spread outwards, adding a dizzying array of new suburbs to an already labyrinthine centre. Londoners, who could increasingly get about by bus, train and the new-fangled underground railway, which opened in 1863 (see page 141), increasingly needed guides to help them navigate around a city where word-of-mouth or half-remembered directions would no longer serve. Into this breach stepped men like Edward Stanford, who began his career as an assistant to a mapseller, and took over the business when his master got into financial difficulties in 1852. From 1858 he began producing his own maps, beginning with one of Europe and culminating in a series of detailed maps of London. This one, produced in 1928, 14 years after Stanford's death, combines clarity with a clear love of the cartographer's art.

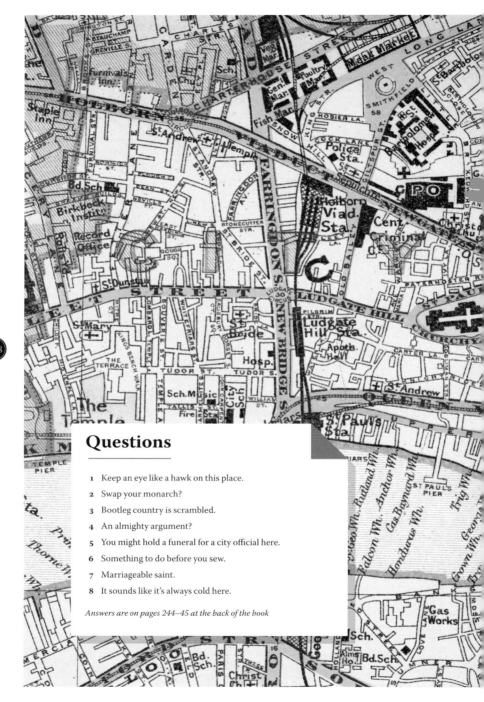

Questions

1   Keep an eye like a hawk on this place.

2   Swap your monarch?

3   Bootleg country is scrambled.

4   An almighty argument?

5   You might hold a funeral for a city official here.

6   Something to do before you sew.

7   Marriageable saint.

8   It sounds like it's always cold here.

Answers are on pages 244–45 at the back of the book

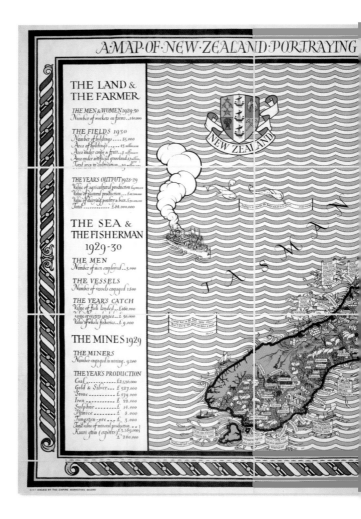

NEW ZEALAND

1930

MACDONALD GILL

T his 1930 map of New Zealand is a riot of green, grazed on by an assortment of agricultural animals interspersed with scrolls naming the country's growing cities. It is a typical product of Macdonald Gill, one of the leading practitioners of illustrated mapping in the first half of the twentieth century. Having cut his teeth on work for London Underground, with the joyously vibrant *Wonderground Map* of London, his work in the 1920s included a *Highways of Empire* map that caused a traffic jam when a poster containing it

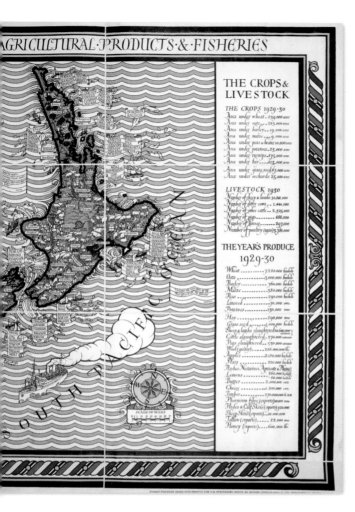

AGRICULTURAL·PRODUCTS·&·FISHERIES

THE CROPS &
LIVESTOCK

THE CROPS 1929-30
Area under wheat - 259,000 acres
Area under oats .. - 283,000 acres
Area under barley .. - 51,000 acres
Area under maize .. - 9,000 acres
Area under peas & beans 10,000 acres
Area under potatoes - 23,000 acres
Area under turnips,175,000 acres
Area under hay ....515,000 acres
Area under grass seed 67,000 acres
Area under orchards 25,000 acres

LIVESTOCK 1930
Number of sheep & lambs 30,841,000
Number of dairy cows - 1,446,000
Number of other cattle - 2,525,000
Number of pigs 488,000
Number of horses 297,000
Number of poultry (1926)3,781,000

THE YEAR'S PRODUCE
1929-30

Wheat .... 7,240,000 bushls
Oats ....5,000,000 bushls
Barley .... 760,000 bushls
Maize .... 350,000 bushls
Peas .... 290,000 bushls
Linseed .... 30,000 cwt.
Potatoes .... 250,000 tons
Hay .... 590,000 tons
Grass seed .... 1,000,000 bushls
Sheep & lambs slaughtered 10,560,000
Cattle slaughtered ... 570,000 carcass
Pigs slaughtered ... 530,000 carcass
Wool (greasy) .... 226,000,000 lb.
Apples .... 2,150,000 bushls
Pears .... 220,000 bushls
Peaches, Nectarines, Apricots & Plums
.... 260,000 bushls
Lemons .... 40,000 bushls
Butter .... 40,000 cwt.
Cheese .... 2,500,000 cwt.
Timber .... 370,000,000 s.ft.
Phormium fibre (exports) 21,000 tons
Hides & Calf Skins (exports) 932,000
Sheep Skins (exports) .. 30,000,000
Tallow (exports) ..... 22,500 tons
Honey (exports) ....600,000 lb.

SOUTH PACIFIC

was put up on Charing Cross Road. That map was commissioned by the Empire Market Board, an organisation set up to promote trade between Britain and her imperial (and former imperial) possessions, and it was the same body that commissioned the New Zealand map, with the aim of promoting the country's agricultural riches. Framed with boxes detailing New Zealand's arable, pastoral, horticultural and mining production for the past two years, the map reinforces the message in graphic form, with icons representing the country's key agricultural

produce and scrolls establishing the sites of its best stocks of various types of fish. To complete the sense of bucolic ease, Gill includes a quote from a poem, 'The Song of the Cities', written by Rudyard Kipling about Auckland during his visit to New Zealand in 1891 – having stopped off at Samoa on the way to visit Robert Louis Stevenson:

'Last, loneliest, loveliest, exquisite, apart—
On us, on us the unswerving season smiles,
Who wonder 'mid our fern why men depart
To seek the Happy Isles!'

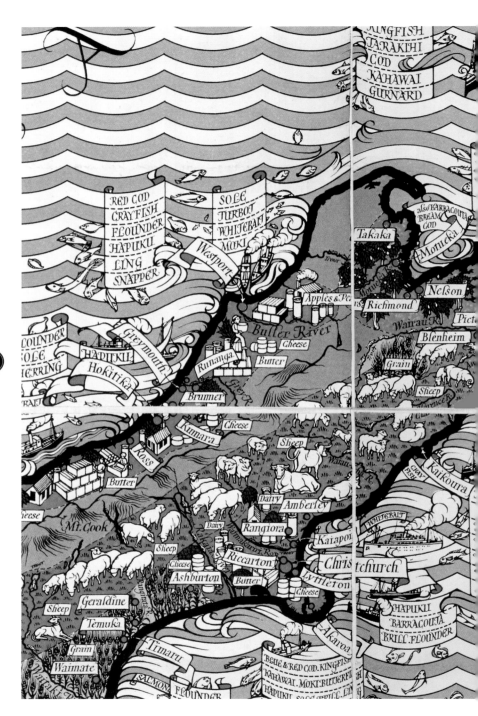

KINGFISH
TARAKIHI
COD
KAHAWAI
GURNARD

RED COD
CRAYFISH
FLOUNDER
HAPUKU
LING
SNAPPER

SOLE
TURBOT
WHITEBAIT
MOKI

also BARRACOUTA
BREAM
COD

Takaka

Motueka

Westport

Nelson

Apples & Pears

Richmond

Trout

Wairau R.

Picton

Butter River

Blenheim

Cheese

Grain

FLOUNDER
SOLE
HERRING
?RAB

Greymouth

HAPUKU
Hokitika

Runanga

Butter

Grey Creek

Sheep

Clarence R.

Brunner

Cheese

Kumara

Cheese

Ross

Sheep

Waiau R.

Kaikoura

Butter

Dairy

Amberley

GRAY FISH

Mt. Cook

Dairy

Rangiora

WHITEBAIT

Sheep

Rangitani R.

Riccarton

Kaiapoi

Christchurch

Cheese

Ashburton

Butter

Lyttleton

Cheese

Geraldine

Cheese

Sheep

Rangitata R.

Akaroa

HAPUKU
BARRACOUTA
BRILL. FLOUNDER

Temuka

Grain

Timaru

Waimate

SALMON
FLOUNDER

BLUE & RED COD. KINGFISH
KAHAWAI. MOKI. BUTTERFISH
HAPUKU. SOLE. BRILL. LING

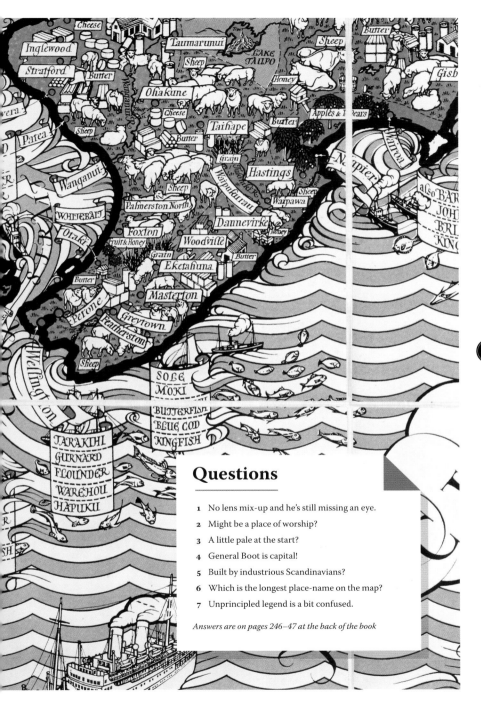

Questions

1 No lens mix-up and he's still missing an eye.
2 Might be a place of worship?
3 A little pale at the start?
4 General Boot is capital!
5 Built by industrious Scandinavians?
6 Which is the longest place-name on the map?
7 Unprincipled legend is a bit confused.

Answers are on pages 246–47 at the back of the book

GERMAN AUTOBAHN

1930s

HEINZ BÜTTGENBACH

T he railways had played a vital role in binding together the industrial countries of Europe in the nineteenth century, and with the growth of automobile ownership in the early part of the twentieth century, governments turned to the construction of new roads to further this process. In Germany, Adolf Hitler's National Socialist government prioritised the building of a high-speed road network, beginning with a stretch between Frankfurt and Darmstadt in 1935. Tens of thousands of workers were devoted to the project, helping to stimulate employment after the lean years of the Great Depression. In the late 1930s, to help publicise the new system, a map was produced, the *Karten-Wunder,* a 13-sheet compilation enclosed in a Bakelite case, with each map consisting of nine sliding panels. The sheet for northwest Germany covers some of the country's most historic towns, which are shown to be connected by the solid dark-green lines of the already completed sections of the autobahn and with dashed dark-green lines indicating those parts of the network which were yet to be completed.

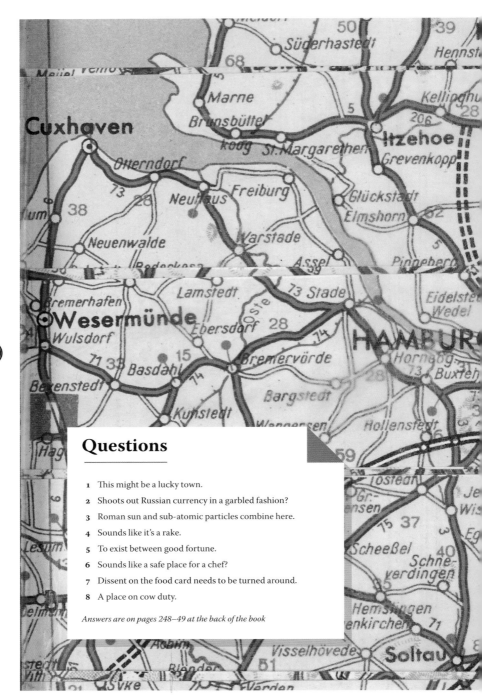

Questions

1   This might be a lucky town.

2   Shoots out Russian currency in a garbled fashion?

3   Roman sun and sub-atomic particles combine here.

4   Sounds like it's a rake.

5   To exist between good fortune.

6   Sounds like a safe place for a chef?

7   Dissent on the food card needs to be turned around.

8   A place on cow duty.

Answers are on pages 248–49 at the back of the book

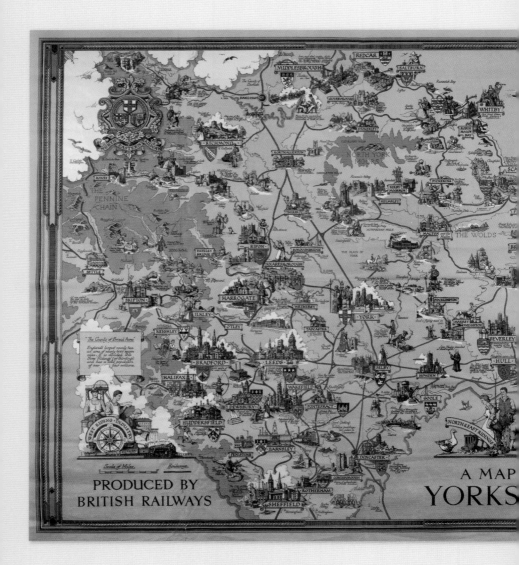

PRODUCED BY
BRITISH RAILWAYS

A MAP
YORKS

YORKSHIRE RAILWAYS

1949

ESTRA CLARKE

The railways had played a key role in making rapid and relatively comfortable travel available to far-wider sectors of society ever since the opening of the first regular passenger line between Stockton and Darlington in 1825. They brought the country together, too, because travel times were greatly reduced and awareness of the country outside people's particular localities increased. With the railways came maps, starting with *Bradshaw's Railway Map of Britain* in 1839. This railway map of Yorkshire, produced for British Railways by Estra Clarke, herself a Yorkshirewoman, is a fine example of the genre. A talented artist and cartographer, she produced several illustrated maps in the 1940s and 1950s, including city maps of York and Canterbury, and this piece covering the whole of Yorkshire. Brown lines representing the railways knit together the county like skein and the landscape is densely populated with figures representing aspects of Yorkshire history, including a Roman legionary and an archbishop at York, and Captain Cook peering out to sea at Whitby.

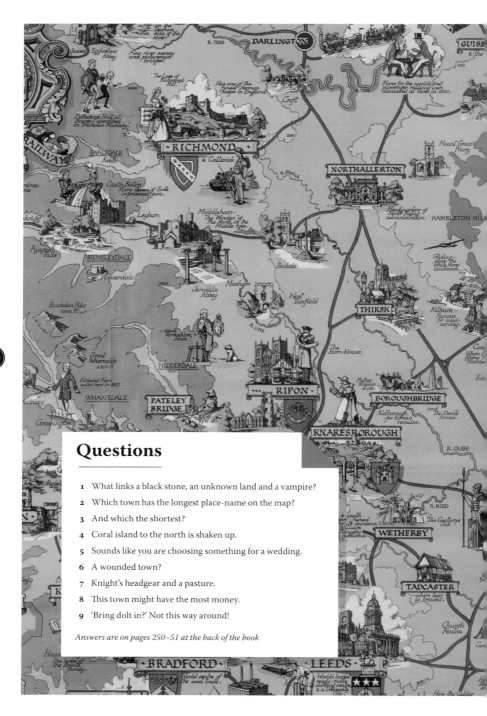

Questions

1   What links a black stone, an unknown land and a vampire?

2   Which town has the longest place-name on the map?

3   And which the shortest?

4   Coral island to the north is shaken up.

5   Sounds like you are choosing something for a wedding.

6   A wounded town?

7   Knight's headgear and a pasture.

8   This town might have the most money.

9   'Bring dolt in?' Not this way around!

Answers are on pages 250–51 at the back of the book

STOKESLEY

Roseberry Topping

Lythe

WHITBY
Here lived Abbess Hilda, Cædmon & Captain Cook.

Danby Beacon

Tom Ferres

Glaisdale & Beggar's Bridge (1621)

Runswick

ROBIN HOOD'S BAY

Sleights

D HILLS

NORTH YORK MOORS

Goathland

Fylingdales Moor

Ravenscar

Cloughton

Once a Roman Signal Station King Richard III had a house here.

SCARBOROUGH

Earthworks Tumuli, and prehistoric remains.

Saltersgate - The Hole of Horcum & turf cakes.

vaulx Abbey

Farndale

PICKERING
The Church has fine mediæval wall paintings.

KIRBY MOORSIDE

Forge Valley

Hackness

HELMSLEY

Byland Abbey

Thornton Dale

R. DERWENT

FILEY

Holiday Camp.

Cromwell's body lies at Newburgh Priory.

HOWARDIAN HILLS

R. RYE

MALTON and Old Malton

THE WOLDS

Strange birds were brought to Bridlington from the New World in 1500.

Be

BRIDLINGTON
with The Priory Church and Bayle Gate.

AIN OF RK

Castle Howard

Kirkham Abbey

Sledmere

DRIFFIELD

Long was Village noted this coast.

Eboracum founded by the Romans in A.D. 71, centre of The Church in the Middle Ages, now a great railway and tourist centre.

Stamford Bridge

A Norwegian champion held the bridge against Harold's army in 1066.

The haunt of smugglers in 18th Century.

HORNSEA

POCKLINGTON

YORK

R. DERWENT

- had a flying man in 1733.

The Mere - Yorkshi largest l

Guy Fawkes born here. Dick Turpin hanged here.

MARKET WEIGHTON

Carvings in the Church of St. Mary inspired Lewis Carroll's March Hare.

BEVERLEY
Administrative capital of the East Riding.

John Wesley preached at Eastrington.

Kingston-upon-Hull

SELBY

HULL
The third largest Port in the United Kingdom. Docks cover a river frontage of seven miles.

HOWDEN

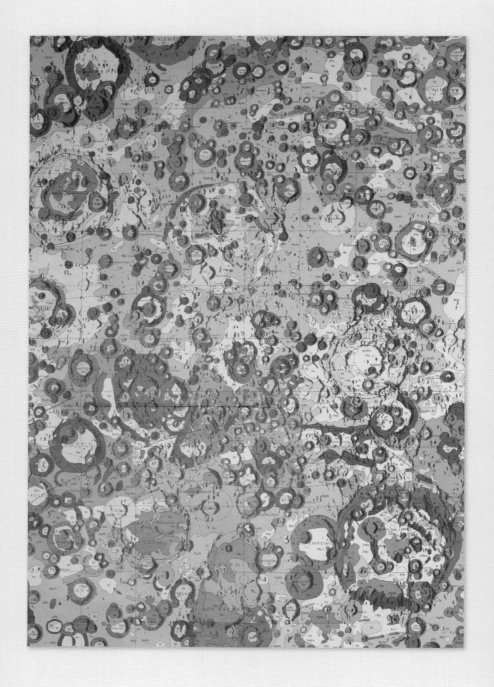

THE MOON

1978

UNITED STATES GEOLOGICAL SURVEY

The moon, and what might be found there, has been an endless source of fascination for those gazing at the night sky. Almost as soon as telescopes enabled more accurate observation of the lunar surface, people began to draw maps of it, starting with William Gilbert, the discoverer of magnetism, in 1603. As telescopes improved, these became more detailed, but the age of satellites marked a sea change in the accuracy of moon maps, beginning with observations sent by the Soviet Union's *Luna 2* and *Luna 3* probes in 1959. This 1978 map produced by the United States Geological Survey covers part of the far side of the moon (the side which always faces away from the Earth and so was never visible before the space age). It uses data gathered during the Apollo missions, in particular *Apollo 8* in December 1968, whose astronauts became the first humans to see the 'dark side', and the Soviet *Zond* probes – in particular *Zond 5*, which three months earlier carried the first Earth-based life forms to the moon's orbit and back, in the shape of two tortoises. The map contains detailed geological data of an area near the lunar equator, colour-coded according to the rock-types to be found there. Many of the craters which pockmark the surface, evidence of ancient asteroid strikes, are named for prominent scientists.

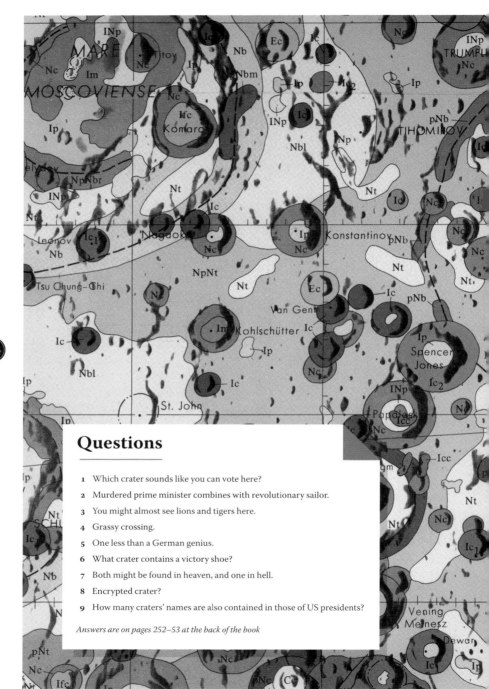

Questions

1   Which crater sounds like you can vote here?

2   Murdered prime minister combines with revolutionary sailor.

3   You might almost see lions and tigers here.

4   Grassy crossing.

5   One less than a German genius.

6   What crater contains a victory shoe?

7   Both might be found in heaven, and one in hell.

8   Encrypted crater?

9   How many craters' names are also contained in those of US presidents?

Answers are on pages 252–53 at the back of the book

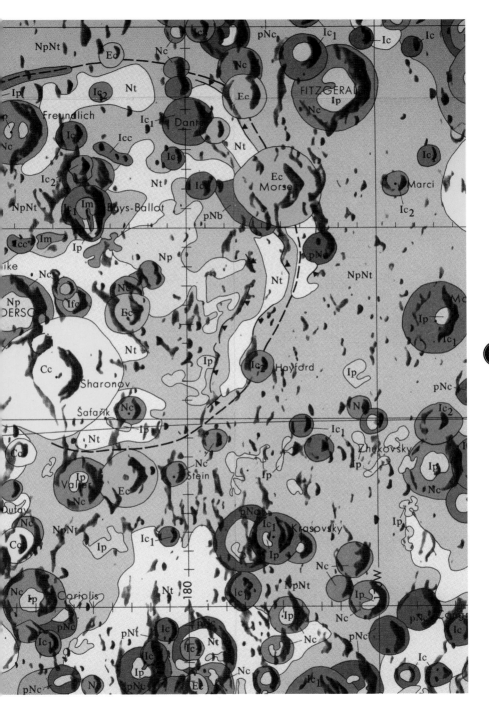

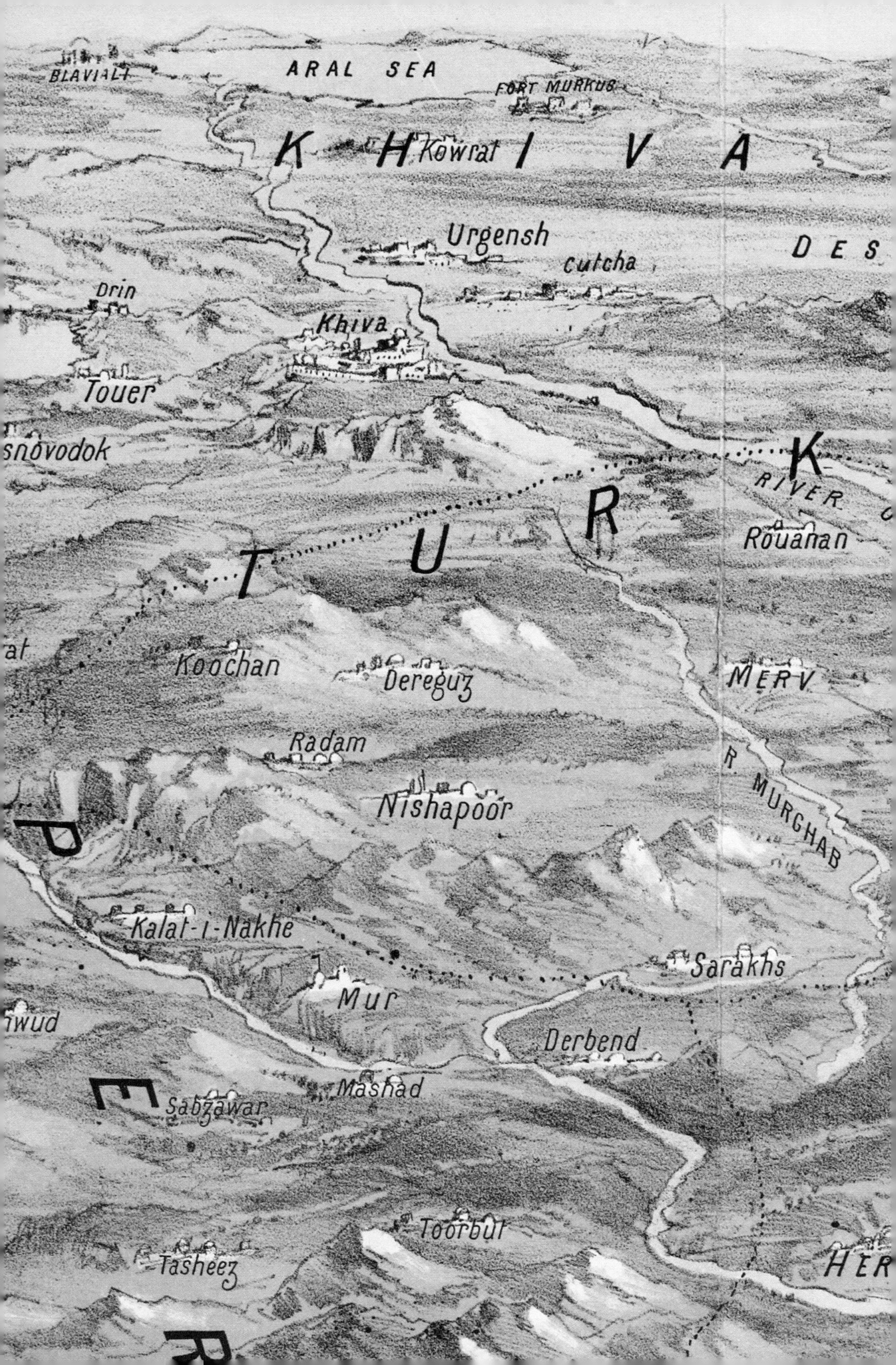
BLAVIALI
ARAL SEA
FORT MURKUS
KHIVA
Kowrat
Urgensh
DES
cutcha
Drin
Khiva
Touer
snovodok
K
RIVER
TURK
Rouanan
at
Koochan
Dereguz
MERV
Radam
R. MURGHAB
Nishapoor
P
Kalat-i-Nakhe
Sarakhs
Mur
wud
Derbend
E
Mashad
Sabzawar
Toorbul
Tasheez
HER
R

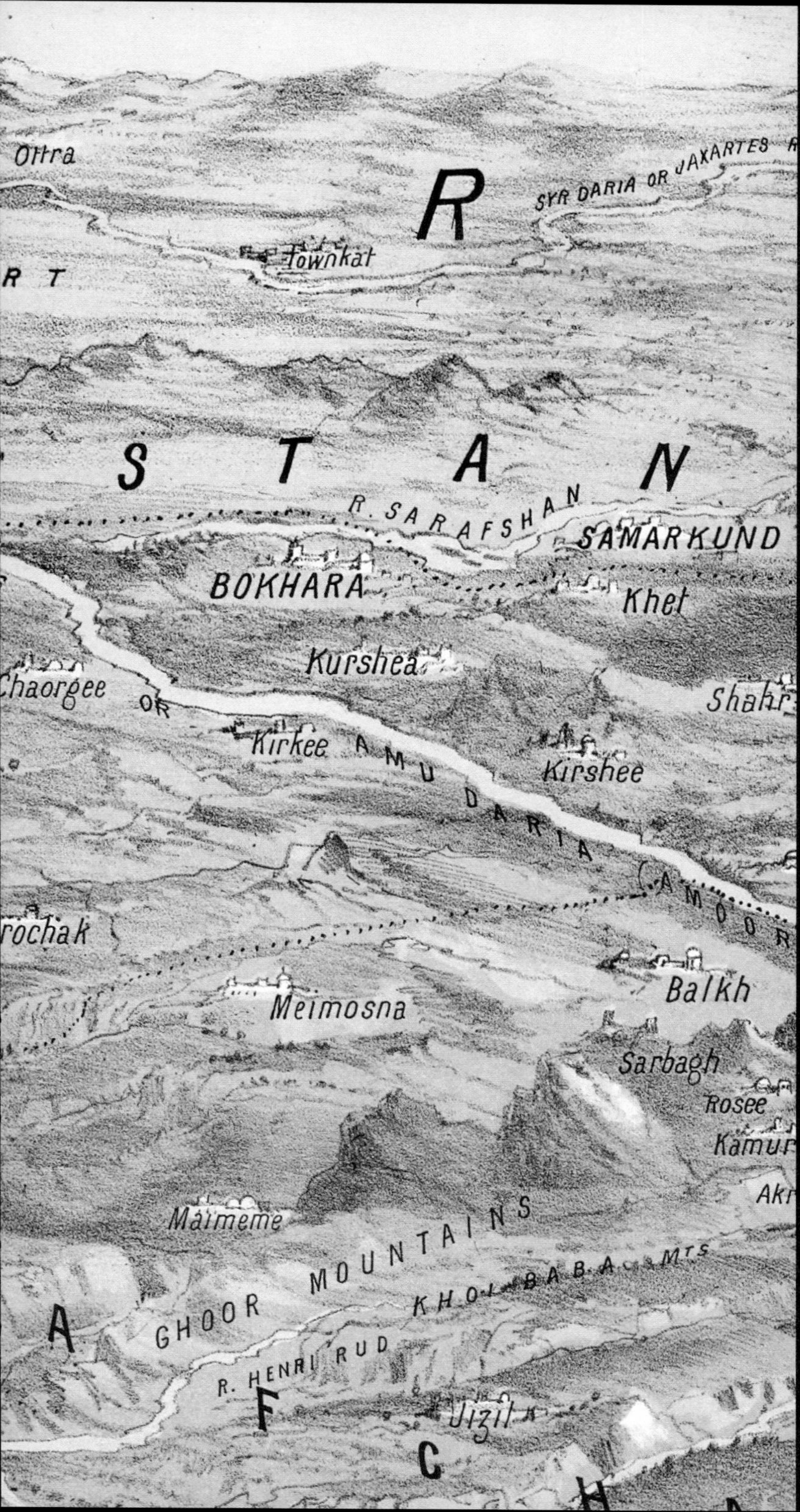

Ottra

R

STAN

Townkat

SYR DARIA OR JAXARTES R

R. SARAFSHAN

SAMARKUND

BOKHARA

Khet

Kurshea

Shahr

Chaorgee   OR

Kirkee   AMU   DARIA

Kirshee

AMOOR

rochak

Meimosna

Balkh

Sarbagh

Rosee

Kamur

Akr

Malmeme

GHOOR MOUNTAINS

KHOJ-BABA MTS.

A

R. HENRI RUD

F

Uizil

C

H

ANCIENT ROME

PIRRO LIGORIO

1 | Capitolium (the name derives from the Latin *caput*, meaning both 'head' and 'summit'). The Capitolium was the most sacred of all Roman temples, dedicated to the 'Capitoline Triad' of deities, Jupiter, Juno and Minerva (equivalent to Zeus, Hera and Athene in the Greek pantheon). The shrine stood on the south summit of the Capitoline Hill, next to the Palatine Hill, the place where, according to tradition, Romulus had founded the city of Rome in 753 BC and which was also the site of Rome's first murder. Romulus's brother Remus had wanted to found the city instead on the Aventine Hill and as part of their quarrel crossed the sacred boundaries of the new city, which his brother was marking with a plough furrow, whereupon Romulus struck and killed him. The Capitolium was dedicated in 509 BC, the first year of the Roman Republic (after the overthrow of the last of its kings, the tyrannical Etruscan Tarquinius Superbus). This temple burned down in 83 BC and was rebuilt by the Roman general and statesman Sulla, who had white marble columns shipped from the shrine to Olympian Zeus in Athens. This new structure suffered two further fires in AD 69 and AD 80, before the emperor Domitian ordered the building of a new temple, which lasted until the end of the Roman Empire in the fifth century. The neo-classical Capitol building in Washington, DC, is the home of the United States Congress. Completed in 1800, it reflects an interest in Rome and the Roman constitution on the part of the Founding Fathers and the name was selected on the insistence of Thomas Jefferson.

2 | Circus Maximus. The Romans were addicted to public spectacles (which were used, in part, by their rulers to keep the lower orders subdued, with the prospect of the thrill of the games outweighing the excitement of riot or revolution). The Circus Maximus was not a circus as we understand it (no lions, ringmasters or clowns), but a horse racing circuit,

its shape – an elongated, flattened circle – giving rise to its name. Races were held here from the very earliest times in honour of Consus, a primitive Roman horse deity, and gradually permanent structures were built, including starting gates in 329 BC. Later, seven huge wooden eggs were added on the central *spina* or barrier to indicate the number of laps the chariots had run. Other sports included elephant races, although in 55 BC some of them broke down the barrier between arena and crowd and started to trample the horrified spectators. Shortly afterwards, Julius Caesar renovated the Circus, enlarging it to the current size of 2,037 feet (621 metres) in length and 387 feet (118 metres) in width (and added better barriers). Like many large Roman structures, the Circus Maximus suffered several catastrophic fires, notably in AD 64 when the Great Fire under Nero, which destroyed much of the centre of Rome, broke out there. The arena had a capacity of around 200,000 spectators, around one-fifth of that of the entire city. The last recorded games there were held in 549, under the rule of the Ostrogothic king Totila.

3 | Rupis Tarpeia (anagram of 'pure apiarist'), or Tarpeian Rock, was the site of one of the less glorious episodes in Rome's history. Worried that there were not enough women for his new city to prosper, Romulus organised a raid on the neighbouring Sabines and kidnapped a large number of their women whom he forced to marry his followers. When the Sabine king Titus Tatius came with an army to take his revenge, he was granted access to the Capitoline fortress by its commander's daughter, Tarpeia. She had been promised the reward of that which the Sabine warriors wore 'on their left arms'. Tarpeia had thought that this meant their gold bracelets, but instead the victorious Sabines crushed her to death with their shields (which they also bore on their left arms). The Roman later used the rock – with its 82-foot (25-metre) drop – as an execution site for notorious traitors, who were simply flung off it, their bodies dashed to pieces on the way down. Among those who suffered this fate were: Marcus Manlius Capitolinus, who despite being a war hero – he had held out for months on the Capitoline against invading Gauls in 390 BC, the occasion on which the garrison was awakened by cackling geese and so able to throw back the invaders at their first assault – was thrown off the rock on suspicion of conspiring to become king; and Simon bar Giora, one of the leaders of the Jewish revolt against the Romans in AD 66–73, who was captured during the fall of Jerusalem in AD 70.

4 | The Lupercalis (*lupus* being the Latin for 'wolf'), or Lupercal, indicated twice on the map, was the site of a very ancient Roman shrine said to mark the cave where Romulus, the founder of Rome, and his twin brother Remus were suckled by a she-wolf. The baby twins had been thrown in the River Tiber when their grandfather Numitor, the king of Alba Longa, was overthrown by his brother Amulius, who saw Romulus and Remus as possible future threats to his rule. Swept out of the river near the site of what would become Rome, the twins were found and looked after by a wolf until some time later a herdsman named Faustulus came across them and raised them to adulthood. The wolf was clearly an important symbol in very early Roman religion, possibly even a tribal totem, because one of the most ancient religious festivals of the city was the Lupercalia ('wolf festival'), held every 15 February. The rites associated with this – as with other antique Roman festivals – were so lost in the mists of time that those who undertook them understood little of the meaning of their often-bizarre requirements. At Lupercalia, a goat and a dog were sacrificed, and then the knife – dripping with their blood – was pressed against the head of the Luperci, the priests dedicated to the festival. At this point, apparently, it was necessary that two young men laugh, to avoid bad luck. The hide of the goat was then cut into strips and the Luperci processed around the Palatine beating any women they came across with these makeshift hide-whips (which were supposed to grant fertility).

5 | Arcus Constantini (anagram of 'satanic icon turns'). The triple Arch of Constantine, at 69 feet (21 metres) high and 85 feet (26 metres) wide, is one of Rome's grandest monuments. It was erected by the emperor Constantine in 315 to commemorate his victory over the usurper Maxentius at the Battle of the Milvian Bridge three years beforehand. This marked a key stage in the resolution of a complex civil war that had threatened to split the empire asunder, but ended in 324 with Constantine as undisputed ruler of the whole empire. Constantine later said that just before the Milvian Bridge he had seen a fiery symbol (possibly a cross) in the sky, accompanied by the words *In Hoc Signo Vinces* ('In this sign conquer'). Those of his advisers who were adherents of the upstart Christian religion interpreted this to mean that the Christian God had helped him win, and encouraged him to tolerate Christianity (which he did by an Edict in 313) and eventually to become Christian himself. Constantine's understanding of the theological niceties of his new religion was probably a little shaky: a year after the Battle of the Milvian Bridge he was still issuing coins with depictions of the Sol Invictus ('unconquered Sun'), a distinctly pagan deity. Although grand, the arch was in part borrowed: many of the friezes that adorn it were in fact stripped from earlier monuments which celebrated victories by emperors Trajan (reigned 98–117) and Marcus Aurelius (reigned 161–180).

6 | Rostra. The Rostra – just like a modern rostrum – was a platform from which Roman orators spoke, addressing crowds assembled in front of the nearby Senate house. It gained its name from the six *rostra* – or beak-shaped ship's rams – which were captured during the Roman naval victory against the Latin League at Antium in 338 BC and then used to decorate the speaker's platform.

7 | Amphitheatrum Flavium. The Amphiteatrum Flavium or Flavian Amphitheatre, is better known as the Colosseum, and is one of ancient Rome's most famous monuments. Begun by the emperor Vespasian in AD 70, it was dedicated by his son Titus in AD 79 with inaugural games, which lasted 100 days, and during which 5,000 wild beasts were killed. The arena could hold around 50,000 spectators, who entered through a complex of gates (or *vomitoria*, which literally 'threw up' the crowd at the end of the games), their assigned entrance and seat indicated by the token that allowed them entrance. A system of awnings could protect the back rows of spectators from rain or beating sun (although the richer attendees, right at the front, were deprived of this consolation). Gladiatorial contests, the most well-known feature of the games held within the Colosseum, had their origin in the third century BC as funerary games to honour the dead, but became big business under the late Republic and early Roman Empire, with rich Romans sponsoring games and having their own gladiatorial schools as a way of raising their profile in a bid to achieve political office. The last gladiatorial contests took place in the Colosseum in 404 and thereafter it was used only for *venationes* or beast shows, in which often lightly armed hunters were left to fight off lions, leopards and other wild animals (in many cases it was in effect a form of execution). Even these ended in 523, after which it was used as a quarry for brick for aristocratic palaces and in part converted to a fortress by the Frangipani family before its restoration in the nineteenth century.

CORNWALL

CHRISTOPHER SAXTON

1 | Twelve. There are Black Rocks just south of Chappelland (to the southwest of Foy) and north of Padstow (where there is also a Gull Rock), and 'The 9 Stones' lie between Bodman [Bodmin] and Columbe Magna. The 9 Stones is a prehistoric stone circle, dating from around 2000 BC, also known as the Nine Maidens or Nine Sisters (in Cornish Naw-voz).

2 | At the base of the map, where the cartographer has used the Latin term *meridies* for south. Meaning 'mid-day', it was also employed to designate the cardinal direction south, since the sun appears to the south at midday in the northern hemisphere. At the top of the map, *septentrionalis* is used for north, derived from *septem* ('seven') and *trio* ('ox'), the Roman name for the constellation Ursa Major, referring to the idea that the stars are plough-oxen grouped around Polaris, the North Star.

3 | Cornubia ('cor' and 'nubia') – on the cartouche surmounted by the royal coat of arms at the top of the map. Cornubia was the Latin name for Cornwall, taken from the Cornovii, the Celtic tribe which lived west of the Tamar, whose name in turn derives from the root *corn-* ('horn'), referring to the horn-shaped Cornish peninsula (and which also appears in Kernow, the Cornish name for Cornwall). Nubia is the historic name for the region to the south of pharaonic Egypt.

4 | Tintagell [Tintagel], whose early medieval fortifications have long been identified (without any secure evidence) as the Camelot of King Arthur. In 1136 the medieval chronicler Geoffrey of Monmouth, in his *History of the Kings of Britain*, declared it to be the birthplace of the king. Although Tintagel was an important trading centre in the sixth century – when King Arthur was supposed to have lived – much of the ruin visible today was in fact built in the 1230s by Richard, Earl of Cornwall, the brother of Henry III.

5 | Camel, lizard, mouse and crow – Camleforde (modern-day Camelford), Lezard point, Moushole (Mousehole) and Crowan, north of Helston. Camelford was the birthplace of the British naval officer and explorer Samuel Wallis (1728–95) who narrowly missed being the first European to set foot on Tahiti when a bout of illness confined him to his cabin as his ship the *Dolphin* anchored off the island on 18 June 1767, allowing his first officer Tobias Furneaux to claim the honour. Lizard Point is the southernmost point in England, which lies within Landewednack parish, its most southerly parish. Nearby at Pen Olver is the point from which Guglielmo Marconi transmitted a wireless message 186 miles (300 kilometres) to the Isle of Wight in January 1901, preparatory to his much more famous feat ten months later in sending the first trans-Atlantic signal. The origin of the name Mousehole is obscure, although the topography of the place, nestled right down a precipitous slope at the sea's edge, has given rise to the idea that it really was named for a mouse's refuge. Crowan is named for St Crewenna, one of a host of Irish holy men and women who came to Cornwall in the sixth century, and of whom almost nothing is known.

6 | Saint Earth (now St Erth), named for the Irish saint Ercus (or Erc), a disciple of St Patrick, who was very active in evangelising southwestern Ireland, including Limerick, in the late sixth century before crossing over to Cornwall.

7 | Sct Michaels Insul – St Michael's Mount near Penzance is a tidal causeway island. Being the site of a Benedictine monastery established between 1135 and 1144, which became a popular pilgrimage site (sparked by the story that the archangel Michael had made an appearance there), the island has history which mirrors that of its sister island in Normandy, where the archangel was similarly said to have manifested himself

– Mont Saint Michel hosted a monastic community from the eighth century and was also a tidal island. After the Norman Conquest in 1066, William the Conqueror – who had been supported by the Norman monastery – gave the Cornish St Michael's Mount to the Norman monks, who made it their daughter house. The Cornish monastery was closed down during Henry VIII's Dissolution of the Monasteries in the 1530s, whereas the Norman priory survived until the French Revolution.

8 | Grampound ('gram' and 'pound'). The village is named for the bridge – *grand-pont* ('big bridge') in Norman French – over the nearby River Fal. Although now having only around 650 inhabitants (if Creed, on the other side of the river is included), Grampound was a prosperous place in the past. It sent two members to Parliament until 1821 when, during the campaign against 'rotten boroughs' – whose shrunken populations allowed rich local landowners to bribe the small numbers of electors with ease – that preceded the Great Reform Bill of 1832, it had its parliamentary representation removed.

9 | Saint Agnes – the saint for whom the village is named was the subject of 'The Eve of St Agnes', a poem by the Romantic poet John Keats (1795–1821). The patron saint of girls, Agnes was martyred during the persecution of Christians by the Roman emperor Diocletian around 304. Aged about 13, her Christianity was betrayed by a jealous neighbour and she was condemned to be sent to a brothel. The men there refused to touch her, save one youth who tried to rape her and was struck blind (but subsequently healed when Agnes prayed for him). She was later martyred by being beheaded after the stake at which she was supposed to be burned alive stubbornly refused to take light. By tradition, young women would pray to the saint on St Agnes's Eve in the hope that the identity of their future husband would be revealed. John Opie was born near the village in 1761. He was a carpenter's son, whose artistic talents were discovered by a local physician and he rose to become a fashionable portraitist and painter of historical scenes. Among the subjects portrayed by the 'Cornish Wonder' were Charles James Fox, Edmund Burke and Mary Shelley.

WESTMORLAND AND CUMBRIA
CHRISTOPHER SAXTON

1 | Carlisle ('carl' and 'isle'), which began life as a stronghold of the Celtic Carvetii tribe and then as the Roman fort of Luguvalium, built in AD 73 on the site of the current city museum. It grew sufficiently important to survive the Roman withdrawal in 411 and the generalised urban collapse that accompanied it in England. St Cuthbert came to Carlisle in 685 to visit the queen of King Ecgfrith of Northumbria and marvelled at the towering stones of nearby Hadrian's Wall, which was then still almost complete. In the Middle Ages Carlisle became a bulwark of the English defence of the north against Scottish invasions and was used as a base by Edward I for his invasions of Scotland between 1298 and 1303. Occupied by the Jacobites during Bonnie Prince Charlie's foray into England in 1745, Carlisle's castle suffered its final siege as they retreated, although it retained a military garrison of the Border Regiment as late as 1959. 'Carl' is a Germanic word meaning 'warrior'. The huscarls were the personal household troops of the Anglo-Saxon monarchs, who had their last day of martial glory at the Battle of Hastings on 14 October 1066.

2 | Cardew ('car' and 'dew'). A small hamlet southwest of Carlisle, Cardew is most remarkable for Cardew Hall, a sixteenth-century stone farmhouse that was the place of birth of Cumberland's most eminent early historian, John Denton, who compiled his history of the county between 1600 and 1610, and of Susanna Blamire, one of the greatest female poets of the Romantic movement, whose song 'And Ye Shall Walk in Silk Attire' was sufficiently well known to be quoted by Charles Dickens in his *The Old Curiosity Shop*.

3 | Raughtonhead (12 letters long). Despite its long name, Raughton Head (now spelled as two words) is a small hamlet, whose name may mean 'Moss Farm'. Even so, it sent 72 of its sons to World War One, of whom 13 died in service and who are commemorated

on a war memorial in the hamlet, together with the 19 local men who fought in World War Two.

4 | The River Eden (running through Carlisle). The Garden of Eden was the earthly paradise in which, according to the Book of Genesis, Adam and Eve, the first people, lived before God expelled them when Eve tasted of the forbidden fruit of the Tree of Knowledge of Good and Evil. Its name may derive from the ancient Sumerian word *edin*, meaning 'plain' and which possibly refers to the fertile area between the Tigris and Euphrates in which the earliest civilisation flourished. The River Eden, in contrast, derives its name from a Celtic word *ituna*, which may mean 'water'. It was first mentioned by the Greco-Roman geographer Ptolemy in the first century AD and runs for 90 miles from the Yorkshire Dales to the Solway Firth near Bowness.

5 | Burgh (modern Burgh by Sands). A burgh is an alternative name for a fortified settlement or castle. Burgh by Sands was the site of Aballava, one of the most westerly of the forts on Hadrian's Wall (the wall line finally petered out at Bowness, a few miles further down the Solway Firth estuary). The fort was home to an eclectic mix of garrisons during its three-century-long life, including several detachments from what is now the Netherlands and a unit from Mauretania Tingitana (modern-day Morocco). The wall and fort have long since disappeared, although fragments of it were reused and can be seen embedded in the structure of the parish church of St Michael. It was there that the body of Edward I lay in state for ten days in 1307 after he died in the nearby marshes while embarked on a final campaign against the Scots.

6 | Uprightbye ('upright'-bye), now Upperby. Formerly an independent settlement, Uprightbye (or Upperby) is now a suburb of Carlisle. The most famous local, George MacDonald Fraser, the author of the *Flashman* novels, was born in the next-door village of Currock. Fraser's series tells the derring-do adventures of Harry Flashman, a hero whom Fraser plucked from the pages of Thomas Hughes's *Tom Brown's School Days* and made all his own, and its canvas ranges from British India's North-West Frontier with Afghanistan to Germany at the time of Bismarck, Singapore, the Crimea, south India and New Orleans. Fraser is said to have written the novels in a bid to escape from the world of journalism (he was Deputy Editor of the *Glasgow Herald* in the late 1960s), but he retained a firm sense of the region of his upbringing, reflected in *The Steel Bonnets* (1971), an account of the border reivers, raiders who took advantage of the instability and lack of central control on the troubled Anglo-Scottish border to run practically independent bandit fiefdoms, which were only finally brought to heel after the union of the crowns of England and Scotland in 1603.

7 | Kirkoswald (kirk-'Oswald'). Oswald was ruler of the Anglo-Saxon kingdom of Northumbria between 633 and 642. Although destined for the throne, he was forced to flee on the death of his father Aethelfrith in 616, when his uncle Edwin seized the crown. During his time in exile, he came into contact with Christianity on the holy island of Iona and converted, becoming an ardent champion for the new religion. When Edwin died in battle against the British king Cadwallon of Gwynedd in 633, Oswald returned to Northumbria, was acclaimed king and defeated and killed his uncle's nemesis the next year at the appropriately named Battle of the Heavenfield near Hexham. When he himself was killed in battle against the resolutely pagan Penda of Mercia in 642, his body was transferred briefly to Kirkoswald, which then took his name. His remains suffered the fate of many early medieval saints – he was canonised soon after his death and then dismembered, with the head going to Durham cathedral, while an arm was said to have been stolen by some monks of Peterborough Abbey and interred there. The village is the site of the ruins of Kirkoswald Castle, built in 1201 by Randolph Engayne, but destroyed by a Scots army under Robert the Bruce in 1314. Afterwards rebuilt, it came into the hands of the locally powerful Dacre and Howard families, before falling into ruins in the early seventeenth century.

8 | Newton in Ardale ('Newton'). Isaac Newton was one of England's most famous scientists and the formulator of the theory of gravity, which he published in his *Principia Mathematica* in 1687. The village gained its name (meaning 'new town') when it was established in the early sixteenth century after a storm had caused sands to inundate and partially destroy the coastal hamlet of Beckfoot, in response to which most of its inhabitants chose to move inland to a new, safer home.

IRELAND

GIOVANNI BATTISTA BOAZIO

1 | Caterlogh (anagram of 'great loch'). Spelled also as Ceatharlach, and in its modern anglicised form Carlow, the town's name is sometimes interpreted as meaning 'place on the lake' (although, oddly, there is not one nearby) or, more plausibly, 'place of cattle'. Its most remarkable feature was the four-tower keep built by the Norman magnate William the Marshall. This survived a succession of attacks on it, including assaults by Art MacMurrough in 1405, by Rory O'More in 1577, by Oliver Cromwell's son-in-law Henry Ireton in 1650 and by Wolfe Tone's United Irishmen in 1798. It was finally reduced to rubble by a certain Dr Middleton, who decided to convert it to a lunatic asylum in 1814. He used such a large charge of dynamite that he succeeded in demolishing most of the castle structure (except a portion of the curtain wall and two towers), rendering it useless. Perhaps a better result would have been achieved had the lunatics been in charge of the asylum.

2 | Dublin (*Dubh linn* means 'black pool') – the Irish capital derives its name from the Irish words *dubh* ('dark' or 'black') and *lind* ('pool'). In modern Irish it is referred to as Baile Átha Cliath, or 'village by the hurdle ford', from an early crossing of the River Liffey. The city owes its origin to the establishment by the Vikings of a longphort, or fortified harbour-camp, in 841 (which was probably situated near Fishamble Street at the confluence of the Poddle and the Liffey). The Viking kings of Dublin continued to dominate the area, diluting their efforts by regular forays into England in an attempt to unite their realm with the Viking lordship of York. Their defeat by an Irish army under Brian Bóruma in 1014 led to the eclipse of their power and the gradual absorption of Dublin into the mainstream of Irish political development.

3 | Kildare ('kil' and 'dare'). Kildare's name means 'church of the oak' and it began as the site of a monastery founded by St Brigid in the late fifth century.

Unusually, it held both monks and nuns (the source of some scurrilous gossip, although the allegation that Brigid actually proposed to (St) Patrick, and won the right for women to propose to their lovers each Leap Year on 29 February, is likely to be apocryphal). East of the town lies the Curragh, the largest unfenced area of arable land in the country and the site of a racecourse that has been famous for centuries. In 1903 the town lay on the route of the Gordon Bennett Cup, the world's first international motor race, and the forerunner of subsequent international grand prix races.

4 | Drogheda (anagram of 'God heard'). Divided by the River Boyne, Drogheda sat on the border of the old Irish kingdoms of Mide (Meath) and Airgíalla (Oriel) and was for long considered two separate towns until their union in 1412. The town was the site of numerous Irish parliaments, including that in 1495 summoned by Sir Edward Poynings, which passed the law named for him that made all the parliament's Acts invalid until they had been approved by the English king (and which became the subject of particular resentment in Ireland). Drogheda was the site of a notorious massacre in 1649 when Oliver Cromwell attacked the town, held by a Royalist garrison. Around 3,000 people were said to have been killed, including a group who fled to St Peter's Church for sanctuary but were burned to death inside it. Only around 30 of the garrison survived and they were summarily shipped off to the English penal colony on Barbados. Drogheda once again found itself on the losing side when it supported James II against William of Orange, but after the defeat of the Stuart army at the Battle of the Boyne on 30 June 1690 (pre Gregorian calendar) the town surrendered and was spared a similar sacking.

5 | Kelles ('Kells'). The abbey at Kells was long the home of one of the most famous books in Ireland, the Book of Kells, with its fantastically illuminated carpet-pages of intertwined patterning like a glorious golden knot. Produced at the Irish monastery on the island of Iona off Scotland's southwest coast in about 800, the lavishly illustrated Latin manuscript of the four New Testament gospels made its way to Kells after the Iona monks fled following a brutal Viking raids in 806 which killed most of the brethren. Kells itself, which had been founded around 550 by Columba, and became one of Ireland's most prominent abbeys, did not prove to be a safe haven for the book; it was raided by Vikings over a dozen times. The abbey (and the Book of Kells) somehow survived until it was dissolved by Henry VIII in 1551. The book remained in Kells until 1654 when Oliver Cromwell's invading army quartered itself in the abbey church, which led to the book being sent for safekeeping to Dublin, where it entered the collection of Trinity College seven years later and remains to this day.

6 | Trimme ('trim' and 'me'). Trim, in Irish Baile Átha Troim ('town at the elderflower ford') began, like many towns in the region, as a monastery, this one founded by Loman, a nephew of (St) Patrick. Trim Castle was the largest Norman castle built in Ireland and the stronghold of the de Lacy family, which ruled over the surrounding area. It was considered during Elizabeth I's reign as the site of a Protestant university for Ireland (which was in the event founded in Dublin, as Trinity College).

7 | Naas, or An Nás, is the county town of County Kildare. It was once the residence of the Kings of Leinster, and developed as a market town after the English invasion of Ireland in 1169. It was an important ecclesiastical centre, with a priory founded for the Canons Regular of the order of St Augustine in the late twelfth century, joined in 1355 by a Dominican friary. Although a small town, it still returned two members to the Irish parliament until the seats were abolished after the Act of Union with Great Britain in 1801.

8 | Louth (the first letter is 'l', one letter before 'm' in 'mouth'). Louth (in Irish Lú), also known through

its history as Knockfergus and Cluain-Caoin, grew out of a monastery founded in the fourth century by Mocteus, one of the early followers of (St) Patrick. It became such a renowned centre of learning that over 100 bishops were said to have been educated there, but it went into a decline after a series of raids by the Vikings, who first attacked and destroyed it in 838. Rebuilt several times, it was then destroyed three times in fires (in 1075, 1133 and 1148) but still recovered. The town itself proved just as resilient (despite suffering disastrous fires in 1150 and 1166), but the priors of the religious house erected on the ruins of the abbey proved to have poor political judgement. Holders of the office had to be pardoned for treason after entertaining Edward Bruce (the brother of Robert), who invaded Ireland in 1315, and for their support of Lambert Simnell, the son of a humble tradesman, who was crowned king in Christ Church Cathedral, Dublin, in 1487 by masquerading as the Earl of Warwick (the nephew of Edward IV) in a bid to overthrow Henry VII.

9 | Old Laghlin (anagram of 'glad on hill'). The site of an ancient Christian monastery, Old Leighlin was the venue for a Church synod in AD 630 at which it was determined that Easter would be celebrated according to the Roman method of calculation and not the traditional Celtic computation. The argument had raged in ecclesiastical circles for decades – including in those parts of England influenced by Irish traditions (it caused the unfortunate situation in Northumbria, where the royal family was divided on the issue, that the king might be celebrating Easter while the queen was still observing her Easter fast). Laserian, the abbot of Old Leighlin, who had argued for the Roman method, was sent after the synod to Rome to receive instruction from Pope Gregory as to how the decision was to be implemented. Laserian suffered a curious death in 639, after plucking a hair from the eyebrow of the corpse of St Sillan. Viewing such a hair was considered fatal, so by his action his death served as a warning that saved from a similar fate anyone who was subsequently tempted to attack the saint's brows.

THE MEDITERRANEAN
JOAN OLIVA

1 | Pesaro (anagram of 'operas'). A city in the Le Marche region of northern Italy, Pesaro was founded as Pisaurum in Etruscan times. Conquered by the Romans in 184 BC, it enjoyed relative tranquillity under the empire. It was destroyed by the Visigoths under Witigis in AD 536 during the Gothic Wars launched by the Eastern Roman emperor Justinian in a bid to win back the Italian peninsula from the Germanic barbarians who had taken control 60 years beforehand. The city was controlled by a number of leading Italian families during the Renaissance, passing from the Malatesta of Rimini to the Sforza of Milan in 1445, and then to the della Rovere dukes of Urbino in 1512. It became best known for its production of maiolica, a type of tin-glazed pottery that was colourfully decorated with lavish scenes, often taken from mythology. The term is probably a corruption of 'Majorca', where Moorish potters are said to have first developed the technique. Pesaro was the birthplace of Gioacchino Rossini (1792–1868), one of the greatest of Italian composers, who turned from singing to creating operas after his voice broke and among whose best-known works are *The Barber of Seville* and *William Tell*.

2 | Ancona (anaconda with the letters 'AD' removed). Ancona, the capital of Le Marche region, was established by Greek colonists from Syracuse in around 390 BC. It takes its name from *ankon*, the Greek word for elbow, which refers to the shape of the promontory on which it sits. After rule by Romans, Goths, Lombards and, briefly around 840, Arabs, it came under the control of the papacy in 1532. Along with Rome, Ancona was the only city in the Papal States where Jews were allowed to live, and the city still has two synagogues.

3 | Salerno ('sale' at the beginning). Founded by the Etruscans in the sixth century BC, Salerno was re-established in 194 BC as the Roman colony of Salernum. It became the capital of the Norman principality established in southern Italy by Robert Guiscard in 1076. It was also the site of the Schola Medica Salernitana, Europe's earliest medical school, which dates from the late ninth century and played a key role in the translation of medical texts from Arabic into Latin (some of them having their origins in Greek originals, such as the works of the fourth-century BC physician Hippocrates, for whom the Hippocratic oath was named). During World War Two, Salerno was one of the main Allied landing points during the invasion of mainland Italy in September 1943, during which much of the old town was destroyed (and what was left was seriously damaged during an eruption of Vesuvius in 1943 and two serious floods in the 1950s).

4 | Terracina (the Italian words *'terra'* – the earth – and *'Cina'* – China). Terracina, around 50 miles (80 kilometres) southeast of Rome, was founded by the Volscians (a pre-Roman tribe) as Anxur and later became a favourite getaway from the imperial capital for the Roman aristocracy, with baths, theatres and villas springing up for their amusement. It was the birthplace of Galba, emperor from AD 68 to 69, in a period of instability known as the Year of the Four Emperors. Having served successive emperors with exemplary loyalty, Galba had (with hindsight) the misfortune to be selected as emperor by the praetorian guard following the suicide of Nero. Hardly in the prime of his youth at 71 and crippled with gout, Galba proved to be a lethargic and indecisive emperor, and his popularity ebbed away with alarming speed. Within two weeks of seizing the imperial throne, he was killed by his own praetorians and his head put on a spike and paraded around the Forum. Loyalty may not have been profitable, but ambition had come at a very high price.

5 | Triesti ('tries' and 'ti' – 'it' reversed or turned around). Few cities have had a more colourful history than Trieste, its strategic site at the head of the Gulf of Istria being both a boon and a curse. Roman, Byzantine, Lombard and Frankish masters were succeeded by a brief period of independence from 948 to 1202. It was then annexed by the Venetians, and the constant attempts by the Triestini to wriggle free of their control merely led to the city coming under Austrian control in 1382. A status as an imperial free port and imperial free city in the eighteenth and nineteenth centuries gave Trieste economic prosperity without any illusion of political autonomy. Its position as a diplomatic ping-pong ball was confirmed in 1918 when the city was handed to Italy as a reward for Italian participation on the Allied side in World War One. Tens of thousands of Slovene-speaking Triestini fled into the newly formed Kingdom of Yugoslavia, creating a legacy of bitterness that was to erupt spectacularly in 1945 when, at the end of World War Two, Yugoslavia demanded Trieste. From 1947 to 1954 the city lived in a diplomatic twilight zone as the Free Territory of Trieste, divided in turn into an Area A (including the city itself), with largely Italian administrators, and an Area B, with Slavic-speaking governors. Predictably, when the system was wound up in 1954, the first area was awarded to Italy and the second to Yugoslavia. Trieste found itself stranded at the edge of the Iron Curtain, its historical role as a port and entrepôt stunted by Cold War rivalries. Only the collapse of communism in eastern Europe in the late 1980s, followed by the accession of both Slovenia and Croatia to the European Union, opened up those trade routes again, and began to bring back a sense of prosperity to the historic port.

6 | Fiumen (anagram of 'fine mu'). Fiumen (or to Italian-speakers, Fiume) is now the Croatian city of Rijeka. After it fell into the hands of the Habsburgs in 1466, Fiumen formed part of the Austro-Hungarian Empire (and from 1870 it was attached to the

Hungarian part of the Dual Monarchy). After the end of World War One the city became the subject of a bitter dispute between Italy and Yugoslavia over which country it should be awarded to. Right-wing Italian opinion was inflamed and in September 1919 the Italian nationalist poet Gabriele D'Annunzio marched in with a scratch militia and occupied it, claiming the city for the Kingdom of Italy. The Yugoslav and Italian governments sidestepped the issue by agreeing that Fiume should be a free state, but its Lilliputian state of independence only aggravated the spiral of anarchy that then engulfed it. In 1924 Italy stepped in and imposed central control, and Fiume remained Italian until 1945 when Yugoslav partisans occupied it at the end of the war.

7 | Lotranto (*LOTR*, acronym of *Lord of the Rings*, and ANTO, acronym of the Austrian National Tourist Office) or L'otranto, now Otranto, is Italy's most easterly town. Known to the Romans as Hydruntum, it was one of the main embarkation points for Greece. Its exposed position on the Adriatic coast made it highly vulnerable to invaders. It was occupied by the Norman Robert Guiscard in 1086 and in 1480 was captured by an Ottoman fleet that looked, for one terrifying moment, as if it was about to extend Turkish control into the Italian peninsula. A crusade was called, but it was internal Ottoman dynastic politics that saved the day when Sultan Mehmet II (the conqueror of Constantinople) died while on his way to lead a campaign in Italy and his successor Bayezid II ordered the abandonment of the city after an occupation of just over a year.

VIRGINIA

JOHN SMITH

1 | Jamestown, named for James I of England (and VI of Scotland), Cape Henry (named in 1607 for James's eldest son, Henry Frederick Stuart, who was then expected to succeed his father) and Cape Charles (named after James's second son Charles, who did inherit the throne in 1625 and unleashed a series of civil wars which engulfed England, Wales, Scotland and Ireland and ultimately led to his execution by beheading in 1649). Cape Henry was the point where the 104 colonists despatched by the Virginia Company aboard the *Susan Constant, Godspeed* and *Discovery* first made landfall in April 1607. It was only a few weeks later that the expedition's leaders sent a party north up the James River to find a more suitable spot for a permanent colony. They came across the site for Jamestown, sheltered from attack by coastal raiders and not at the time occupied by the local Tsenacommachah Native Americans. Although reinforced by a subsequent fleet, in the winter of 1609–10, almost 90 per cent of the by then 500 colonists in Jamestown perished during the 'starving time'.

2 | In Payankatank (Payanka-'tank'). The Payankatank were one of the roughly 30 sub-groups which were subordinate to the locally dominant Tsenacommachah, led by Powhatan. In 1608, just after the arrival of the Europeans, they were attacked by Powhatan, resulting in 24 of their warriors being killed and the rest deported to be replaced by members of the Kecoughtan tribe.

3 | Chesapeack (anagram of 'cheap cakes') or Chesapeake Bay. Named for the local Chesapeake tribe, who were wiped out by Powhatan just before the European colonists arrived, because Tsenacommachah prophets foretold that out of their land would arise a people who would destroy the Tsenacommachah. The mouth of the bay was the site of an important battle during the American Revolutionary War (the

American War of Independence) in which a French fleet under the Comte de Grasse defeated a British one led by Thomas Graves, securing control of the bay and completing the encirclement of Cornwallis at Yorktown. The engagement is also known as the Battle of the Capes. Chesapeake town on the edge of the bay is the second largest in the state of Virginia by area, including in its bounds the gloomily named Great Dismal Swamp.

4 | Cuttatawomen (anagram of 'can mutate two'), halfway up the Chesapeake. Early records describe it as the home of the Cuttatawomen tribe, a small group with only about 30 warriors.

5 | Smyths Isles, near Cape Charles. John Smith was one of the early leaders of the Jamestown colony (although he had been locked up for mutiny during the voyage and was only released when a sealed letter with instructions for the colonists was opened on arrival in the Americas and it was found he was intended to be the colony's governing council). While exploring upriver north of Jamestown he was captured by a raiding party sent out by Powhatan. Although Smith's accounts of his brief captivity became more elaborate over the years, the most enduring one is that he was about to be put to death and was only saved by the entreaties of Powhatan's daughter Pocahontas, who later became an icon of European–Native American co-operation. Smith only stayed at Jamestown two more years and returned home to England after being injured in a gunpowder explosion in 1610.

6 | Acquintanacsuck (15 letters), a small Native American village at the head of the Patuxent River. The village was visited in 1621 by John Pory, an intrepid traveller, who had previously acted as an English diplomat in Constantinople and Savoy. The first speaker of the Virginia Assembly, he was invited to

Acquintanacsuck by its chief, Namenacus, who greeted Pory and his companions with a meal of boiled oysters. Relations, though, later soured: the promised trade did not materialise and Namenacus was accused of trying to murder Pory.

7 | Keale's Hill, just east of Charles Bay. The highest point in the immediate vicinity, the hill must have been an obvious landmark as Smith began to survey the area. He was in the habit of creating place-names for members of the colonising party and ships' crews, and so this may have been named for Richard Keale, one of Smith's soldiers, who later made a living as a fishmonger in the infant colony.

8 | Toppahanock ('top'-pahanock). Now called Tappahanock, it is the oldest settlement in Essex County, Virginia. One of Smith's initial landing places, he found Native American resistance there too strong and so moved on to the site for Jamestown. The native name means 'rise and fall of water', but when an English trader named Jacob Hobbs set up a post here it became known as 'Hobbs Hole'. In 1682 when the Colony of Virginia ordered county towns to be established on the spot, it was allied with New Plymouth, but the name reverted to the native form Tappahanock in 1705. Hobbs Hole survives as the name of a local golf course.

PARIS

JAN ZIARNKO

1 | Nostre Dame (anagram or rearrangement of 'notes dream'), or Nôtre-Dame. Notre Dame has long been a holy place. In Roman times the site of a pagan shrine to Jupiter, a church dedicated to the Virgin Mary was built there as early as 365. The Merovingian king Childebert I built a second chapel on the site in 555, and the whole complex was then replaced by a cathedral constructed under the auspices of Maurice de Sully, the bishop of Paris. The foundation stone for this was laid in 1163 by no less an ecclesiastical figure than Pope Alexander III, then in exile in Paris after his election was disputed by a rival antipope supported by the Holy Roman Emperor. The church has experienced many modifications and seen many historic events, including the preaching of the Third Crusade by Heraclius, Patriarch of Jerusalem, in 1185; the coronation of Henry VI (the only English king to be crowned king of France) in 1431; and the coronation of Napoleon Bonaparte in 1804. The tragic fire in April 2019, which destroyed much of the medieval woodwork in the roof and the cathedral's famous spire, means that, more than 850 years after its construction, the church of Notre Dame is about to experience yet another rebirth.

2 | Rue de la Coutellerie ('Cutlery Street'). Like many medieval cities, Paris was characterised by micro-quarters in which various types of craftsmen clustered. The Rue de la Coutellerie is named for the knifemakers (or cutlers) who established workshops there from the time of Henri II (1547–59). Before that, it was named Rue des Recommanderesses, for the women who would recommend valets, chambermaids and nurses, a type of medieval employment agency. The road was widened in the 1850s. In 1853 the owners on one side had their properties expropriated and demolished; if their neighbours on the other side of the road felt smug, they were wrong to, for the next year the houses on the other side of the road were confiscated and they, too, were flattened.

3 | Le Cloistre ('the cloister'), now Rue du Cloître-Notre-Dame. The street derives its name from the 'cloister' or enclosed area where nuns or monks lived, and which became applicable more widely to the immediate area around a large ecclesiastical building that served the domestic needs of its clergy. Originally the road was closed by two gates and contained two additional churches, of Saint-Jean-le-Rond and Saint-Denis-au-Pas (so called because it was separated from Notre Dame by only a step or *pas*).

4 | Rue du Coq ('Cock Street'). Also called the Rue du Coq-Saint-Jean after an inn sign here, the road became a dead-end alley after the cutting through of the Rue de Rivoli in 1854. The time was long past by then when cocks might be heard crowing in the centre of Paris.

5 | Place Maubert ('Mau'-bert). The Mau Mau was a Kenyan revolutionary movement that conducted a six-year long guerrilla campaign against British rule from 1950, which led to the deaths of 100 Europeans, 2,000 Africans loyal to the British and 11,000 Mau Mau rebels, as well as the eviction of 20,000 Kikuyu, the tribe which made up the largest reservoir of Mau Mau support, into detention camps. The Place Maubert has a very venerable history, possibly deriving its name from the Abbé Aubert who permitted butchers to set up their businesses on the site in the twelfth century. The combination of discarded offal from the butchers and general waste dumped on the square gave it a reputation for being a foul place, and a law of 1392 decreed that all the waste was to be gathered nightly and placed on the Place de Grève (whose inhabitants were probably not best pleased at the measure). Place Maubert was at the heart of the medieval academic quarter of the Sorbonne, but also became a place of execution, mainly of Protestants and printers who disseminated Lutheran and Calvinist tracts. Prominent among them was Étienne Dolet, who later became a symbol of those martyred in the cause of free thought. A statue was erected to him on the square in 1889.

6 | Rue Saint-Jacques ('St James Street'). One of the oldest roads in Paris (along the line of the old Roman cardo maximus), it formed one of the city's main spinal roads until the construction of the Boulevard St Michel in the 1850s. Pilgrims leaving France for the long road to the shrine of Santiago di Compostela in northwest Spain would gather and depart from here. It was home to the Sorbonne, the oldest French university, founded in 1253, and the site of the first printing press in France in the 1470s.

7 | L'Otelle (nowadays the Hôtel de Ville). Not a hotel (or even a hostel), but the town hall of Paris since 1357, when Étienne Marcel, 'provost of the merchants' (the de facto mayor of the city), bought a property named the House of the Pillars because of the portico that led to it. The core of the current building was begun in 1533 when Francis I decided the French capital needed a grander administrative headquarters, although the building work dragged on for almost a century before it was finally completed in 1628. Perhaps the most dramatic moment in the building's long history came on 27 July 1794 (9 Thermidor according to the French Revolutionary calendar) when Maximilien Robespierre, one of the most hard-line revolutionaries and a member of the Committee of Public Safety, was arrested by his opponents. During the fracas, he was shot in the jaw (some alleged by his own hand) and the next day he was guillotined along with 28 of his associates. The Hôtel became the headquarters of the Paris Commune, the revolutionary government that briefly took power after the French surrender to the Prussians at the end of the Franco-Prussian War in 1870–71. At the overthrow of the Commune on 24 May 1871, the building was set on fire, destroying an archive of 60,000 precious volumes and leading to the Hôtel

de Ville's reconstruction in its present form. It was here that General de Gaulle announced the liberation of Paris on 25 August 1944.

8 | Rue Galande (anagram of 'a gun dealer'), a corruption of Garlande. The street is named for a prominent family in medieval Paris who held property here – Auzeau de Garlande was the seneschal to Philip I (1059–1108) and Louis VI 'the Fat' (1108–37), and his brother Étienne de Garlande held the same office in the 1140s. Rue Galande possesses one of the oldest street signs in Paris, a bas-relief showing the legend of St Julien l'Hospitalier ('Julien the hospitaller'), also known as St Julien le Pauvre ('Julien the poor'). Julien came from a well-to-do Roman family, but during his boyhood developed an unfortunate tendency to sadism after crushing a mouse that was disturbing his concentration during Mass. While on a hunting expedition to slaughter an entire valley full of deer, Julien brought one stag to bay that cursed him to murder his own parents. He eventually became the leader of a group of bandits and, haunted by the ghosts of all the animals he had killed, he murdered his parents when he found them in his own bed and thought his father was a stranger sleeping with his wife. Mad with grief, he took up a life of penance carrying travellers across a river. One day he was asked to transport a leper. Despite the risks of catching the disease and an enormous storm that blew up, Julien staggered across bearing the man, but the leper further demanded that Julien give him his house, which he did. The stranger then revealed himself to be Jesus Christ and Julien was redeemed. One mouse had caused a great deal of mischief.

THE WORLD

CLAES JANSZOON VISSCHER

1 | Troia (Troy) – now Truva in Anatolia, modern-day Turkey – is considered to be the probable site of the events recounted by the Greek poet Homer in his epic *The Iliad*. The story of the Trojan horse does not in fact appear in Homer's work, but in later continuations, including that by the Roman poet Virgil. The Trojans are said to have been tricked by the besieging Greeks, who burned their camp and pretended to sail away, leaving just one man and a giant wooden horse behind. The solitary straggler claimed that he had been abandoned by his comrades and that the horse was an offering to the goddess Athena for the Greeks' safe return home. Unknown to the Trojans, 40 men led by the formidable warrior Odysseus were hiding inside. When Laocoön, a Trojan priest, voiced his suspicions, he was strangled by a huge sea serpent sent by the god Poseidon, and the Trojans then dragged the horse into the city. That night, the Greek warriors emerged from the horse and let the rest of their countrymen, who had turned their ships around, into Troy. The city then fell to them amid a terrible sacking. The episode gave rise to the noun 'Trojan horse', meaning something that breaches one's defences through trickery, and the expression 'Beware of Greeks bearing gifts' (a form of which – *Timeo Danaos et dona ferentes*, 'I fear Greeks even when bearing gifts' – is the warning that Laocoön unsuccessfully delivers to the Trojans).

2 | Thessaloni (anagram of 'hailstones'). Now known as Thessaloniki, the city was also called Salonica in the Middle Ages. It was named for Alexander the Great's half-sister, who was married to Cassander, one of his generals who inherited the throne of Macedonia in 305 BC. A prosperous town in Roman times, it became an early centre of Christianity and then the second city of the Byzantine Empire. The city endured one of the darker moments in its history in 390 when the emperor Theodosius massacred 10,000 of its inhabitants in the hippodrome in revenge for a failed uprising. In the later

Middle Ages it endured a see-saw of control between Byzantines, Bulgarians, Crusaders and Venetians before finally being captured by the Ottoman Turks in 1430. Its cosmopolitan character was further enhanced by the arrival of many Jews expelled from Spain after the Christian capture of Granada in 1492, and by the early sixteenth century they made up half the population. In 1881 Thessaloniki was the birthplace of Kemal Ataturk, the founder of the modern Turkish Republic, and only finally reverted to Greece in 1912, when the Ottoman garrison surrendered, by chance on the feast day of St Demetrios, the city's patron saint.

3 | Isla Brava (*brava* means 'brave') – is the smallest of the inhabited islands of the Cape Verde archipelago. Although discovered in 1462 by the Portuguese explorer Diogo Afonso, it had very few settlers at the time of Visscher's map – only when a volcanic eruption on nearby Fogo in 1680 persuaded that island's population to relocate did it reach a substantial number of inhabitants. In the eighteenth century American whaling ships recruited crews here and a community of Cabo Verdeans grew up in New England. As a result, the island acquired one of the Unites States' most far-flung consulates when one was opened on Brava in 1843.

4 | Tripoli on the Black Sea coast of modern-day Turkey. Tripoli (or Tripolis) was originally founded by colonists from Miletos in 656 BC, and was also known as Ischopolis. It is now the small fishing port of Tirebolu, and is situated a good way west of where Visscher places it. The other famous Tripoli on the map is the capital of modern Libya, which was founded by Phoenicians in the seventh century BC as Oea, then fell into the Greek sphere of influence as Greek settlers moved west from Cyrenaica, later became Carthaginian, before finally falling to the Roman Empire in the second century BC. Its subsequent masters have include Vandals, Byzantines, a succession of Arab dynasties, a brief Spanish interlude, the Ottoman Turks, Italians and an eight-year flirtation with the British Empire before independence in 1951. One famous Tripoli that is not on the map is Lebanon's second city, founded some time before the eighth century BC by the Phoenicians. Among its varied history is being given as a present by Mark Anthony to Ptolemy Philadelphos in 34 BC and later being the centre of the County of Tripoli, one of the crusader states in the Levant from 1109 to 1289.

5 | Constantinopoli (Constantinople or modern-day Istanbul). This city with many names was founded in AD 330 near the site of the ancient town of Byzantium (which itself dated from the mid-seventh century BC) by the emperor Constantine, who wished it to act as the capital of the eastern portion of the Roman Empire. This it did, standing against the tides of history until, its imperial possessions having shrunk virtually to the suburbs of the city, it fell to an Ottoman Turkish siege in 1453. Its last emperor, Constantine XI, is said to have torn off his imperial regalia and flung himself into the final, desperate defence. His body was never recovered. Officially known as Kostantiyye under the Ottoman Empire, it was colloquially referred to as Istanbul (possibly from the Greek *eis tin polin* – 'to the city') or Stamboul. The name was officially changed to Istanbul under the Turkish Republic in 1930. The city has also been called a variety of names by its neighbours or enemies, including Tsargrad ('City of the Caesars') by the Bulgarians and Miklagard ('Great City') by the Vikings.

6 | Berenice – is near modern Benghazi in Libya and was renamed for Berenice II, the queen of Ptolemy III, who was a native of the area. It had previously been called Euhesperides because its great fertility reminded early settlers of the Gardens of the Hesperides, which were reputed to lie in the far west, and from which Hercules, for his 11th labour, had to steal the resident nymphs' golden apples. Berenice had a troubled love life: she was married to Demetrius the Fair of Macedonia in 250 BC, but found that her husband was having an affair with her own mother, Apama. In revenge she had Demetrius assassinated while the adulterous couple were in bed. Her marriage to Ptolemy united her kingdom with Egypt, creating a powerful empire stretching across North Africa. She was reputedly a formidable horsewoman, winning a victory at the Nemean Games in 245 BC.

7 | Samaria, on the border between Judea and Galilee, was the ancient centre of the Samaritans, who held to a form of Judaism they claimed to have been preserved by a select few in Israel while the rest of the Jewish people were in exile in Babylon. They believed that Mount Gezirim, near Nabulus, was the sacred place of the Jews and the proper site of the Temple rather than Jerusalem, and were shunned by mainstream Jewish opinion. Their numbers dwindled until by the twelfth century there were only around 2,000 – and today there are just 800. The parable of the Good Samaritan contained in the gospel of Luke tells of a traveller who is beaten and left for dead. Various other travellers, including 'a priest', came along the road and saw him but ignored him and passed by on the other side. When a Samaritan came along he went to his aid, his act commanding particular praise because he is helping someone from a community who would normally have treated him as an adversary.

8 | Babylon ('baby'-lon) is a city of extreme antiquity, founded around 2300 BC and was the capital of Hammurabi (1792–1750 BC), who created one of the world's earliest law codes. It gave rise to the expression 'an eye for an eye, a tooth for a tooth' for its retributive and seemingly cruel penalties (including being buried alive for breaking into a house by making a hole in the wall, and being burned alive for taking advantage of a fire by stealing from the affected property). Babylon was centre of a great empire, and its last ruler was Nebuchadnezzar, by tradition responsible for the building of the Hanging Gardens of Babylon, but it then fell to the Persians in 539 BC and its political importance declined. Alexander the Great died of a fever in the palace of Nebuchadnezzar in 323 BC after a gruelling journey back from his final campaign in India.

FRANCE'S POST-ROADS

NICOLAS BEREY

1 | Château Gaillard is marked on the map as Chau Gaillaird ('gail' – sounds like 'gale' – and 'laird'). Château Gaillard (or 'cheeky castle') got its name when Richard I (the Lionheart) of England, who had ordered it built to guard the approaches to English-held Normandy from French attacks, saw what his engineers had achieved and deemed it 'cheeky', a provocative challenge thrusting towards the heartland of the French monarchy. It was doubly so, because a treaty between Richard and Philip II of France explicitly forbade the building of fortifications on the site. Richard was so proud of Gaillard and its impregnability that he announced he could defend it even if its walls were made of butter. He did not enjoy his triumph for long, because he died in 1199, the year after the castle's completion, when a wound from a crossbow bolt he sustained while besieging Châlus became infected. The French had the last laugh in another way, when the castle fell to them just five years later in March 1204, after a seven-month siege and at the start of a campaign that saw them reconquer the whole of Normandy. Gaillard later served as the residence for the nine-year-old David II of Scotland, who was forced to flee his homeland after the English victory at Halidon Hill in 1333 and spent eight years immured in the fort with his bride, Joan, who was just three years older (David was peculiarly unlucky – in 1346, five years after his return to Scotland, he was captured by the English at Neville's Cross and spent the next 11 years incarcerated in the Tower of London). Château Gaillard changed hands a number of times between England and France in the Hundred Years' War before becoming definitively French in 1449. It was partially demolished at the start of the seventeenth century.

2 | Angers. The capital of the Maine-et-Loire département, Angers was the birthplace of the Angevin dynasty in the Middle Ages. It began life as the *oppidum* (a hillfort proto-town) of the Andecavi

tribe, and after the Roman invasion by Julius Caesar in the 40s BC was renamed Juliomagus (or 'the market of Julius'). The counts of Anjou gradually consolidated their control in the area in the tenth and eleventh centuries, and became sufficiently powerful for Henry I of England to see them as opportune allies against the kings of France. His first attempt at a dynastic union failed when his eldest son William, destined for the match, drowned in the sinking of the *White Ship* in 1120. Instead, Henry's daughter Matilda married Geoffrey Plantagenet, the heir to the county of Anjou. In 1151 their son, also Henry, became successively Duke of Normandy (a territory his father had acquired) and Count of Anjou on his father's death, and then the following year gained control of Aquitaine by his marriage to Eleanor, its heiress, together with Gascony and Poitiers. In 1154, on the death of Stephen, with whom his mother and her allies had tussled over England in a protracted civil war, he added the English crown to his burgeoning domains. The Angevin Empire, as his collection of territories are known, was one of Europe's largest and most powerful states, but it lasted only until its total collapse in 1204, when King John proved himself utterly unsuited to life as a military leader and lost almost the whole of northern France in a single campaigning season.

3 | Orleans ('*or*' being French for 'gold' and 'leans'). Orleans began as Cenabum, the *oppidum* of the Carnutes tribe, but was destroyed by Julius Caesar in 52 BC. It was then rebuilt and refounded again in the third century AD, when it was renamed Civitas Aurelianum in honour of the emperor Aurelian (r. 270–275). It was the scene of one of the most significant military defeats in English history, inflicted by Joan of Arc, a young peasant girl who had heard what she believed to be saints' voices urging her to go to the royal court and inspire the dauphin Charles, heir to the French throne, to continue what many considered a hopeless resistance to the English. Despite their initial suspicion of the teenage girl parading around the siege-works in armour, the French commanders found that she was having a pleasing effect on morale and a previously disheartened besieging force was roused to greater efforts. Nine days later Orléans fell to the French, leading to a wholesale revival in their cause and the conquest of most of the English territories in France. Joan was less fortunate: she was captured by Burgundian troops allied to the English outside Compiègne in 1430, handed over to the English authorities, tried for heresy and, when she refused to recant, was burned at the stake at Rouen on 30 May 1431.

4 | Chaalons (modern Châlons) – anagram of 'cash loan'. Châlons-en-Champagne (renamed in 1995 from Châlons-sur-Marne) derives its name from a corruption of the Cataullani, the Gaulish tribe in residence at the time of Caesar's conquest. It stands near the site of a battle that saved the Roman Empire, although only for a decade or two, and prevented a very different style of nomadic conqueror from emerging as triumphant. In 451 an unlikely alliance formed between Visigoths (themselves Germanic barbarians who had migrated westwards from southern Ukraine over the preceding century) and what survived of the Roman army in Gaul (which was very little). The coalition delivered a rebuff to the vast army of Attila the Hun, whose forces had been spreading terror on the Roman borderlands almost unchecked. Although it was not the stinging defeat Roman historians claimed it to be, it did stop the Huns' momentum; they turned back eastwards and then paused after a final sack of Aquileia in northeast Italy in 452 (refugees from which are said to have founded the original settlement at Venice). Attila died on his wedding night early in 453, when he choked to death on his own blood after either a severe nosebleed or the rupture of arteries in his oesophagus. After so much bloodshed, it was his own blood that killed him. Attila's sons proved better at squabbling than leadership and within a year the vast Hunnish empire had fallen apart.

5 | Soissons = gained its name from the Gaulish Suessiones tribe and was renamed Noviodunum (or 'new fort') after the Roman conquest. It was one of the last parts of Gaul to remain in Roman hands, acting as the capital of the 'Kingdom of Soissons' ruled by the last Roman military commander in Gaul, Aegidius, and then his son, Syagrius, who held it as a Roman enclave in the north after the provinces in the south were overrun by the Visigoths. It even survived the fall of the Roman Empire in the West by ten years, only finally falling to the Frankish king Clovis in 486.

6 | Vitry, or Vitry-le-François, was founded in 1545 by Francis I to replace the nearby town of Vitry-en-Perthois, which had been razed the previous year by the Holy Roman Emperor Charles V during a war with France. Francis, a true Renaissance king, ordered the architect and engineer Girolamo Marini to design it along modern lines, which explains its regular grid pattern in the centre in contrast to the organic muddle of most medieval urban topography.

7 | Bayeux, where the most famous artefact is the Bayeux Tapestry, a 231-feet-long (70-metre) strip of linen, probably created around 1080, which tells the story of the Battle of Hastings with a distinct Norman bias (it lays great emphasis on scenes where Harold Godwinson is alleged to have sworn to support Duke William of Normandy's claim to the English throne, so making Harold an oathbreaker when he accepted the crown after Edward the Confessor's death in January 1066). Its most famous scene is the image of an Anglo-Saxon warrior plucking an arrow from his eye under the inscription 'Here King Harold was Killed'. It is not wholly clear if the warrior shown was Harold, but it helped perpetuate the myth that this was how the last of the Anglo-Saxon kings perished. The tapestry is embroidered in another sense, too, because it is in fact not a tapestry at all but an embroidery – the patterns that make up the story were not woven directly into the fabric on the loom, but stitched onto the linen cloth later.

8 | Sens ('sense' without the ending 'e') was named for the Gaulish Senones tribe, whose name may be derived from a Celtic word meaning 'old'. Its cathedral, begun around 1135, was one of the first of the new wave of Gothic churches built in France. Sens was also the scene of the trial of Peter Abelard, a talented but rather prickly poet and theologian who had a talent for getting himself into trouble. In 1114 he managed to fall madly in love with Héloise, the niece of Fulbert, a canon of Paris cathedral and one of his patrons, and the ensuing scandal forced him into monastic life. He spent his time compiling works on logic and a great work on theology called the *Theologia*, which was deemed to be contrary to the Church's teachings on the Trinity. He was tried at Sens in 1121 and, when condemned, forced to burn his book in public. After alienating a succession of abbots, he spent five years confined to a hermitage at Nogent-Sur-Seine before contriving to become abbot of a community of nuns headed by none other than his long-lost love Héloise. His happiness was abruptly terminated in 1141 when he got into another theological wrangle with the well-connected Bernard of Clairvaux (founder of the Cistercian order), was condemned, excommunicated and his books once again burned. Heartbroken, he died soon after.

THE NORTH SEA

ROBERT DUDLEY

1 | Ipswig (anagram of 'swig pi'). Ipswich (spelled here Ipswig) is one of England's oldest towns, having its origins in a seventh-century town called Gipeswic (the 'wic' designating a trading settlement). It was an important centre of the Anglo-Saxon kingdom of East Anglia and came under the control of the Vikings when they overran the east of England in 869. Recaptured by Edward the Elder, the son of Alfred the Great, in 917, it grew prosperous in the Middle Ages on the back of the wool trade. Ipswich's most eminent son was Thomas Wolsey, who from humble beginnings as a butcher's son rose through the ranks of the Church to become Henry VII's royal chaplain and then, through his ability to flatter the ambitions of Henry, became Archbishop of York in 1514 and a cardinal the next year. Wolsey's fall was as rapid as his rise had been meteoric. Henry's desire for a male heir led him to want to set aside his first wife, Catherine of Aragon, who had not produced one. Despite his high standing in the Church, Wolsey could not – to the unbridled fury of his royal master – persuade the papal authorities to grant the king an annulment of his marriage. Ordered back to London from York, where he had taken refuge after being stripped of his government offices, Wolsey fell ill and died at Leicester in November 1530, saving Henry the trouble of having him executed. The fine house he had built at Hampton Court thus fell into royal hands and became a favoured Tudor palace in west London. The artist Thomas Gainsborough, a local Suffolk boy, lived in Ipswich between 1752 and 1759, painting local merchants and dignitaries, before his career really took off after his move to Bath and then to London.

2 | Edam is the name for the dam across the local river E (or Ije), which was built in the thirteenth century. It was a prosperous trading town until flooding caused the harbour to be partially sealed with lock gates in 1569, resulting in its silting up. Edam was thrown back on its other resources, notably the cheese for which it was to become world famous. A semi-hard cow's cheese, its slow maturing qualities made it a popular choice for export, including to the Dutch colonies which grew up after the establishment of the Dutch East India Company in 1601. Known in Dutch as the VOC, or Vereenigde Oostindische Compagnie, or more popularly as 'Jan Compagnie', it was a powerful mercantile company, almost a government in its own right, which carried the flag of the Dutch United Provinces to the Spice Islands of Indonesia, to Sri Lanka, to the Americas (where they held the future New York from 1624 to 1664) and even, for a brief period between 1630 and 1654, to a slice of northern Brazil.

3 | Hoorn (with an 'o' less makes 'horn') takes its name either from its horn-shaped harbour or being a 'corner' of land along the indented north Holland coast. Founded in 716 at a time of growth in emporia, or trading settlements, throughout northwestern Europe, it reached the height of its prosperity in the seventeenth century. Jan Pieterszoon Coen, one of the most famous officers of the Dutch East India Company (the VOC), was born here. He twice served as governor-general of the company's territories in Indonesia (between 1617 and 1629). His aggressive tactics muscled out the VOC's English and Portuguese rivals, securing monopolies over the clove trade in the Moluccas and the nutmeg trade from the Banda Islands. In 1619 he conquered the site of modern Jakarta, where he established the VOC's headquarters for the entire East Indies, which became known as Batavia (after the Latin name of the Netherlands). He was also VOC governor-general in 1623 at the time of the Amboina Massacre – the arrest, torture and execution of ten English East India Company merchants on Ambon. The Dutch explorer Willem Schouten was also born in Hoorn, and when he discovered and rounded the southern tip of South America in 1616, he named it Kap Hoorn (Cape Horn) after his hometown.

4 | Delfe (anagram of 'ed elf'). Eight miles northwest of Rotterdam, Delft was founded in 1076 and grew to become one of Holland's most important commercial centres. Its best-known product was Delft Blue, a tin-glazed pottery with a characteristic hue, which offered a more economical alternative to expensive imported Chinese porcelain. Delft served as the de facto capital of the Dutch provinces during their rebellion against Spanish rule from 1568, and the United Netherlands' first leader, William the Silent, Prince of Orange, was assassinated here in 1584. It was the birthplace of Antonie van Leeuwenhoek (1632–1724), the father of microbiology, whose pioneering work with the microscope enabled him to view bacteria for the first time; and also of Hugo Grotius, whose *On the Law of War and Peace* (1625) laid the foundations of modern international law, providing a legal framework within which states could relate to each other, which would restrain the untrammelled use of warfare. In one form or another, Grotius's ideas have continued to shape the architecture of international relations to this day.

5 | Orford-nes (Or-'ford'[a river crossing]-nes, now Orfordness or Orford Ness). A long shingle spit on the Suffolk Coast, Orford Ness was formed by a centuries-long drift of gravel from further north. Its isolated location led to its acquisition by the War Department in 1913 as a mooted base for several airfields and testing sites. It was used by the Atomic Weapons Research Establishment in the 1960s for testing the components of atom bombs and then as a base for the RAF Explosive Ordnance Disposal unit. It is now a nature reserve, run by the National Trust, containing one of Europe's best-preserved areas of coastal vegetated shingle.

6 | Amsterdam (anagram of 'smart mead'). The capital and most populous city of the modern Netherlands, Amsterdam was first recorded in 1275 when Count Floris V of Holland granted its residents immunity from tolls. Its merchants acquired a dominant position

in northern Holland (helped by their acquisition of a monopoly of beer imports from Hamburg in 1323 and the wealth accumulated from the wool trade with England). When the Spanish captured its rival port of Antwerp in 1585 during the Dutch Revolt, refugees (including many merchants) flooded into Amsterdam, securing its position as the rebels' new chief city. It became the headquarters of the Dutch East India Company, and the site of the Netherlands' first stock exchange. Among its many monuments is the Anne Frank House on Prinsengracht, where the teenage Jewish girl hid with members of her family and friends from Nazi persecution during World War Two. Finally betrayed to the Gestapo in August 1944, she was transported to Auschwitz and then to Bergen-Belsen concentration camp, where she died, probably of typhus, around February 1945. Her diary, preserved and then published after the war in an edition of just 3,000 copies, has since been translated into 60 languages and is probably the most famous book of all time by a Dutch author.

7 | Alborow ('lend' it an 'l' and an 'r' to make 'all-borrow'). Now spelled as Aldeburgh (or 'old town'), this was a thriving fishing village in Tudor times and became prosperous enough for Henry VIII to grant it a charter as a borough in 1539, before the treacherous sands offshore shifted again and blocked the harbour, putting an end to its precocious growth. The *Pelican*, the ship in which Sir Francis Drake completed his circumnavigation of the globe in 1580, was built here. One of a flotilla of five vessels to set out, it was the only one to return, with 56 men aboard, and cemented Drake's reputation as a daring captain, which he subsequently milked for all it was worth in being allowed by Elizabeth I to raid Spanish possessions in the New World and to attack Cadiz – provocations which in no small measure contributed to the launching of the Spanish Armada against England in 1588. Centuries later Aldeburgh was home to the composer Benjamin Britten, whose works included *A Young Person's Guide to the Orchestra* and *Peter Grimes*, and he founded the Aldeburgh music festival in 1948. Britten lived in the town for the last 20 years of his life, from 1956.

RUSSIA

JOAN BLAEU

1 | Moscua (anagram of 'cam sou'), or Moscow, is first mentioned in a Russian chronicle in 1147 and within nine years the growing settlement had received a protective wooden wall. Unfortunately, this did not stop it (and probably aided it) being burned down by the Mongols during the invasion of 1237 when Russia fell under their rule, a period known as the 'Tatar Yoke'. The city became the capital of the Grand Duchy of Moscow in 1283, and by the 1480s, under the rule of Ivan IV, it threw off Mongol rule and completed the conquest of the other neighbouring principalities. It continued to be Russia's capital until Peter the Great moved the seat of government to St Petersburg in 1712. Moscow regained its position after the 1917 rebellion, which overthrew the tsar and brought the communists to power, and it acted as capital of the Soviet Union and then (from 1991) once more of Russia. The Cam is the river that runs through the English university town of Cambridge. A sou is a French coin, derived from the Roman gold solidus, which was taken up as a currency division by the Frankish ruler Charlemagne in the late eighth century. It was debased over time, becoming eventually a low-value bronze coin in the eighteenth century. It was abolished altogether by the revolutionary government in 1795, when the Franc was introduced (although the term remained in use as slang for a five-centime coin).

2 | Nisi Novegorod ('Nisi', from Decree Nisi, and '*nove*'), or Nizhniy Novgorod. Situated at the confluence of the Volga and Oka rivers around 250 miles (400 kilometres) east of Moscow, Nizhniy Novgorod was founded in 1221, as the Muscovites began to press eastwards and colonise the fringes of Siberia. It became formally part of the Grand Duchy of Moscow in 1392 and an important centre for trade into Siberia and Central Asia; the annual Nizhniy Novgorod Fair, established in 1817, became

Russia's most important. Among the city's notable residents was the writer Maxim Gorky, born there in 1868. His real surname was Peshkov, but he adopted the pen-name Gorky (meaning 'bitter') in reference to his own troubled life and the trials of working-class Russians which his works portrayed. He became a committed Marxist, but opposed the communist seizure of power in 1917. In exile for a decade, he was induced to return by Stalin in 1928 and became an establishment figure and the leader of the Socialist Realist literary movement, which acted – in effect – as propaganda for the Soviet regime. Nizhniy Novgorod was renamed Gorky in his honour in 1932 and only reverted to its former name in 1990, after the collapse of the communist regime. A Decree Nisi is a document in British law that a divorce will become final within a set time, unless the parties come to some other agreement. '*Nove*' is the Italian for nine.

3 | Smolenska (anagram of 'ask lemons'), or Smolensk, is one of Russia's oldest cities. It is mentioned in a *Russian Primary Chronicle* entry for 863, when the Scandinavian chieftains Askold and Dir were among the Vikings who had been invited by Slavic tribes to restore order to the area the year before, but instead bypassed it and pressed on to Kiev (which then became the capital of a Viking-Slavic state known as Kievan Rus). On the border between Russia and Lithuania (a powerful state in the Middle Ages), control of Smolensk see-sawed between the two, being captured by the Russians in 1340, the Lithuanians in 1408, the Russians again in 1514, the Poles in 1611, and only finally becoming Russian in 1654. It was the site of a battle during Napoleon's invasion of Russia in August 1812 (and lay along the route of his retreat with the ragged remains of his Grande Armée four months later). Smolensk was the birthplace of Yuri Gagarin, who on 12 April 1961 became the first man to reach Earth orbit in his *Vostok 1* spacecraft, shocking the United States, which had underestimated the Soviet Union's technological ability, and igniting the Space Race.

4 | Weliki Novgorod (or 'Old' Novgorod). Weliki, or Veliky, Novgorod was already in existence in 859, when it was mentioned in the *Russian Primary Chronicle.* It had a unique form of government from 1019, when it was ruled not by a prince, duke or tsar, but by an elected assembly, being in effect a republic. It grew rich on trade, becoming the eastern conduit into Russia for the merchant towns of the Hanseatic League. In 1478 Ivan III (the Great) finally snuffed out Novgorod's independence and thereafter the town experienced a relative decline in importance.

5 | Thorn, or Toruń, was founded in 1233 by the Teutonic Knights, a Christian chivalric order established in Germany, which acted as a spearhead for settlement by German-speaking peasants and for crusades against the pagan peoples of Prussia and Lithuania. Gradually, the crusading movement lost its impetus and the conversion to Christianity of the rulers of Poland and Lithuania removed much of the Teutonic Knights' raison d'être, while the union of those two states created a powerful new rival which rapidly encroached on the Knights' territory. In 1410 the Grand Master of the Order Ulrich von Jungingen was defeated and killed by a Polish-Lithuanian army at Tannenberg, 100 miles (160 kilometres) northeast of Thorn. Most of the Teutonic Knights' other leaders also perished and, although the peace signed at Thorn deprived them of only a little of their lands, the order went into a sharp decline. In 1454 Thorn revolted against the Teutonic Knights and became part of the Kingdom of Poland. Thorn was annexed by Prussia following the Second Partition of Poland in 1793 and was only returned to Poland following World War Two. The city was the birthplace in 1473 of the astronomer Nicolaus Copernicus, who in 1543 published one of the most important scientific works of all time, the *De revolutionibus orbium coelestium* (*Concerning the Revolutions of the Heavens*), which contained a definitive statement of his heliocentric theory (that the Earth orbited around the sun, and not the other way around).

6 | Vilna is a city of many names. Now known (in Lithuanian) as Vilnius, it is also called (in Russian) Vilna and (in Polish) Wilno, reflecting a complex political history since its establishment in the tenth century. In 1323 it became the capital of the Grand Duchy of Lithuania and was the subject of one of the more quixotic of English military expeditions when Henry Bolingbroke, the future Henry IV, and a number of English knights joined in a siege of the city during an intervention by the Teutonic Knights in a Lithuanian civil war. The incident was alluded to by Geoffrey Chaucer in 'The Knight's Tale', part of his *Canterbury Tales,* in which the knight is said to have 'the border bigonne, Aboven all nations in Pruce' (or Prussia). Coming under Polish control in the mid-sixteenth century, Vilnius was annexed by Russia in 1795 as part of the Third Partition of Poland. The city belonged briefly to the Republic of Lithuania that was established in 1918 during the chaos that followed the Russian Revolution, but reverted to Poland in 1922, then suffered a turbulent World War Two in which Lithuanian, German and Soviet occupation alternated, and ultimately ended up in the Soviet Union before it became the capital of independent Lithuania in 1991.

7 | Cargopol (anagram of 'carp logo'), or Kargopol, is a regional administrative headquarters of a subdivision of the Arkhangelsk *oblast.* It was first mentioned in a document from 1146 and grew rich from its position on the main route from Moscow to Russia's growing Siberian territories, from the sixteenth century, and the port of Arkhangelsk to the north. Alexander Baranov, the first governor of Russian-held Alaska from 1799, was born in Kargopol. He named its main settlement Novo Arkhangelsk (although it subsequently became Sitka) and it was the headquarters of an expanding Russian colony, whose tendrils touched as far south as northern California, until it was sold to the United States in 1867 for $7.2 million. The transaction at the time was dubbed 'Seward's Folly' after the then Secretary of State who was considered to have struck a bad deal, although the subsequent discovery of enormous mineral resources in Alaska, and its strategic position facing Russian Siberia mean that, with hindsight, it was one of the greatest bargains of all time.

PATAGONIA

SIR JOHN NARBROUGH

1 | Port Famin. Now San Juan de la Posesión in Chile, Port Famin gained its unfortunate name from the attempt by the Spanish to build a fort here in 1584, which ended in disaster as soldiers and colonists starved or froze to death in the bleak landscape. Ironically, Narbrough notes that there is 'Good Fresh water here', and that, despite some rocks close to the shore, it was relatively easy to make landfall there.

2 | Port Gallant (port is a 'harbour', gallant means 'chivalrous'). A sheltered harbour, Narbrough simply noted in his journal that to the west of this was 'very high Land, whose topps are Covered with snow'.

3 | San Jeroms River. Jerom refers to Jerome, one of the first translators of the Bible. An able Christian polemicist, he retired to Palestine after a bid to be elected pope failed, and in 382 began a new translation of the Bible into Latin. Up to that date the faithful had had to rely on a rather defective 'Old Latin' version or the Septuagint, a Greek translation, which derived its name (meaning 'Seventy') from the tradition that it had been composed by a panel of 72, with six members drawn from each of the 12 Tribes of Israel. Jerome's translation departed so significantly from the established version that traditionalists were outraged and when a section of the Book of Jonah was read out in Oea (now Tripoli in Libya), it caused a riot. Narbrough found this San Jeroms channel to be a useful cut between the labyrinthine islands off the tip of Patagonia. He thought its 'several brave' coves were rather like the wet dock at Deptford back home, and one of them he called Mussle Bay, for the great quantity of good mussles which could be gathered there.

4 | Conoa Bay (contains 'cyan' and 'boa'). Narbrough named this for the canoes which he saw in abundance in the Magellan Strait. He described them as being 'of the rind of the trees' bound together with splinted sticks. He noted they were around 18 feet long and four feet (5.5 by 1.2 metres) wide and could carry up to ten people. Narbrough was generally sympathetic to the Patagonians, but he had difficulties communicating with them. He commented that they said the word '*ursah*' repeatedly, but that 'what it meant I could not understand, nor one word they spake'.

5 | Cape Holland. A cape is a type of cloak, and Holland, or the Netherlands, is one of the 'Low Countries'. Now known in Chile as Cabo Holland, it forms a sparsely populated region of Patagonia, one of a number of outcroppings and bays which Narbrough sailed by but did not stop to investigate.

6 | Cape Coventry. One theory has it that the English expression 'to be sent to Coventry', or to be ostentatiously ignored, stems from the English Civil War, when particularly disliked Royalist prisoners were sent to the strongly Parliamentarian town, where they were liable to find life rather uncomfortable. Cape Coventry, now Cabo Coventry, was probably named by Narbrough for Sir William Coventry (1627–86) who served on the Navy Board as a Commissioner from 1662 to 1667, and was also the MP for Great Yarmouth between 1661 and 1679. He fell from grace after objecting to his being lampooned as 'Sir Cautious Trouble-All' in a play penned by George Villiers, the 2nd Duke of Buckingham and a favourite of Charles II. When Coventry died in 1686, he left £3,000 in his will for the redemption of Englishmen who had been carried off into slavery by the Barbary Corsairs of North Africa. The cape named after him is a desolate place, which Narbrough passed over quickly, noting only that it was one of several nearby promontories that had a 'small wood growing on them, some grasse, some are rocks, there is broken ground amongst them'.

PENNSYLVANIA

THOMAS HOLME

1 | Springfield ('spring'-field). In common with many towns and cities in Pennsylvania, Springfield (spelled Springfeild on the map) was founded by Quakers who either accompanied or supported William Penn's establishment of the colony. It was the destination of one of the first roads laid down in the colony, leading from Philadelphia. It has one of the earliest Quaker meetinghouses in the state, established in 1801. On the map the manor of Springfield is assigned to Gulielma Maria Penn, the wife of William Penn. Born Gulielma Maria Postuma Springett, she was a wealthy heiress and daughter of a lawyer who fought for Parliament during the English Civil War. She married Penn in 1672 but never visited the land that in theory belonged to her, remaining at their house at Warmingshurst in Sussex while her husband set up the colony in 1682–84.

2 | Haverford (anagram of 'had fervor') was given its name by the community of Welsh Quakers who settled this part of Pennsylvania (including next-door Radnor Township). It was so-called in memory of Haverfordwest, the county town of Pembrokeshire in Wales. Founded in 1682 Haverford Township was predominantly agricultural and long the site of a number of saw and powder mills.

3 | Fair Mount. Now the site of the Philadelphia Museum of Art, Fair Mount was originally outside the city limits of Pennsylvania and earmarked by William Penn to build his own manor house. In the end he built it at Falls, just to the north of the city, where the grand Pennsbury Manor was reconstructed in the 1930s. By the nineteenth century, the urban sprawl had begun to encroach on what had become Fairmount and it was the site of several reservoirs and the Fairmount Water Works, which, curiously, were one of the places in the United States that Charles Dickens was particularly keen to see when he visited in 1842. He describes them approvingly as 'no less ornamental than useful, being tastefully laid out as a public garden, and kept in the best and neatest order'.

4 | Trial Holme. The area described as belonging to 'Trial Holme' was in fact assigned to Captain Thomas Holme, a member of the very first assembly of the colony that met in 1682 under the presidency of William Penn. He was subsequently appointed surveyor-general of Pennsylvania and produced this, the first map of the colony – it was felt particularly urgent to establish an accurate survey, as there were tensions with Lord Baltimore's Colony of Maryland to the west, and several people had been killed in clashes. He was subsequently appointed to be Commissioner of Property for the colony, a position he held until his death in 1694.

5 | Samuel Clarridg (anagram of 'cruel madrigals'). Samuel Clarridg (or Clarridge) was a firebrand Irish Quaker, whose refusal to compromise on his faith led to him into a number or scrapes with the law. He was imprisoned in Dublin three times, in 1660, 1662 and 1669, for attending Quaker meetings. He lobbied to have the restrictions on Quakers in Ireland lifted and had 2,000 primers printed to instruct Quaker children in their faith. His position as a prosperous merchant to some extent protected his position (and in 1672 he was allowed a licence to trade in Dublin without taking the customary oath, which, as a devout Quaker, he could not do). He became embroiled in a scandal in 1676 when he got his maid pregnant, and he was nearly expelled from the Quaker community. Although he never visited Pennsylvania, he was an early investor and bought 5,000 acres of land, much of which, however, he soon sold to Thomas Holme.

6 | Philadelphia – received its name from the Greek words *philos* ('love') and *adelphos* ('brother'), a reference to Penn's vision that the colony should be a place of fraternal love (it is still nicknamed 'the City of Brotherly Love'). William Penn received a land grant from Charles II in 1681 for what would become the Colony of Pennsylvania (the land was officially in repayment for a loan made by his father Admiral William Penn). As almost the entire eastern seaboard of New England had already been allocated, Penn was given land which had recently been captured from the Swedes and Dutch. He early identified the site for Philadelphia as the colony's chief settlement, but his plan for a symmetric, regular grid of eight blocks soon broke down, as houses spread out towards the Schuylkill River. It rapidly grew to become one of the most prominent towns in the 13 Colonies, an important trading port and a hotbed of American patriot sentiment, which hosted the First and Second Continental Congresses in 1774 and 1775 and the signing of the Declaration of Independence in 1776. It was the capital of the United States for ten years, from 1790 to 1800, while the permanent federal capital at Washington, DC, was being prepared.

7 | Moreland (Mannor of Moreland) was named for Nicolas More, who was given a large tract of land by Penn when he arrived in Pennsylvania in 1682. Although trained in medicine, he set himself up in business as a merchant and was respected enough by his peers to be appointed first chief justice of the supreme court of Pennsylvania in 1684 (aided by his false claim to have been a lawyer in London). Unfortunately, he proved an arrogant and rather erratic chief justice, and the shortcomings in his legal ability soon became apparent. In 1685 he was impeached before the assembly on several charges, including intimidating a witness, mistreatment of his fellow judges and the unlawful constitution of juries. He was found guilty and thus has the dubious honour of being the first ever judge to be impeached in what would become the United States.

8 | Dellaware ('dell' – wooded valley – and 'aware') River. At around 300 miles (480 kilometres) in length, the Delaware is one of the eastern seaboard's principal rivers. It was named for Thomas West, Baron de la Warr, who was the first governor of Virginia from 1609 to 1618. What became the state of Delaware originally formed part of the Colony of Pennsylvania, until the two were legally separated in 1776.

THE ATLANTIC

PIETER GOOS

1 | Ravenna ('raven') had its heyday in the last days of the Western Roman Empire. Its position, surrounded by marshes on one side but with a port allowing easy access to the Adriatic, made it the perfect capital for Honorius, emperor from 395, just as the Germanic barbarians pressing on the imperial boundaries began to flood into the imperial heartland in Italy. When finally they succeeded in deposing the last emperor, the hapless teenager Romulus Augustulus (named with unintentional irony for Rome's first king and its first emperor), it was Ravenna they took as their capital. The Ostrogothic king Theodoric captured the city in 493, restoring a temporary peace and post-imperial twilight to Italy: his mausoleum is one of Ravenna's most splendid monuments. Once the Byzantines (the Eastern Romans) retook it in 540, it became the capital of the Exarchate of Ravenna, until the city fell to the Lombards in 751. The mosaics of Emperor Justinian and his wife Theodora in the Church of San Vitale are among the glories of early medieval art.

2 | Sevilia (anagram of 'visa lie'). Seville was established by the Tartessians, an ancient culture of Andalusia, in around 800 BC. The city was occupied by the Phoenicians and then by the Romans, who captured it in 206 BC during the Second Punic War and gave it the name Hispalis (of which Seville is a corruption). It was an important centre of the Visigothic kingdom, which ruled the Iberian peninsula from the mid-fifth century and fell to invading Arab Muslim armies in 712. It formed part of the Islamic Emirate of Córdoba and its successor states until it fell to the resurgent Spanish Christian forces of Ferdinand III of Castile in 1248. Seville became Spain's most prosperous city during the Age of Exploration, serving from 1503 as the headquarters of the Casa de Contratación ('Trade House'), responsible for controlling all trade with Spain's

new colonies in the Americas. The writer Miguel de Cervantes spent time in Seville's city jail in 1597. A royal tax collector, he had the misfortune to deposit the money he had collected in overdue taxes from Granada in a bank that then went bust. Unable to hand over what was due, he was slung into prison. He made good use of the time that he was incarcerated, however, by using it to dream up the stories which formed the heart of his great picaresque novel *Don Quixote*, and so guaranteeing him far greater fame than he could ever have hoped for as a civil servant.

3 | Palermo ('paler'-mo) sometimes refers to itself, with self-deprecating pride, as Europe's most-conquered city. After its initial foundation by the Phoenicians around 734 BC, it experienced rule by Greeks, Romans, Byzantines, Aghlabid Arabs, Normans, German Hohenstaufens, Spanish and Franco-Spanish Bourbons, before becoming part of the Kingdom of Sardinia in 1860 (and of the unified Kingdom of Italy the following year). Perhaps the city's most glorious epoch was during the reign of the Norman Roger II from 1130 to 1154. A cultured and tolerant monarch he encouraged literary and scientific exchanges between Muslim and Christian scholars, creating a hybrid culture that produced the *Tabula Rogeriana* (*Book of Roger*), a map of the world compiled by the Arab geographer Muhammad al-Idrisi, and churches which show the influence of Arab-Norman architecture, such as the red domes of St John of the Hermits and the richly inlaid carvings of Monreale Cathedral.

4 | Ragusa ('Rag' and 'USA'). A resolutely independent town on Croatia's Adriatic coast, Ragusa (now Dubrovnik) managed to retain its autonomous status through centuries of attack by more powerful neighbours such as the Byzantine, Ottoman and Venetian empires. Founded around 614 by refugees from the Slav and Avar sack of nearby Epidauros, it at first came under the rule of the Byzantine Empire, but the weakening of Byzantine control in the northern Balkans meant that it gradually detached itself from central control. The growing wealth of its merchants brought it to the attention of Venice, which came to regard it as a dangerous rival and in 1205 the Venetians, having suborned the army of the Fourth Crusade to take Constantinople instead of heading for Jerusalem, turned its forces on Ragusa, which was then subject to them until 1358. Thereafter the city engaged in a delicate balancing act between Venice and the Ottomans, until in 1804 Napoleon's armies marched in and extinguished its independence, an act confirmed at the end of the Napoleonic Wars by the Congress of Vienna, which, in the face of bitter complaints by the Ragusans, awarded it to the Austro-Hungarian Empire. Rag or ragtime is a musical genre originating in the Southern states of the USA. Popular in the last decades of the nineteenth and the first two decades of the twentieth century, it had a characteristic syncopated or 'ragged' beat and among its finest exponents was Scott Joplin, the composer of 'Maple Leaf Rag'.

5 | Valencia ('vale'-ncia), Spain's third largest city, was founded by the Romans in 138 BC as Valentia Edetanorum (after the local Edetani tribe). It was conquered by the Visigoths in 413, and fell briefly back into Byzantine Roman hands between 554 and 625, before its conquest by the invading Arabs in 714. In the late eleventh century, when the Christian kingdoms of Spain were beginning to expand, opening up a somewhat lawless frontier with the Muslim emirates to the south, soldiers of fortune and adventurers flourished there. One of them, Rodrigo Díaz de Vivar, nicknamed El Cid, carved himself out an independent territory in the region of Valencia, finally conquering the city in 1094 with his mixed Spanish–Arab army. He defended against all-comers for five years, until his death during a siege by the Muslim revivalist Almoravids in 1099, although it is unlikely that his wife Ximena placed his corpse on his horse and pretended he still lived as a means of preventing his army's morale collapsing, as portrayed by Sophia Loren and Charlton Heston in the 1961 Hollywood version of the tale. The city was the site of the first printing press in Spain, established in 1493.

6 | Lisbona (anagram of 'albinos'). Lisbon's origins are lost in antiquity, although it was probably founded by the Phoenicians about 1200 BC (and not by the legendary Greek hero Odysseus, or Ulysses, from whom its original name Olisipo, or Ulyssipio, was said to derive). It was successively ruled by the Romans, the Sueves (a Germanic group), the Visigoths and the Arabs, before asserting its independence in 1147 as the capital of an independent county of Portugal. The Portuguese forces that besieged it were helped by English crusaders on their way to the Second Crusade, beginning ties of friendship that culminated in 1386 with the Treaty of Windsor between the two countries, making Portugal, it is said, England's (and Britain's) oldest ally.

7 | Montpelliers, anagram of 'triples lemon', or Montpellier, is a relative newcomer as southern French cities go, being first mentioned in a document only in 985. It became the seat of a university, with a notable medical faculty, from 1180. Among its students was the mystic Nostradamus, who was expelled in 1529 for having practised as an apothecary, a manual trade of which the university authorities disapproved. He eventually turned to the occult and from 1555 published a series of *Prophecies* and *Almanacs* containing predictions in verse of future events. His subsequent admirers have claimed that he foretold things as diverse as the Great Fire of London, the French Revolution and the atom bomb attack on Hiroshima. His quatrains, though, are sufficiently dense and delphic that, with a will, almost any historical event can be retrospectively read back into them.

8 | Argiera (anagram of 'air rage'), an early Spanish form for Algiers. Established by the Phoenicians in the early first millennium BC, Algiers was refounded by the Berber Ziyid dynasty in 944 (its Arabic name Al-Jaza'ir refers to the four islands which originally lay off the coast). Briefly occupied by the Spanish from 1510 to 1529, it then was then recaptured by Aruj and Hayreddine Barbarossa, the first of the Barbary Corsairs, pirates who plagued the western Mediterranean for over three centuries. Among their victims was the writer Miguel de Cervantes, who was held captive there for five years and only rescued when the Trinitarian friars raised the exorbitant ransom the pirates had demanded. The Barbary Corsair menace only lessened after the United States twice went to war with them (1801–05 and 1815–16) in one of the fledgling republic's first foreign conflicts, and the threat ceased completely after the French occupied Algeria in 1830.

THE PHILIPPINES
PEDRO MURILLO VELARDE

1 | Subic (one letter difference from 'cubic'). The municipality of Subic lies alongside the bay of the same name, one of the earliest points in the Philippines explored by the Spanish, where they landed in 1542. The town itself was founded in 1607 by Augustinian friars, but it came to prominence as a naval base only after the British occupation of Manila in 1762 during the latter stages of the Seven Years' War, which prompted the Spanish authorities to investigate alternatives to the port at Manila. Under American rule from 1898, Subic became an important naval station, and particularly so during the Vietnam War. American forces finally withdrew in 1992.

2 | Balayan ('Bala' and 'Yan'). Bala is a market town in Snowdonia, North Wales, and the birthplace of Betsi Cadwaladr, the founder of Welsh nursing, who worked alongside Florence Nightingale at the military hospital in Scutari during the Crimean War (1853–56). Yan was one of the last of the so-called Warring States to be conquered by the state of Qin (in 222 BC), just before the unification of China under its first emperor Qin Shih Huangdi. Balayan was the capital of one of the Moro sultanates, the Islamic states which dominated parts of Mindanao from the thirteenth century. They resisted the Spanish and it took a series of wars from 1578 until the late nineteenth century to subdue them.

3 | Manila (anagram of 'animal') dates from pre-Spanish times, coming to prominence as a Muslim sultanate under Rajah Ahmad from 1258, and growing rich on the levying of customs dues from traders heading up the Pasig river. Miguel López de Legazpi, the first Spanish governor-general of the Philippines, seized it in 1571 and made it into the capital of the new colony. It remained in Spanish hands, save for a two-year-long British occupation in 1762, until 1898,

when Spain's defeat in the Spanish–American War led to its acquisition by the United States. It became the capital of the independent Philippines in 1946.

4 | Abucay ('Abu' and 'cay') was the site of the first printing press in the Philippines. Established in 1593 by Domingo de Nieva, a deacon from Salamanca, it drew on the expertise of a Chinese printer, Keng Yong. As a result, the earliest books were printed using the technique common in China of engraved wooden blocks (so that the pages could not be recomposed), and printing using movable type was only introduced in 1606. Among its earliest productions was the *Doctrina Cristiana,* a catechism for missionaries.

5 | Alabat (anagram of 'at a lab'). Many of Alabat Island's inhabitants belong to a group known as Negritos, widely scattered throughout Southeast Asia (including the Andaman Islands, southern Thailand and Malaysia), who may represent the original indigenous inhabitants of the region before the arrival of Malay-speaking rice farmers. Alabat is home to one of the world's most endangered languages, Inagba-Alabat, which in 2015 had only 30 recorded speakers.

6 Lampon ('lamp' and 'on') provided a convenient port on the east coast of Luzon for travellers arriving on Spanish galleons from Acapulco in Mexico (which shipped in silver from the Spanish-owned mines in the New World on the westbound leg and shipped out spices on the eastbound voyage).

7 Antipolo ('anti' and 'polo') is believed to have got its name from the locally abundant *Artocarpus blancoi,* or tipolo tree, a type of breadfruit. It is the most important pilgrimage site in the Philippines, having been the home of an image of the Virgin Mary (known as 'the Virgin of Antipolo') since 1626.

LONDON

JOHN ROCQUE

1 | Red and gray – Red Lyon Square (today Red Lion Square) and Gray's Inn. The square took its name from the Red Lion Inn, which stood on the square and was where the body of Oliver Cromwell and several other regicides were displayed overnight on the orders of a vengeful Charles II, before being taken to Tyburn (the site of the public gallows) where they were posthumously hung, drawn and quartered for their part in the execution of his father, Charles I. The square was first laid out in 1684 by Nicholas Barbon, who pioneered London's first fire insurance and fire brigade system (if you did not have his insurance, his firemen would let your building burn). The laying out of the square was accompanied by pitched battles between Barbon's workmen and the lawyers of Gray's Inn, who objected to the loss of their view. It was already known as a lodging place for the legal profession in the 1370s, and those connected to it included William Cecil, Lord Burghley, Elizabeth I's chief minister and spymaster, and Lord Shawcross, the chief Allied prosecutor at the Nuremberg War Crimes Tribunal.

2 | Jockeys Fields. This area was redeveloped around 1720, and it is not clear what its use was before, but the exercising of horses is one strong possibility.

3 | High Holbourn (today High Holborn). The continuation eastwards of Holborn (which takes its name from the Holebourne, a minor tributary of the Fleet, one of London's vanished rivers), it housed the first church of the order of Knights Templar in London before their growing numbers forced the building of a larger round church off Fleet Street in the 1180s. Among the noted early residents of the street was the poet John Milton, author of *Paradise Lost*, who lived here in the 1660s.

4 | Two. Spread Eagle Court, just east of Gray's Inn, and Eagle Street, north of High Holbourn. The latter was the birthplace of Martin van Butchell, a particularly eccentric dentist who broke out of his father's business as a maker of royal tapestries to fix the teeth of well-to-do Londoners. His prices were high (80 guineas for a set of false teeth) and he refused, unlike most of his competitors, to make house calls. His lasting fame, however, came from his long flowing grey beard, the pony on which he made his way about London and, above all, from having had his wife embalmed after she died in 1775 and put on display in his living room, equipped with glass eyes and garbed in her wedding dress. Van Butchell claimed that in doing so he was only fulfilling a clause in their wedding contract. He had her removed to the Hunterian Museum only when he remarried and his new wife, rather understandably, objected to the presence of her dead predecessor in the marital home.

5 | Liquorpond ('liquor' and 'pond') Street. Appropriately enough, this street has housed several breweries during its history and an 1832 directory lists four pubs along the road, namely the Duke of York, the Globe and Dolphin, the White Hart and the curiously named Tippling Philosopher. Among the other residents were a pawnbroker, an 'a la mode beef house', a pork butcher, an ivory turner, a coach builder, a bootmaker, a dealer in coal, several bakers, a pastry cook and a French polisher – an apt microcosm of nineteenth-century London society.

6 | Theobald's ('bald') Row (now Theobald's Road). The road takes its name from James I's house at Theobalds in Hertfordshire. It formed part of the route taken by the royal entourage, with 200 heavily laden carts, as the king made his way to the country. The name of its modern continuation, Kingsway, displays the connection more clearly.

7 | Hatton ('hat' and 'ton') Garden. The area gained its name from Hatton House, a residence built for Sir Christopher Hatton, the Lord Chancellor and favourite of Elizabeth I. Although the house had been demolished by 1720, it still retained a green space around it and shops were forbidden to be built there in an effort to retain it as a high-class quarter. Its famous residents included Giuseppe Mazzini, the Italian revolutionary who spent several years in exile in London in the 1840s (where he also founded a school for impoverished Italians) and Hiram Maxim, the inventor in 1884 of the automatic gun bearing his name which could fire up to 600 rounds a minute – and which gave Britain such an advantage in colonial warfare that it led Hilaire Belloc to compose the cynical lines 'Whatever happens we have got, the Maxim gun, and they have not'. By the late nineteenth century Hatton Garden had become a centre for the diamond trade, a reputation it still retains.

8 | Saffron Hill – named for the spice that was introduced into England in the thirteenth century, the use of which became essential to disguise the taste of rotten meat, which was common in the era, and was grown in a garden here. Saffron Hill formed part of Sir Christopher Hatton's estate, but gradually went into decline and part of it was used as a prison during the English Civil War. By the nineteenth century it had become a rookery, one of the teeming sets of lanes and alleys in which London's poorest inhabitants dwelled, their lives made even worse by the presence of the Fleet Ditch, an open sewer. Criminality flourished here, and Charles Dickens made it the setting for Fagin's lair in *Oliver Twist*. Much of the road was demolished in the 1840s when the station at Holborn Viaduct was constructed

9 | Ely Court. A small gated lane, this enclave (now Ely Place) is officially part of Cambridgeshire and

the Metropolitan Police are in theory only allowed to enter with permission. Ely Court/Place gained this status from being the site of the palace of the Bishops of Ely from the thirteenth century to 1772. It was the scene of a gargantuan feast in 1531 when Henry VIII, Catherine of Aragon and their guests consumed 100 sheep, 51 cows and 4,000 unfortunate larks. The royal family must have taken a liking to the place, for Elizabeth I forced the bishop to lease it to Sir Christopher Hatton for a nominal rent of £10 a year and a rose plucked at midsummer. After being occupied by Hatton's descendants it reverted to the Crown in 1772 and it is from this link, as Crown rather than ecclesiastical property, that it acquired its special status as being outside the jurisdiction of the City of London.

10 | Lincoln's Inn Fields. This was formerly the playing fields for the students from the nearby legal establishment at Lincoln's Inn (which were known as Purse Field and Cup Field). It was the site in 1586 of the hanging, drawing and quartering of Anthony Babington and his accomplices (who had been found guilty of a plot against Elizabeth I's life that ultimately drew in and led to the execution of her cousin Mary Queen of Scots). Mid-seventeenth century developers wanted to build housing on Purse Field, and after a protracted legal battle it was agreed in the 1630s that the other section should remain permanently a park. Among those who lived in houses overlooking the square were Nell Gwynne, the mistress of Charles II, who first set eyes on her while she sold oranges inside the theatre of the King's Company on Bridges Street. Abraham Lincoln, the sixteenth president of the United States, bears a surname that indicates his distant ancestors may have come from Lincoln, although his great-grandfather Samuel Lincoln, the first of the family to migrate to the Americas, was born in Norfolk. The president himself never visited Britain.

THE ARCTIC
PHILIPPE BUACHE

1 | 'Kamtchatka'. The 750-mile-long (1,200-kilometre) Kamchatka peninsula is in the far east of Russia. By the mid-seventeenth century, Russia's expansion through Siberia had brought it to the Pacific Ocean, but it was not until 1697–99 that the peninsula was explored by the Siberian Cossack Vladimir Atlasov. Resistance from local tribes, including several revolts, hampered expansion and Russian control over Kamchatka was not secured until 1739. The town of Kamchatka was founded by the Danish explorer Vitus Bering in 1740 during his second voyage of discovery in Russia's far east – he named it Petropavlovsk, after his patrons Tsar Peter the Great and his brother Paul. Bering explored much of the area portrayed by Buache, and became the first Russian to sight North America, when he glimpsed part of the coast of Alaska near Kodiak Island. He did not, sadly, receive the credit for his exploits, dying (possibly of scurvy) in December 1741 after his ship became marooned on an uninhabited island in the Commander Islands off the coast of Kamchatka.

2 | 'Archipelago de St. Lazare'. Buache depicts a group of islands he calls 'St. Lazare' roughly in the position of the Alexander Islands south of Juneau, Alaska. Two of them – Chichagov and Baranov – were named in 1804 by the Russian naval officer and explorer Yuri Lisansky after Admiral Vasili Chichagov, who explored part of the north coast of Siberia, and Alexander Baranov, a Russian merchant who founded Novo Arkhangelsk (now Sitka); Baranov became the first governor of Russian Alaska. According to the gospel of John, Lazare, or Lazarus, was the brother of Mary and Martha, whom Jesus raised from the dead four days after his death and who was later honoured as a saint (his alleged tomb in Bethany became a pilgrimage site).

3 | Quivira (sounds like 'quiver'). Although the Spanish had found (and seized) vast quantities of gold during their conquest of the Aztecs of Mexico and the Inca of Peru, explorations further into North America had proved disappointing. In 1540 Francisco Vásquez de Coronado heard rumours of the 'Seven Cities of Gold' said to lie in the interior. The following year he organised an expedition to locate them, penetrating into the Great Plains north of Arkansas, and searching in vain for a city named Quivira, which always seemed to be just beyond the horizon. His informants encouraged him on with ever-more-fabulous tales of the gold cups said to hang down from trees there, ripe for the plucking. Finally, Coronado did reach a settlement he was told was Quivira, but it was a poor place, a village of straw-thatched huts, whose inhabitants had no gold at all. Searches for the other 'Cities of Gold', including Teguaio, which is also marked on the Buache map, proved similarly fruitless.

4 | Cap Blanc (cap blanc means 'white cape'), now Cape Blanco, Oregon, is one of the most westerly points in the United States. It was renamed Cape Orford by the British explorer George Vancouver in 1792, but the original name stuck. Buache places it, along with Cap Mendocino, at the entrance to an inlet into the 'Mer de l'Ouest' or 'Western Sea', the last relic of a belief common among the more-imaginative sixteenth- and seventeenth-century cartographers of North America that there was a vast inland sea somewhere in its western interior.

5 | Fou-sang (anagram of 'sofa gun') is one of Buache's more-creative touches. The Buddhist monk Hui Sen was said to have sailed eastwards from China in the late fifth century and to have found an island, which he named Fou-sang after the mythological place

where the sun was said to rise. Eighteenth-century antiquarians took measurements of the distances cited by Hui Sen and determined that Fou-sang must lie on the west coast of North America. Faced with a gap in his knowledge, Buache placed Fou-sang there, although no trace of the early horseriding culture Hui Sen described, or indeed of the Chinese explorers, has ever been found.

6 | Lac de Fonte (anagram of 'cadet felon') is named for Bartholomew de Fonte, a Spanish admiral who allegedly made a voyage in 1640 during which he sailed up the west coast of North America and discovered a network of bays, lakes and rivers that led eastwards

towards Hudson Bay. He sailed into this system of waterways and encountered a ship that had come in the opposite direction from Boston. The account, published in 1708 in a magazine called *Memoirs for the Curious*, did much to fuel speculation that there really was a Northwest Passage (a navigable channel that linked the Atlantic and Pacific oceans). Unfortunately, the de Fonte account was fabricated, and there is no evidence that such a person ever existed, let alone made the discoveries attributed to him (many of them demonstrably nonexistent). Buache adapted these 'discoveries' and his map includes Lac de Fonte and a string of imaginary waterways reaching tantalisingly from Alaska almost to Hudson Bay.

NORTH AMERICA
JOHN MITCHELL

1 | Augusta. The title taken by Julius Caesar's adoptive son Octavian when he became the first Roman emperor in 27 BC was Augustus (meaning 'revered'). The feminine form Augusta was used as an honorific for empresses and senior female members of the imperial family. The place called Augusta was established in 1736 by James Oglethorpe, the founder of the colony of Georgia (who had managed to persuade the British government into allowing the setting up of the first new North American colony for half a century). It was named for Augusta of Saxe-Coburg-Altenburg, the wife of Frederick, Prince of Wales, the eldest son of George II. A German princess, she arrived in Britain speaking scarcely a word of English, but because the ruling Hanoverians were also German, her native tongue was actually an asset at court. She never became queen, though, because Frederick died in 1751, and her long-term influence was confined to the enlargement of Kew Gardens, including the building of the Chinese Pagoda in 1762. When new settlement was limited to the area east of the Appalachians in 1763, Augusta attracted large numbers of land-hungry settlers temporarily denied the opportunity of pushing the frontier further west. The Southern Baptist Convention was established in Augusta in 1845 and during the Revolutionary War, after Savannah had fallen to the British, it was briefly the state capital. Augusta suffered less badly than many towns in Georgia during the American Civil War, since it was bypassed during Sherman's March to the Sea. It was the boyhood home of Woodrow Wilson, president from 1913 to 1921, whose vision of a community of nations free to determine their own destiny shaped the peace settlement after World War One and prompted the foundation in 1920 of the League of Nations, a body which, much to Wilson's disappointment, the United States never joined because the Senate failed to ratify the accession treaty.

2 | Saxe-gotha Township was one of the original nine townships authorised after the British Crown took over the colony of South Carolina in 1729. Each extended to approximately 20,000 acres and would-be settlers were offered free land and free transportation to the Carolinas as an inducement. Originally called Congaree, it was renamed Saxe-gotha by the large number of German Lutherans who took up the offer (and also in diplomatic acknowledgement of Princess Augusta of Saxe-Coburg-Altenberg, then the wife of the heir to the British throne and expected to become queen in due course). The settlement never prospered, and no permanent towns were established; by 1800, it had disappeared from the map. Ironically, the town that now stands close to the spot is named Congaree.

3 | Granville (anagram of 'viral glen'). Granville County's lifespan was short. It was originally named Carteret County, and was rechristened in 1708, but retained its new name only until 1768 when it became Beaufort County. It was named in honour of John Carteret, 2nd Earl of Granville, a distinguished British politician who served as Secretary of State for the Northern Department (in effect, the Home Office) from 1742 to 1744 and as Lord President of the Council from 1751 to 1763. His great-grandfather George Carteret (for whom the county was originally named) had been one of the eight Lords Proprietor to whom Charles II granted the original charter of Carolina in 1663.

4 | Charlestown (anagram of 'worn satchel'), now Charleston, was founded in 1680 and rapidly became one of Carolina's most prosperous ports. This wealth attracted the notorious pirate Edward Teach, known to posterity as Blackbeard, who blockaded Charlestown for five days in 1718. Unfortunately, not much valuable cargo was being shipped to the town at the time and so the haul with which he made off was meagre (including a chest of medical supplies he demanded from Governor Johnson as a ransom). Charleston saw the opening shots of the American Civil War on 12 April 1861, when shore-based artillery under the command of Confederate General Pierre Beauregard began shelling the Union-held Fort Sumter out in the harbour.

5 | Saltcatchers ('salt'-'catchers'), named for the nearby river (now the Salkehatchie), was the site of a 750-acre plantation owned from 1768 by the Inglis family.

6 | Cape Fear. Jutting out from the North Carolina coastline into the Atlantic, Cape Fear was a prominent landmark for early explorers of North America. The Florentine Giovanni da Verrazzano made landfall here in 1524, calling the place Selva di Lauri ('Laurel Forest'). Francis I of France, who was keen that the Spanish not retain a complete monopoly on the newfound lands in the west, had despatched the expedition to challenge the monopoly and in a bid to find a passage through to the Pacific and so to China and the fabulously valuable trade with the Spice Islands of Indonesia. Verrazzano was disappointed in the latter, but he did explore virtually the entire eastern seaboard (including Long Island and the area of New York which, through lack of follow-up, failed to become a French colony) as far as Newfoundland. Verrazzano's career was abruptly cut short in 1528 during a subsequent voyage to the Caribbean, when he went ashore at Guadeloupe and was killed and eaten by cannibals. Cape Fear was given its name during the 1585 expedition by the English explorer Sir Richard Grenville, when one of his ships became trapped by a bay behind the cape and the mariners were petrified that it would run aground. The cape, though, is probably best known for giving its name to *Cape Fear*, the 1962 psychological thriller starring Robert Mitchum and Gregory Peck (and a 1991 remake starring Robert De Niro, which made it, in a sense, one of the few geographical features ever to have been nominated for an Oscar).

7 | Coffin Land. Lying offshore from Charleston, Coffin Land, also known as Folly Island, has attracted more than its fair share of legends. The macabre name is said to have derived from the large number of sailors who perished in wrecks nearby, but is more likely to be derived from the Coffin family, wealthy landowners who owned several plantations in Beaufort County on the mainland. In 1832 the *Amelia*, carrying over 100 passengers from New York to New Orleans, was wrecked on Coffin Island. While a group of survivors was marooned, 20 contracted cholera and died, leading to the city authorities refusing to rescue the rest and leaving them in quarantine. They were later awarded substantial damages. Coffin Island holds an even more bizarre secret: in 1987 over a dozen headless corpses were found during construction at the west edge of the island. From their surviving clothing and military insignia, it is probable that they were soldiers of the Union Army's 55th Massachusetts Regiment, an African-American unit, but how they came to be buried there and why they were missing their skulls remains a mystery.

8 | Savannah = was Georgia's oldest town and first capital, established in 1733 by James Oglethorpe and the first colonists. One of North America's first planned cities, it was laid out in a grid around a set of squares and its atmosphere was a curious mix of the liberal and the prescriptive. Hard liquor and slavery were banned in the early decades of the colony and lawyers not allowed to practise there until 1755 (Oglethorpe was said to have an intense dislike of the profession). The city hosted the oldest Jewish congregation in the Southern states and the Methodist reformer John Wesley was invited by Oglethorpe to be the colony's chaplain, arriving in Savannah in February 1736 and serving in his post for just 18 months (he was driven out after a court case involving his refusal to give communion to a woman whom he had previously hoped to marry).

THE TROSSACHS
WILLIAM ROY

1 | Aberfoil (Aber-'foil') or Bridge of Aberfoil (now Aberfoyle) became one of the gateways to the Trossachs after the popularisation of nearby Lake Katrine by Walter Scott in his poem 'The Lady of the Lake' in which he celebrates the dramatic landscape:

'Each purple peak, each flinty spire,
Was bathed in floods of living fire.
But not a setting beam could glow
Within the dark ravines below,
Where twined the path in shadow hid,
Round many a rocky pyramid,'

Aberfoyle was the birthplace in 1644 of Robert Kirk, a Church of Scotland Minister, biblical scholar – he translated the psalms of David and oversaw the printing of the first Bible in Gaelic – and, more curiously for a cleric, a folklorist with a fascination for faeries. In the early 1690s he made a compilation of faery lore called *The Secret Commonwealth*, but one day in 1692, before it could be published, he went walking in the hills and failed to return. Some time later, his dead body was found lying on Doon Hill, the place he had identified as the gateway to the faerie realm. Whispers rose locally that he had been kidnapped by the hidden folk for revealing their secrets and the hill is still supposed to have supernatural connections.

2 | Loch of Monteith (anagram of 'tech of monolith') was known as such in the nineteenth century, but is now called the Lake of Menteith, making it Scotland's only lake. It has been inhabited since ancient times, being the site of eight crannogs – Iron Age lake dwellings in the form of artificial islands built on stilts embedded in the lakebed. The largest of the loch's three islands is the site of Inchmahome Priory, built in 1238 by Augustinian canons under the patronage of Walter Comyn, Earl of Menteith, who had a home

on next-door Inch Talla. Walter clearly did not gain divine approval for his action, as he was said to have died when he fell from his horse and his foot became caught in the stirrup, causing him to be dragged along until his body was cut to pieces – an event Walter Scott invoked in *Rob Roy* as 'Walter Cuming's curse'. Mary Queen of Scot's is said to have taken refuge in the priory in 1547 when, as a four-year-old, she was on the run after the Battle of Pinkie Cleugh against the English (and eventually made it with her guardians to France, where she became engaged to the dauphin Francis, the future Francis II).

3 | Lochend. In the eighteenth century, Lochend, at the foot of the Lake of Menteith, was deep in 'bandit country'. It was here that Robin Og, who had already been outlawed in 1736, took refuge after he abducted the heiress Jean Kay in 1750. He was apprehended and hanged in Edinburgh in 1754. His father was Rob Roy MacGregor, the outlaw and folk hero immortalised by Walter Scott in his novel *Rob Roy*. Already a veteran rebel, as a young man he had joined in the Jacobite uprising led by Viscount Dundee aimed at restoring James II to the throne, and in 1715 he led the Clan MacGregor in the second major Jacobite rebellion. When this again failed, Rob and the MacGregors were excluded from the terms of an amnesty in 1717, which forgave most of the Jacobites, and for several years he led a last-ditch resistance in the Highlands. Outlawed for cattle rustling, he was eventually captured and imprisoned for five years, but after his release in 1727 he settled down to a comparatively quiet old age.

4 | Loch Drunkie. This isolated freshwater loch derives its name from the Gaelic *Drongaidh*, or 'place of the ridge', appropriately enough for its location, surrounded on all four sides by hills and steep ridges.

WESTMINSTER

THOMAS JEFFERYS

1 | Six (Somerset House, Surry Street, Norfolk Street, Essex Street, Northumberland Street and Suffolk Street). Strand became the site of a large number of noble palaces in the later Middle Ages, and many of the surrounding street names are reminders of them. Hence Norfolk Street (now demolished) was named for the Howards, Dukes of Norfolk, who owned Arundel House, which occupied the site from the sixteenth century until its demolition in 1938. Essex Street derives its name from Elizabeth I's favourite Robert Devereux, 2nd Earl of Essex. Somerset House, the sole survivor, lies on the site of a Renaissance palace built for Lord Protector Somerset in 1547, after the demolition of properties belonging to the Bishops of Chester and Worcester (their position much weakened after the Reformation). A royal residence from the time of Elizabeth I until the 1690s, and then used as government offices, Somerset House was the first building in England to have parquet flooring.

2 | Three (Portugal twice, as Portugal Row and Portugal Street; Denmark Street; and, though it is tiny, Holland Street, west of Soho Square). Portugal Row and Portugal Street were named in honour of Charles II's wife, Catherine of Braganza, after their marriage in 1661. Although the marriage was childless (Charles was far more interested in a succession of mistresses, including the actress Nell Gwynne), it proved fruitful in that as part of her dowry Britain received Tangier (which it only held onto until 1684) and Mumbai (which proved a more durable and valuable possession, remaining in British hands until Indian independence in 1947). Portugal Street was the site of the last stocks in London, where passers-by could abuse and hurl rotten food at hapless petty criminals, often convicted debtors, until the stocks were removed in about 1820. Denmark Street is better known as 'Tin Pan Alley' – although partially redeveloped now, it was long the site of a host of

music shops, instrument shops and music publishers, and it is still one of London's prime spots for buying an electric guitar. The Rolling Stones recorded in a studio here and during the heyday of Punk, the Sex Pistols actually lived in a flat behind No. 6. More sedately, the German neo-classical painter Johann Zoffany lived for a time on Denmark Street during a 50-year residence in London that was only broken by a six-year stint in India. On his way back, the artist was shipwrecked off the Andaman Islands and, short of food, the survivors drew lots to determine which one of them the others should eat. Artist and cannibal, Zoffany may be, in the end, the edgiest of the street's former residents.

3 | Strand. Before the building of the Victoria Embankment in 1865, Strand really was at the edge of the river (hence its name, strand or 'beach'). After the fall of the Roman Empire and the abandonment of the old Roman settlement where the City now stands, the Anglo-Saxons recolonised London (which they called Lundenburh), beginning a new town roughly along the length of Strand as far as Aldwych. By the Middle Ages it occupied a middle position between London within the Roman walls and a new centre of royal power at Westminster. As a result many noble palaces were built along its length, most notably the Savoy Palace (on the site of the modern hotel) and Somerset House.

4 | Broad Street (anagram of 'better roads') now forms part of Broadwick Street (together with the eastern part that in 1745 was known as Edward Street). Its moment of fame was rather a baleful one. In 1854 London was hit by a cholera, a disease that had first struck Britain in the 1830s after travelling westwards from Asia. Although not as severe as previous outbreaks, the 1854 epidemic killed more than 600 people in Soho alone and piqued the curiosity of a local doctor, John Snow, who branched out from his principal interest in anaesthesia to question quite why there was a concentration of cholera deaths in such a small area. Snow plotted each death onto a map and found a cluster in a very small area of Soho – on Lexington Street almost 80 per cent of the 49 houses had suffered a fatality. He narrowed the spread of the disease down to users of a water pump on Broadwick Street and concluded that the cholera must originate from contaminated water. In the face of vigorous mocking from medical contemporaries that cholera was instead caused by 'miasma' (or bad air), he persuaded the local parish commissioners to have the pump handle removed. Local residents' outrage at the inconvenience soon lessened when deaths from the dread disease subsided. It was subsequently established that a leak from a sewage pipe near the pump had contaminated the drinking water supply at the Broadwick pump, confirming Snow's theory and establishing him as the father of modern epidemiology.

5 | Knaves Acre. Now subsumed into Great Pulteney Street, Knaves Acre acquired its unsavoury name from being a patch of waste land into which inhabitants of the surrounding house tipped their rubbish (it was also known as Laystall Place, a laystall being a depository where cattle dung was collected at markets).

6 | Golden Square. In common with much of the area of modern Soho, Golden Square was laid out in the later seventeenth century (the original plans were submitted by Christopher Wren in 1670). It became the home of aristocrats – notably one of Charles II's mistresses, Barbara Villiers, the Duchess of Cleveland – and of diplomats, including the Portuguese embassy that once stood on the square, which was replaced in the early eighteenth century by the Bavarian consulate and then by a Catholic chapel. Dickens used Golden Square as a setting for *Nicholas Nickleby*, placing the father of the hero there and depicting a locality much changed from its aristocratic heyday, where: 'Street bands are on their metal in Golden Square, and itinerant glee-singers quaver involuntarily, as they raise their voices within its boundaries.'

7 | Dean Street – may have been named for Henry Compton, Bishop of London from 1675 to 1713, who was also Dean of the Chapel Royal. It once held Caldwell Assembly Rooms, where the child prodigy Wolfgang Amadeus Mozart gave a recital in 1764, aged eight, during a grand European tour arranged by his proud father Leopold. Little Mozart also took time off during his visit to London to compose his first symphony. The German revolutionary and philosopher of communism, Karl Marx, lived between 1851 and 1856 in rooms above what is now the Quo Vadis restaurant, a time during which Marx was so short of funds that he was often behind with the rent and once had to flee to Manchester to avoid his creditors.

8 | Seven Dials (anagram of 'slaves dine'), with its characteristic form of seven streets radiating out as spokes from a central point, was laid out by the MP and entrepreneur Sir Thomas Neale in the 1690s. A hyperactive personality, Neale was practically ubiquitous in the late Stuart court, serving, among other positions, as Postmaster General of the North American Colonies, Master of the Mint and Groom Porter of Charles II. In that position, he was in charge of supervising gambling and lotteries (including managing the king's healthy appetite for the gaming table). As part of his effort to regularise the gambling industry (and perhaps to limit his master's losses), he developed a pair of dice designed to avoid cheating (by being difficult to load). He also devised a new way of raising money for the Exchequer, by instituting Britain's first national lottery, the 'Million Lottery' in 1694, which was intended to bring in a million pounds by selling 100,000 tickets at £10 each (the equivalent of about £2,000 today). The results of the Seven Dials development were in the end disappointing, because it rapidly descended the social scale; by Dickens's time it was a slum, which he commented on in *Sketches by Boz*. There was originally a column at the centre of the crossroads with seven faces each bearing a sundial, but it was removed in 1773 in the mistaken belief that there was a hoard of money hidden inside it. It ended up in Weybridge as a monument to Princess Frederica Charlotte, the wife of George III's son the Duke of York, who spent over 20 years there after her separation from her husband.

9 | Maiden Lane. The street is named not for just any young lady, but after the statue of the Virgin Mary that once stood on its corner. Originally a track between Covent Garden and St Martin's Lane, the street was laid from around 1631. It was hoped, as for many seventeenth-century developments in the area, that aristocratic tenants would move in, but it soon went downhill. All the same, it has had some distinguished residents. The artist J.M.W. Turner was born here in 1775 over the shop where his father, who was a barber, ran his business. His fascination with the elements of nature, fire and the sea were a world away from the crowded urban setting of his childhood (although he never lost the cockney accent which betrayed his roots). The French philosopher Voltaire also spent a year living on the street in 1727–28, a period in which he wrote his *Lettres sur les anglais* (*Letters on the English*), a work in which he comments favourably on aspects of the English Constitution and way of life as a means of attacking their French counterparts. Maiden Lane was long a cul-de-sac, but in 1857 a way was cut through to Southampton Street – so, it was said, that Queen Victoria did not have to suffer the inconvenience of having to turn around when she went to the theatre at the Adelphi.

NEW YORK

BERNARD RATZER

1 | Delancy's Square (anagram of 'as candles query'). The neat square on the map to the north of the developed area of 1770s' New York never came into being. It was part of a projected plan to lay out a grid of new streets on the estate of the De Lancey family, prominent loyalist New Yorkers. The De Lanceys were Huguenots, who had originally come to the Americas as refugees from the Revocation of the Edict of Nantes in 1685, which removed freedom of worship from French Protestants. After the success of the American Revolution, those loyalists who had stuck by the British suffered legal persecution (and Oliver De Lancey, who had raised three battalions of men for the British forces was a particular target). Around 100,000 New York loyalists went into exile, and their property was declared forfeit. Although they were allowed to return in 1792, their property was not handed back and the De Lancey estate was sold off, much of it eventually to form the core of the Bowery district.

2 | Beaver Street is one of New York's oldest thoroughfares. It was already laid out by the 1660s, and was one of the main roads of Dutch-era New Amsterdam, when it was called Markveldt ('Market Field') for the cattle market that took place there. After the British took control of New Amsterdam in 1664 and renamed it New York, many of its street names were also anglicised. The new Beaver Street was named for the aquatic rodents which could still be trapped near the Hudson (and which were a mainstay of the fur trade). It also briefly acquired the nickname 'Petticoat Lane' when it became the haunt of prostitutes serving the soldiers in the fort at the tip of Manhattan Island. It overcame this infamy and eventually the name extended further to the east of the original Beaver Street as the road acquired its current length.

3 | One (Duke Street). Princess Street, Queen Street, King George's Street and Prince Street do not count because they are royal titles. Duke Street is now called Stone Street, and was one of the city's very first streets; it existed as early as the 1630s, when it was called Hoogh Straat ('High Street') and hosted New Amsterdam's first brewery. Under British occupation it was renamed Duke Street (for the Duke of York), but it was completely flattened around 1770 and redeveloped from 1790 with cobbled stone paving that gave the street its current name. After decades of being used principally for nondescript warehouses and storage, it has recently undergone regeneration into a dining district.

4 | Broadway ('broad'-way). Both wide and the famed venue for theatrical performances, Broadway is one of New York's spines, running for 17 miles (nearly 30 kilometres) from the very tip of Manhattan, right to the north of the borough and one four miles (six kilometres) into the Bronx. It was originally a ridge-top trail used by Native Americans and under the Dutch it became a principal trade route into the interior. The long career of the lower end of Broadway as a theatrical district began in 1750, when a theatre was opened up on Nassau Street. The Park Theatre on Park Row was founded in 1798, offering a traditional theatrical repertoire, but the opening of the Bowery Theatre in 1826 on Canal Street, whose shows appealed more to working-class and immigrant tastes, began the district's reputation for populist entertainment which it has retained ever since.

5 | Peck's Slip ('peck' and 'slip'). A peck is one-quarter of a bushel, which is equivalent to two gallons, or around nine litres. The early Manhattan coastline was indented with a complex of tiny waterways that acted as boat slips, which included Peck's Slip, but have long been converted into narrow parks or built over. Peck's Slip was used as a hiding place by George Washington and a contingent of revolutionary soldiers after they failed at the Battle of Long Island in August 1776 to prevent the British occupying New York. Two days later Washington slipped away across the East River with his men, denying the British his capture, which might have put a premature end to the American patriots' cause. In 1838 Peck's Slip was the docking point for the SS *Great Western* as it became the first purpose-built steam-powered vessel to make a crossing of the Atlantic. The initial voyage was somewhat ill-fated, as a fire broke out shortly after setting sail and Isambard Kingdom Brunel, the ship's designer, was injured and had to disembark. Although the damage was limited, most of the passengers booked for the voyage also cancelled and left the vessel, leaving only around half a dozen to complete the crossing. A muted later life saw the Slip eventually becoming the car park for Fulton Fish Market, but it is now in the process of being transformed into a park, after a decade-long planning battle.

6 | Wall Street (anagram of 'we tell tsar'). For the centre of New York's financial district, and one of the most important banking centres in the world, Wall Street is a modest road, running for less than a mile between Broadway and the East River. It gained its name from the small protective wall built there by the Dutch in 1653 to protect against attacks by Native Americans or the British. The wall was taken down in 1699, but the name stuck. The street became the location of the first New York Stock Exchange in May 1792, when 24 brokers gathered under a buttonwood tree (a type of sycamore) to sign an agreement that they would only trade stocks with each other and for

the same commission, to avoid the kind of cut-throat competitiveness that had recently caused a financial panic. They can have had little thought that their rustic beginnings marked the beginnings of an institution that now trades on average about $170 billion of shares daily.

7 | Hanover Square – was named for the House of Hanover, which became the ruling British dynasty in 1714, with the accession of the George I, who had been the Elector of the German state of Hanover. The Great Fire of New York broke out here in December 1835, consuming more than 20 blocks of largely wooden housing in Lower Manhattan. It took 1,900 firemen to douse the flames and the damage, estimated at around $30 million, caused 23 of the city's 26 insurance companies to go bankrupt. Hanover Square later became a centre for commodity trading, with both the New York Cotton Exchange and New York Cocoa Exchange based there.

8 | The Battery. The name harks back to the early defences of New York, when a fortification (Fort Amsterdam, later Fort George) was sited here, complete with a battery of guns to fight off any attempted landings on Manhattan by the British. A new fort was built at Castle Clinton (which still stands) between 1807 and 1811 when it looked as if the British would launch an invasion to reclaim their lost colonies, which they really did in 1814, although their thrust into New York State was stalled in the north at Plattsburgh and they had to be content with a series of raids, in one of which they burned the White House in Washington, DC. In 1855 the area was converted into a park, which it still remains.

CANADA

FRENCH SURVEYORS / JONATHAN CARVER

1 | Trois Rivières was originally named for the triple channel caused by islands in the St-Maurice River – forming 'three rivers' – as it enters the St Lawrence. It is the second-oldest settlement in French Canada, established by the Sieur de Laviolette in 1634 as a fur trading station. It also became an important missionary centre, with a school established by the Ursuline sisters in 1697. It was French Canada's first industrial city; its iron foundry was established in 1738, and by 1747 was producing a million pounds in weight of stoves, nails and other metal implements each year.

2 | La Bouteillerie ('bouteillerie' being a place where bottles are manufactured). Now known as Saint-Denis-de-la-Bouteillerie, this small municipality lies on the east bank of the St Lawrence River. It was the birthplace of Jean-Charles Chapais, who served as a member of the legislative assembly of Canada and was a delegate at the 1864 Quebec Conference called to develop the federal structure for Canada's future government as a Dominion, semi-detached from the British Empire. He became the Dominion's first agriculture minister.

3 | Quebec ('q') is the oldest city in New France and was first explored in 1535 by Jacques Cartier, who visited the Native American village called Stadcona then stood on the spot. The city itself was founded by Samuel de Champlain, who built a fort here in 1608; its strategic position astride the St Lawrence and its eminently defensible citadel made it the obvious choice as the capital of French Canada. It fell, though, to the British in September 1759 after the British general James Wolfe had his men scale the Heights of Abraham, believed by the French garrison (under the Marquis de Montcalm) to be unclimbable. Both commanders perished in the battle. Wolfe was shot as

he moved forward to join his advancing men, his death immortalised in a work by the Anglo-American artist Benjamin West (who made something of a specialty of the niche genre of dying commanders, painting *The Death of Nelson* nearly 40 years later, in 1806). Montcalm died of his wounds the next day, living long enough to know that Quebec had fallen.

4 | Falls of Montmorency (anagram of 'Macron foments folly') is named in honour of the Duc de Montmorency, who was the second viceroy of New France from 1620 to 1625, ably supported by his deputy Samuel de Champlain. Despite his service to the French Crown, Montmorency became embroiled in a plot against Louis XIII in 1632, was captured and, at the orders of the king's chief minister Cardinal Richelieu, beheaded in front of Toulouse town hall. The waterfall has a total height of 272 feet (83 metres), in two drops, making it nearly 100 feet (30 metres) taller than Niagara Falls.

5 | Cape Torment (or Cap Tourmente) is a protected wildlife area that hosts large number of greater snow geese during their migratory flights. Within it lies a historic farm used by Samuel de Champlain to provide a secure food source during the very early years of Quebec. Cap Tourmente was the site of Canada's worst mass killing, in 1949, when Quebec jeweller Joseph-Albert Guay – unable to get divorced and marry his mistress because of Quebec's strict marital laws – sent his wife onto a Canadian Pacific Airlines flight with a bomb in her suitcase, which detonated, killing 23 people. Guay and two accomplices were hanged.

6 | The Pilgrims – this string of islands north of Quebec in the St Lawrence River are so-called because their shape seems to resemble that of a figure praying (with Great Pilgrim as the head, the Middle Pilgrims as the hands, and Long Pilgrim and Little Pilgrim being the body). Long Pilgrim's lighthouse had a resident lighthouse keeper until it was automated in 1957.

7 | Orleans Island was originally named Bacchus by Jacques Cartier because of the abundant wild grapes he found growing there. He had a diplomatic change of mind, however, and rechristened it after his patron Henri, Duc d'Orléans, the son of Francis I. Cartier's patron prospered, ultimately becoming king as Henri II, but died one of the more bizarre deaths of the French royal house. In June 1559, at a great feast celebrating peace with the Habsburgs and the marriage of his daughter to King Philip II of Spain,

Henri took part in the accompanying tournament. He jousted against Gabriel de Lorges, the Comte de Montgomery, and as the two thundered towards each other, Montgomery's lance tilted upwards and shattered as it impacted with the king's visor. Shards of wood penetrated Henri's helmet and lodged itself in his temple and in his eye. Despite the best efforts of the royal surgeons – and those of the queen, Catherine de Medici, who was rumoured to have had criminals executed by having splintered lances pushed into their eyes to give the doctors something to practice on – Henri died 11 days later after the wound became infected.

BOSTON

HENRY PELHAM

1 | Mill Pond (anagram of 'mind poll'). The long-disappeared Mill Pond is a sign of Boston's gradual encroachment into the water over the centuries. It was built in the 1640s, when a group of mill-owners gained permission to dam a cove at the north end of the Shawmut peninsula so that they could use the water to power their mills. The enterprise proved less popular than hoped and eventually the mills were sold off, and the mill gates at the western end of the pond were stopped up. This meant that the previously healthy waterflow through the area became sluggish, leading to a build-up of detritus that found its way into the river, most notably rotting animal carcasses. Eventually, the city authorities grew tired of the stench and in 1807 the whole pond was filled in, using soil scooped from the top of Beacon Hill (which lost 60 feet/18 metres in height as a result). Today this area forms the Bulfinch Triangle district of the city, between Merrimac Street and Causeway Street.

2 | Hancock's Wharf was originally named Clark's Wharf, for the wealthy Boston-born merchant William Clark who built a grand house on North Square in 1711. By the 1760s the wharf had taken the name of Thomas Hancock, another merchant and one of Boston's wealthiest men. His nephew was John Hancock, who inherited his uncle's fortune and became an ardent opponent of British rule after the Townshend Acts in 1767 imposed new customs duties in the 13 Colonies and threatened the livelihood of the American mercantile community. His profile rose when he was tried by the British authorities for allegedly evading duty on madeira wine landed from his sloop *Liberty*; he became a member of the First Continental Congress, and in 1775 was elected its president. His large and flamboyant signature on the United States Declaration of Independence lodged him in the popular imagination (and a 'John Hancock' is sometime used informally as a term for a signature),

although he achieved more concrete fame as the first governor of Massachusetts.

3 | Hudson Point (Hudson's Point) derives its name from Francis Hudson, who operated the ferry from the Shawmut peninsula to Charlestown in the early days of Boston. It was near here that John Winthrop landed with the first colonists late in 1630, after their initial choice of settlement site at Charlestown proved to have insufficient water. Mrs Hudson was the landlady and housekeeper of 221B Baker Street in Sir Arthur Conan Doyle's *Sherlock Holmes* detective novels. Henry Hudson was an English explorer who surveyed the coastline around New York on a 1609 expedition in search of the Northwest Passage, a fabled waterway that would give direct access to the Pacific and enable rapid voyages to East Asia. He sailed up the river that is now named after him (the Hudson) and returned two years later, sailing further north and discovering the inland sea in northeastern Canada now named Hudson Bay. The voyage ended in disaster when his crew mutinied and Hudson, his son and several other crew members were set adrift in a small boat, never to be seen again. The Hudson Motor Car Company was an automobile manufacturer based in Detroit from 1909 to 1957, whose Essex models were an early competitor to the Model-T Ford.

4 | Copley's Hill was named for the artist John Singleton Copley, who owned a large plot of land to the south on what is now Beacon Street. He was one of the most important portraitists in mid-eighteenth century New England and his sitters included many prominent Bostonians, such as the revolutionary Paul Revere. Copley's father-in-law Richard Clarke was an East India Company agent and one of the merchants whose tea was pitched into the harbour by American patriots during the Boston Tea Party in December 1773. In the aftermath, Boston began to be an uncomfortable place for those perceived as having pro-British sympathies, and Copley went on a diplomatic Grand Tour of Europe, from which he never returned. He gained considerable recognition in Britain, and was elected to the Royal Academy in 1779. Unfortunately, his business interests back in Boston did not prosper so well and in 1795 he decided to sell his land (and house) there. The plot had suddenly become more valuable when Boston authorities decided to build the State House there, but Copley's agent was unaware of this and sold it at the bargain rate of $1,000 an acre. When Copley got wind of the deal, he sent his son to Boston to renegotiate the contract, but despite a legal mind that later brought him to the lofty heights of Lord Chancellor, he was unable to break its terms and his father had to settle for the sum of $18,450.

5 | Medford River (or Mystick, now Mystic, River) was an early alternative name for the waterway that in part runs parallel to the Charles River. In its original form it may have been a contraction of 'meadow ford'. The name 'Mystic' is the one that stuck, deriving from the Algonquin word *missituk,* meaning 'great tidal river'.

6 | Noddle (an informal word for 'head') Island is named for William Noddle, who first settled it in 1629. He did not live to enjoy his new home long, because three years later he died when his canoe overturned while paddling down the South River. It then became the home of Samuel Maverick, who has the dubious accolade of becoming New England's first slave-owner when he bought a number of slaves who had been transported from the Spanish-owned Tortugas in the Caribbean in 1638. During the later stages of the American Revolutionary War, the island was used as a hospital by the French fleet, which had come to the aid of the revolutionaries, who christened it 'L'Ile de France'.

7 | Rowe's Wharf (sounds like 'rose'). Now the home of the Boston Harbor Hotel, Rowe's Wharf was built in 1764 by the merchant John Rowe beside the site of an early defensive artillery battery. Originally from Devon, he prospered mightily from smuggling and slave-dealing and was the owner of the tea on the *Eleanor,* one of the ships which became caught up in the Boston Tea Party.

8 | Bunkers Hill (generally known as Bunker Hill) was the site of one of the first major battles in the American Revolutionary War, fought when the British and the American patriot forces clashed in an effort to secure control over Boston. When the revolutionaries heard that the British were planning to occupy Charlestown, they began building entrenchments on Bunker Hill and nearby Breed's Hill in an effort to prevent them doing so. As the British advanced in perfect formation, one patriot officer is said to have ordered his men not to 'fire until you see the whites of their eyes'. The defence was in vain; on the third attempt the British overran the revolutionaries' positions and they retreated over Bunker Hill and back towards Cambridge. Fifty years later, a huge 221-feet-high (67-metre) granite obelisk was erected on Breed's Hill to commemorate the battle, although the construction process was prolonged, taking 18 years to build and forcing the Monument Association supervising the works to sell most of the land for housing to raise the funds to complete it.

EAST BANK OF THE HUGHLY

MARK WOOD

1 | Govindpoore ('govind' – short for government of India – and 'poor'), or Govindpur, became the administrative headquarters of the Mánbhúm subdivision of Bengal. The wider district contained four courts by 1895, and its 196,000 inhabitants (77% of them Hindu) were policed by a force comprised of 83 officers and 681 village watchmen. If British India lacked anything, it was not bureaucratic precision.

2 | Khiderpoore (anagram of 'hiked poorer') was named for James and Robert Kyd, who in 1807 took over control of the government dockyard there. Established in 1780, over the next 40 years its workers built some 237 vessels, including the 74-gun *Hastings* (whose main combat action was against Chinese pirates at the Battle of Tonkin River in northern Vietnam in 1849). The Kyds were a prominent Anglo-Indian family. The brothers' father Alexander Kyd was surveyor-general of Bengal and their cousin Robert founded the Kolkata Botanic Gardens in 1787.

3 | Dom-Doma (*dom* is the Russian word for 'house'; Mont Dom is the third-highest peak in the Swiss Alps – at 14,911 feet/4,545 metres it is 863 feet/263 metres lower than Mont Blanc). Dom-Doma (or Dum-Dum) was the site of the signing of the treaty between the

East India Company and the Nawab of Bengal in 1757 following the Battle of Plassey that restored British control over Fort William and allocated the British tax-collecting privileges, which rapidly eroded the nawab's powers. Dum-Dum housed the main British arsenal in Bengal from 1783 – and its artillery headquarters (until that was removed to Meerut in 1853). It was from here that rumours spread in 1857 that the new paper cartridges introduced by the East India Company's army had been greased with pig and beef fat. As the soldiers had to bite open the cartridges before use, this made them repugnant on religious grounds to both of India's large religious groups. The result of this, and other grievances against the British, was the Indian Mutiny, which very nearly overthrew British control and led to the government in London taking direct control of British-occupied territories there and the ending of rule by the East India Company. It was also at the Dum-Dum arsenal that Captain Neville Bertie-Clay in 1896 devised a bullet with a soft tip that expanded when it hit a target, causing severe internal injuries. So appalling were the wounds inflicted by the dum-dum bullet that in 1899 its use was banned by the Hague Convention, an early agreement on the laws of war, on the grounds that they were 'contrary to the humanitarian spirit'.

VIRGIN ISLANDS

THOMAS JEFFERYS

1 | Three – Moskito (mosquito) Island on Virgin Gorda, Ducks Island east of St Johns and Birds Key by St Johns. Mosquito Bay was the site of a sugar plantation set up in 1720 by Johan Lorentz Carstens, a Danish landowner. Virgin Gorda ('Fat Virgin') is said to have been so named by Christopher Columbus in 1493 because he thought the profile of the island from the sea resembled an overweight woman lying on her side. It was once home to a colony of over 100 Cornish miners, who came in the mid-nineteenth century to work in the Old Copper Mine when the industry back home went into decline. Their reprieve, though, was short, because the Virgin Gorda mine closed in 1862. Moskito Island and nearby Nicker Island (now known as Necker Island) were bought by the entrepreneur Richard Branson (in 2007 and 1978) for development as luxury resorts.

2 | Witch Island. It is unclear how Witch Island got its name, but the tiny islet was long disputed between the United States and United Kingdom, as it sat firmly astride their maritime boundary. In 1977 the United Kingdom relinquished all claims, but the island had by then become known as Flanagan Island. Curiously, the name Witch Island then migrated to what had been Pelican Island, just north of Normands Island, within the British Virgin Islands. Perhaps the witch was a British sorceress.

3 | Fat Hog Bay. Today, Fat Hogs Bay (the slight modern variant on the original name) has several marinas taking advantage of its position overlooking Sir Francis Drake's Bay. This passage was named for the British adventurer, explorer and privateer who took a shortcut through the Virgin Islands during his circumnavigation of the globe in 1577–80 (which, when he arrived back in Plymouth in September 1580, made him the first expedition commander to complete the feat, because his predecessor Ferdinand Magellan

had died in the Philippines halfway through his voyage, killed in an argument between two local tribes).

4 | Salt Island and Ginger Island. Salt Island was named for one of the salt ponds (where salt can be gathered by natural evaporation) scattered around the Virgins Islands. The salt was used for preserving meat and other goods. The salt-gatherers who lived here lost their livelihood with the advent of refrigeration in the late nineteenth century, and the Salt Pond on the island today is owned by the government. By tradition, the inhabitants of the island would send rent of a pound of salt to the British monarch each year, a custom that was renewed in 2015 (although there are now only a handful of residents). The coast of Salt Island is the site of the wreck of the Royal Mail steamship *Rhone*, which was driven onto rocks during a severe storm in 1867 with the loss of 123 passengers and crew. The uninhabited Ginger Island is largely overgrown and with limited anchorage, but spectacular diving. One of the main dive spots is called 'Alice in Wonderland'.

5 | Jost van Dykes (anagram of 'yaks vend jots') is believed to have been named for a Dutch buccaneer who used the small island's harbours as a hideout for his privateers. The whole Virgin Islands archipelago became a nest of pirates from the sixteenth century, as the Spanish, English, Dutch, French and Danish all tussled for control, leaving a power vacuum within which criminality flourished. Only after the Dutch established a permanent base on Tortola in 1648 and the British captured it in 1672 did the islands slowly begin to return to a state of comparative tranquillity. Although tiny, Jost van Dyke, as it is now called, was the birthplace of Dr William Thornton, the designer of the Capitol in Washington, DC, and of Dr John Lettsom, who founded the Medical Society of London in 1773. His best-known academic monograph was a long way from the rural isolation of his upbringing, dealing with *Diseases of Great Towns and the Best Means of Preserving them,* and he clearly had something of a sense of humour, writing a well-known piece of doggerel about himself:

I, John Letsom
Blisters, bleeds and sweats 'em
If after that they please to die
I, John Letsom

6 | Four – Spanish Town, English Keys, Dutch Head, Frenchman's Keys and Frenchman's Rock (or five if you count Normands Island, now Norman Island). Spanish Town on Virgin Gorda is the second-largest town on the British Virgin Islands and was the capital of the colony from 1680 to 1741, when the administrative headquarters was moved to Road Town on Tortola. This and the other locations are a reminder of the complex colonial history of the Caribbean, and the Virgin Islands in particular. The islands were first sighted by Columbus on his second voyage in 1493, but it was not until 1555 that the Spanish sent an expedition to subdue them. Central control, though, was lax, and St Croix, the first island to be settled, was inhabited by a rag-tag bunch of English, French and Dutch buccaneers. A formal Spanish expedition then seized it in 1650, only to be driven out a few months later by the French, who held it (save a nine-month period when they sold it off to the Knights of Malta) until 1733, when it became Danish. A brief British interlude during the Napoleonic War ended with the restoration of Danish rule in 1815 before St Croix and the other westerly Virgin Islands were purchased by the United States in 1917. The eastern Virgin Islands, including Tortola and Virgin Gorda, were settled by the British in 1680 after they drove out the Dutch pirates who had flourished there. They remain a British Overseas Territory. Normands Island (now Norman Island) is reputed to have been the inspiration for Robert Louis Stevenson's *Treasure Island,* published in 1883. It was certainly the location of a real-life pirate story: the crew of the Spanish treasure ship, *Nuestra Señora de Guadalupe,* mutinied off the North Carolina coast in 1750 and made off in two small boats, one of which wended its way, first to St Croix, and then to the more-remote

Normands, where they buried the loot. Much of it was recovered when the governor of the island offered an amnesty and a one-third share to anyone who returned a part of the treasure, but some was rumoured to have remained buried, and may be there still. Normands Island's small neighbour to the east – 'the Dead Chest' – really did inspire Stevenson. He found the name in a book by Charles Kingsley about the West Indies and adapted it for his resounding pirate song: 'Fifteen Men on the dead man's chest – Yo-ho-ho and a bottle of rum! Drink and the devil had done for the rest – Yo-ho-ho and a bottle of rum!'

7 | Four – Coopers Island, Fisherman's Head (on Tortola), Brewers Bay and, less reputably, Virgin's Gangway of the Freebooters. Coopers Island is one of many of the modern British Virgin Islands which acts as a dive centre (although the presence of a brewery and a rum bar there may make it particularly popular). The name of Brewers Bay on Tortola is a reference to the nearby sugar plantations and rum distilleries which once stood nearby. Virgin's Gangway of the Freebooters is an alternative name for the Sir Francis Drake's Channel, because it offered a swift passage to buccaneers on the run and seeking refuge on one of the smaller and less accessible of the islands.

8 | Guana ('iguana' minus the 'i') was settled in the 1720s by two Quaker families, part of a Quaker community which for four decades settled in the Virgin Islands and helped improve conditions for slaves on the sugar plantations there. Among its members were William Thornton and John Lettsom (see answer 5), as well as Richard Humphreys, who endowed Cheyney University in Pennsylvania, one of the first higher education colleges for African Americans.

9 | Anegada (anagram of 'an adage'). Although one of the larger of the British Virgin Islands, Anegada, nicknamed the 'drowned island', is only 28 feet (8.5 metres) above sea level at its highest point, and during high tides is completely submerged. Its mysterious quality as a disappearing land mass made it the subject of myths and rumours about buried pirate treasure said to be secreted away somewhere in its frustratingly shifting sands.

CAERNARFONSHIRE

ROBERT DAWSON

1 | Carnarvon (or Caernarfon) – means 'the fort in Arfon', with Arfon in turn deriving from the Welsh for 'facing Anglesey'. It was the centre of the *cantref* of Arfon, a subdivision of the medieval Welsh kingdom of Gwynedd. An early Norman stone castle stood here, but was replaced by the current imposing fortress after Edward I's conquest of Wales in 1283. Edward's castle dominated North Wales and withstood all Welsh attempts to take it, in particular a siege in 1402 during the uprising of Owain Glyndŵr. It proved less resistant to more-modern military techniques, though, and changed hands between Royalists and Parliamentarians three times during the English Civil War of the 1640s. The Earldom of Carnarvon was created by Charles I in 1628 but went extinct twice before it was bestowed on Henry Herbert in 1793 as a reward for long service in various Whig administrations. His great-great-grandson George Herbert, the 5th Earl, was a keen Egyptologist, a hobby he was able to indulge in thanks to the handsome dowry that accompanied his wife Almina, the illegitimate daughter of the banking magnate Alfred de Rothschild. The Earl of Carnarvon bankrolled Howard Carter on several digs in Egypt, before receiving a licence to dig in 1914. By 1922 the earl's patience had run out and he warned Carter that this would be the final season he would fund. Fortunately for posterity – and less so for the earl – on 4 November Carter found steps leading down to the tomb of Tutankhamun, the boy pharaoh whose burial place had been overlooked by previous archaeologists. Carnarvon came to Egypt to witness the entrance to the burial chamber and the fabulous treasures which it contained. He remained in Egypt several months and in March 1923 suffered a mosquito bite, which became infected, leading to pneumonia, blood-poisoning and his death. The event gave rise to the story of a 'pharaoh's curse', which struck all those who had first entered the tomb (although in fact many of them, including Carnarvon's own daughter, lived to a ripe old age).

2 | Bryn Bras ('bras', item of clothing). The small settlement of Bryn Bras is most remarkable for the farmhouse, which was remodelled between 1828 and 1840 by Thomas Williams, a local lawyer, to create an extravagant neo-Norman folly, complete with turrets, castellations and a great hall. Possibly in part designed by Samuel Beazley, an architect whose real love was the design of theatres, including the Lyceum and remodellings of the Drury Lane and Adelphi theatres in London. He was a better architect than a poet, as his self-written tomb epitaph demonstrates:

> *'Here lies Samuel Beazley,*
> *Who lived hard and died easily.'*

3 | Llanbeblig (anagram of 'baling bell') has one of the oldest Christian sites in Wales; the church is dedicated to Peblig, or Publicius, and was founded in 433. He was said to have been the son of Macsen Wledig, the hero of a Welsh epic poem (identified with Magnus Maximus, a usurping Roman emperor who reigned from 383 to 388 over Britain , Gaul and Spain, but who died when he tried to expand his domain into Italy and was defeated and executed by the legitimate Emperor Theodosius). In the poetic version Macsen has a dream in which he travels over the sea and through a mountainous land to a noble hall where he sees a beautiful maiden. When he wakes, Macsen is driven to distraction by the vision and neglects his subjects, leading to rumbles of discontent. He sends out messengers to find the land and woman of his dreams, but it takes them years to locate her. As a condition of their marriage, the princess insists Macsen come to Snowdonia, which he does, spending seven years building roads and castles and enjoying marital bliss. He then returns to Rome to find that he has been deposed in his absence by a new emperor. He is forced to call on the brothers of his wife Helen, who take the city and in return are granted sovereignty over Britain and Wales. The story was supposed to boost Welsh claims to sovereignty by giving it an external validation. The English, sadly, took no notice.

4 | Llanrug (a 'rug' is a type of carpet), to the east of Caernarvon had the highest proportion of Welsh-speakers of any locality in the 2011 census (at 88 per cent). The village's name means 'the church in the heather' and it was occasionally known as 'Llanfihangel-yn-Rug' for its saint Mihangel (or Michael), to whom the local church, with its fifteenth-century roof, is dedicated.

5 | Plas Llanfaglan (anagram of 'flag annals pall'), which means 'church of Baglan', is home to a derelict church dedicated to Baglan ab Dingad, which was noted for a fine stone lychgate built by the church warden in 1722. Legend had it that Baglan, the son of a sixth-century Breton prince, could carry fire in his bare hands without being burned (a sign of moral purity). He was instructed by Cadoc, a hermit, to build a church where he found a tree 'with three fruits'. Rather than doing as he was told, Baglan started to construct the church at a

nearby, more-level site, but each night rain washed the foundations away. Finally, Baglan realised that to stand in the way of the divine will was futile and he then built the predecessor of the church we see today.

6 | Waun Fawr was a stop on the North Wales Narrow Gauge Railway, which opened in 1877 and closed in 1937. It was reopened in 2000 when the railway revived and now acts as a stop just on the border of the Snowdonia National Park.

7 | Segontium. There are very many ('legions') places on the map, but only Segontium, as a Roman fort, was the home of a legion. The fort at Segontium was one of the oldest Roman military installations in Wales, built by governor Agricola in AD 77–78 during the first Roman advance against the Ordovices in the north of the country. It was rebuilt in stone in the second century AD and held a garrison of an auxiliary cohort (around 500 men), which at the end of the second century consisted of the Cohors I Sunicorum, recruited in what is now Belgium. Segontium remained in use until the late fourth century. According to the medieval chronicler Nennius there was a tomb here to 'Constantine' (by which he probably means Constantius Chlorus, the father of Constantine the Great), although since Constantius died in York in 306, this is unlikely.

LONDON

GEORGE CRUCHLEY

1 | Canada (Canada Wharf). Canada Wharf and Saw Mills is a reminder of the trade once carried out from Surrey Docks to Canada, particularly in timber which was cut here. The last remaining sawmill in the area (over the river in Rotherhithe) only closed in 1986.

2 | Cuckolds Point. Situated just after the Thames takes a sharp turn southwards, Cuckolds Point has a curious history. For many years a post with a pair of horns was mounted here, the sign of a cuckold – a man whose wife has cheated on him. Legend has it that while King John was out hunting by the river, he came across the attractive wife of a miller and was on the point of seducing her when her husband returned home. The king saved himself only from the outraged man by revealing his identity, and as compensation for his offence gave the miller all the land between Cuckolds Point and Charlton. Every year, on St Luke's Day, a 'Horn Fair' was held in Charlton and a procession with participants wearing horns would make their way from Cuckolds Point to Charlton's parish church. Cuckolds Point was the source of much ribald humour and a popular Royalist ballad during the English Civil War made a dig at the morality of the Parliamentarians with the rhyme: 'And when they reach Cuckold's Point they make a gallant show./Their wives bid the Musick play Cuckolds All in A Row.' Daniel Defoe was less than impressed by the Horn Fair, referring to the 'yearly collected rabble of mad-people at Horn Fair' and the 'all manner of indecency and immodesty that could be experienced there'. The fair was suppressed in the 1870s, but a version of it has recently been revived.

3 | Ropemakers Fields. Rope Street, Rope Walk and nearby Ropemakers Fields are reminders of one of the industries which Limehouse's maritime heritage brought to the area. Samuel Pepys, while Secretary to the Admiralty, visited the ropeworks in the area in 1664, as did Tsar Alexander II of Russia in 1871.

4 | Gun Lane (anagram of 'nu angle' – sounds like 'new angle', and nu is the 13th letter of the ancient Greek alphabet). Gun Lane is perhaps a reminder of the armaments industry, which the naval heritage of Limehouse and the docklands in general brought to the area (and in the 1890s it was renamed Grenade Street, continuing the theme with a more up-to-date weapon).

5 | Narrow Street once marked the medieval river wall of the Thames and, despite its restricted width (in contrast to nearby Broad Street), was one of the busiest areas of the docklands, lined with lime kilns, cuts, chandlery businesses and (from 1769) the Limehouse Cut, which allowed smaller ships to enter the Regents Canal (or their cargoes to be reloaded onto canal boats). Charles Dickens's godfather Christopher Huffam operated a business making sails from nearby Newell Street, and the author was a frequent visitor to the area, picking The Grapes public house as the model for The Six Jolly Fellowship Porters in *Our Mutual Friend.*

6 | Lavender Dock was built around 1702 on the site of an earlier windmill. The name comes from Lavender Street (the previous name of Queen Street, just inland, which is in turn now called Rotherhithe Street), which was probably taken from the lavender once grown in nearby market gardens. At the time of the Cruchley map, the dock was occupied by Job Cockshott who ran a shipbreaking business, and who for a time was a business partner of Richard Trevithick, the Cornish mining engineer and pioneer of locomotive steam engines. In 1808 Trevithick's *Catch Me Who Can* engine became the first train in history to carry fare-paying passengers when it ran on a demonstration track just south of today's Euston station. Unfortunately, the train derailed and the enterprise was a flop. To recoup his losses, Trevithick went into business with Cockshott at the Lavender Dock Yard, trying to adapt his engine to place it into an old Lord Mayor's Barge, with the intention of creating a steam-powered vessel to ply the Thames. The attempt was a failure and in 1809 Trevithick went bankrupt.

7 | Lower Shadwell (anagram of 'herald slew owl'). Shadwell was one of London's first suburbs, just outside the City walls and was granted to the Canons of St Paul's in 1228. It became the centre of a maritime culture, with wharves, tanneries, smiths and ropemaking businesses. Just north of Lower Shadwell is the church of St Paul's whose strong connections with the sea led to it being nicknamed 'The Church of the Sea Captains'. It was here that Captain James Cook, the discoverer of Australia, had his first child – also called James – baptised in 1763. The younger James followed his father into the Royal Navy, but drowned in 1794 while on his way in a small open boat to take up his first command, of the *Spitfire* in Portsmouth.

8 | Two – Devon in Devonport Street and Surrey in the Grand Surrey Outer Dock. The Surrey Commercial Docks were part of the first wave of dock-building that transformed this area of East London in the nineteenth century. Although the London Docks had already been opened (in 1805) and the East India Docks were completed in 1806, the Surrey Docks, finished the next year, were the first south of the river. They specialised in timber and were part of a system of waterways, including canals, that was supposed to reach down as far as Portsmouth. The Surrey Docks were badly damaged in World War Two during the Blitz and by the 1960s had become unviable. The dock basin was filled in in 1967 and the whole area was redeveloped from the 1990s as the new district of Surrey Quays.

AUSTRALIA

JOHN TALLIS

1 | Mount Babbage. At 980 feet (299 metres) and lying in the eastern part of South Australia (and not, as shown on the 1851 map, in New South Wales), Mount Babbage is named for the geologist, botanist and explorer Benjamin Herschel Babbage. During the early part of his career Babbage worked on several projects to improve the water supply in English towns, and in 1850 was invited by Patrick Brontë, father of the novelists Anne, Charlotte and Emily, to inspect the sewers of Haworth, where he and his family lived (Babbage found them to be in an appalling state). He arrived in South Australia in 1851 and was tasked by the Colonial Secretary Earl Grey with the carrying out of a mineralogical survey of the colony. During his surveys in 1856 Babbage found that Lake Torrens was not in fact a single lake and that Lake Eyre is divided into a northern and southern section; he also discovered the mountain later named for him, which he initially called Mount Hopeful. Babbage's progress was so slow that in 1858 he was recalled and replaced by Peter Egerton-Burton (an altogether more-determined type, who pioneered the first overland crossing from Adelaide to Perth in 1872 – an expedition so gruelling that all his men came down with scurvy, and Egerton-Burton lost an eye). Benjamin Babbage's father was Charles Babbage, the mathematician and inventor, who in the 1820s devised and partially built the Difference Engine, a pioneering mechanical computational device, and also designed a more sophisticated version, the Analytical Engine, which could be programmed with punch cards. Despite the fact that it was never built (being too complex for the engineering of the time), he thus has a claim to be the father of computing.

2 | Port Lincoln (the colour being 'Lincoln green'). Situated at the southeastern end of the Eyre peninsula, Port Lincoln has a harbour area three times the size of Sydney. The port was given its name in 1802 by the explorer Matthew Flinders, in memory of his native

Lincolnshire. It was in the running as the first capital of South Australia, but its limited supply of fresh water led to its being rejected in favour of Adelaide. The town grew slowly from its first settlement in 1839 until it was incorporated as a municipality in 1921, but thereafter its economy grew steadily on the back of Australia's largest tuna fleet and tourism, in part attracted by the town's annual Tunarama festival. 'Lincoln green' is a bright green colour traditionally produced by the dyers of Lincoln by mixing woad (which is blue) and yellow weld. It became associated in popular tradition with the garments worn by the folk hero Robin Hood and his band of outlaws.

3 | Kangaroo Island. Just over 90 miles (145 kilometres) long, Kangaroo Island is Australia's third-largest island (after Tasmania and Melville Island). It was discovered by Matthew Flinders in 1802, and named for the large numbers of kangaroos he found there. It became the haunt of sealers and whalers, and was a stopping-off point for the fleet that brought the first settlers to South Australia in 1836. A popular tourist spot, Kangaroo Island is also noted for its honey, said to be produced by the world's last surviving colony of pure Ligurian bees.

4 | Melbourne (anagram of 'rouble men') was one of Australia's earliest settlements outside New South Wales. Port Phillip Bay, on which it lies, was discovered by Lieutenant John Murray in 1802 and the town was formally established in 1836 after a number of earlier, illegal squatter settlements. The discovery of gold in 1851 brought the colony of Victoria, in which it lay, a spurt of growth and Melbourne became large and prosperous enough – with a population of 500,000 by the 1890s – to challenge Sydney as the capital of the new Federation of Australia. Melbourne did indeed become the seat of the new federal parliament in 1901, but its victory was pyrrhic, because the capital was moved definitively to the purpose-built city of Canberra in 1927. Melbourne was the host city for the Olympics in 1956, the first time the games had been held outside Europe and it is the venue of the annual Melbourne Cup, Australia's most-renowned horse race.

5 | Encounter Bay, on the south coast of the Fleurieu peninsula, is named for the meeting there in 1802 between the English explorer Matthew Flinders and his French counterpart Nicholas Baudin. Both were charting the area for their respective governments with a view to establishing a colony. Although the two explorers were amicable enough, considering the fact that they believed their countries to be at war (unaware of the peace treaty signed at Amiens a few weeks before), they were each suspicious of the other's intentions. Baudin continued eastwards, surveying as far as Sydney and Tasmania, before returning home. He died of tuberculosis on Mauritius in September 1803 and this, together with the preoccupation of Napoleon's government with the renewed war with Britain, meant that in the end no French colonising expedition was ever sent to Australia.

6 | Northumberland (in Cape Northumberland, 14 letters). Around 240 miles (385 kilometres) southeast of Adelaide, Cape Northumberland was named in December 1800 for Lieutenant Henry Percy, the 2nd Duke of Northumberland, who fought at the Battles of Lexington and Concord in 1775 at the start of the American Revolutionary War. It was the site of one of Australia's most notorious shipwrecks in 1859. The steamship *Admella*, on its way from Port Adelaide to Melbourne, hit submerged rocks in shallow waters off the cape and began, slowly, to sink. The survivors clung to the wreck for a week, in full site of the shore, as successive rescue attempts failed. In the end 89 of the 113 aboard died, drowned as they slipped into the waters from exhaustion, or from the effects of drinking salt water as the supply of fresh water ran out. Finally,

a rescue lifeboat managed to pull up beside the *Admella* and the survivors were carried to safety at Portland, 60 miles (95 kilometres) to the east.

7 | Paramatta (now Parramatta). Today a suburb of Greater Sydney, Paramatta was founded in 1788 as the first inland settlement of the new European colony. It was originally called 'Rose Hill', but the name was soon modified to a version of that used by local Aboriginal people. It was the site of the first successful farm to grow grain in Australia and housed the residence of the governors of New South Wales until the 1850s. In 1803 Paramatta was the scene of the attempted execution of Joseph Samuel, convicted for the brutal murder of a police constable. The rope used for the hanging – which was carried out by driving a cart away from underneath the condemned man – snapped. A second rope slipped off Samuel's head, and a third one snapped. Finally, the increasingly restive crowd demanded his release and the governor, Philip Gidley King, granted him clemency and commuted his sentence to life imprisonment. The 'man they could not hang' ran out of luck in 1806, when he escaped with several companions from a mine where he had been sent to do hard labour; he stole a boat, which was later found floating upturned, and was presumed drowned.

8 | Mount Kosciusko (or Kosciuszko). At 7,310 feet (2,228 metres), Mount Kosciuszko is the highest peak in Australia. It was named by the explorer Pawel Strzelecki in 1840 in honour of the Polish patriot Tadeusz Kosciuszko, apparently on the grounds that its shape resembled Kosciuszko's tomb in Krakow. Kosciuszko had led an uprising in 1794 against the Russian occupation of the eastern part of Poland, following the Second Partition of the country. After its failure he spent the rest of his life in exile in the United States, Austria and Switzerland, but his body was transported to Poland in 1818 where, in death, he was greeted as a hero.

THE FRANKLIN SEARCH
LADY JANE FRANKLIN

1 | Wollaston Land (anagram of 'owl talons'), now called the Wollaston peninsula, is situated on the south edge of Victoria Island. It lies largely within the Kitikmeot region of Nunavut, the Canadian territory established in 1999 with the country's largest concentration of indigenous peoples. It was first seen in 1826 by Sir John Richardson during his expedition eastwards from the west coast of Canada, and was named by him after Dr William Hyde Wollaston, a chemist who discovered the elements palladium and rhodium. Wollaston was further explored by John Rae in 1849 as part of his expedition to discover the fate of Franklin.

2 | Baring Island (Ba-'ring'), now Banks Island, was first sighted by Sir William Parry in 1820, during his expedition in search of the Northwest Passage. The feat was achieved only in 1903–06 by the Norwegian explorer Roald Amundsen (the first man to reach the South Pole) and the presence of ice sheets in winter meant the route only became regularly navigable in 2009, as global temperatures rose. Parry named it Banks Island in honour of the naturalist Sir Joseph Banks, who had accompanied James Cook on the voyage that discovered eastern Australia in 1770 (during which Banks made the first written record of a kangaroo). Banks Island was dubbed Baring Island by Robert McClure during his 1850 expedition in search of Franklin. After an initially successful survey, his ship, the *Investigator*, was closed in by pack ice, and McClure and his crew had to endure three years trapped near Victoria Island before they were rescued. Ruins on the island indicate that it was settled by Thule Inuit people around 500 years ago, and by pre-Dorset Palaeo-Eskimos around 1500 BC.

3 | Melville Island. Sparsely vegetated Melville Island is a key breeding ground for the brant goose.

It was discovered by Sir William Parry in 1819, who experienced a forced overwintering there when the sea froze around his ship. He named the island for Robert Melville, 2nd Viscount Dundas, who was First Lord of the Admiralty at the time (his main task in office was to fight vested interests who, after the British naval victory at Trafalgar in 1805, argued that, with Britain's maritime supremacy assured, there was no need to invest any further money in the Royal Navy). Petroleum-bearing deposits were identified on Melville as early as 1913 by the Icelandic-Canadian explorer Vilhjalmur Stefansson and the island now has a major gas field. The American novelist Herman Melville is best known for *Moby Dick*, his classic of the sea, published in 1851, which recounts the obsessive quest of Ahab, captain of the whaler *Pequod*, to take revenge on Moby Dick, a sperm whale which nearly killed him on a previous voyage.

4 | Fort Confidence, at the northeastern tip of Great Bear Lake, was established in 1837 as a winter base by Thomas Simpson and Peter Warren Dease, who were exploring the area on behalf of the Hudson's Bay Company. It was rebuilt in 1848 to serve as a base for John Rae's expedition in search of Franklin. It is the setting for several scenes in *The Fur Country*, one of Jules Vernes's less well-known novels, in which the heroes are trapped on drifting ice (a fate which in fact befell several real Arctic explorers) before their eventual rescue by a Danish whaling ship.

5 | Prince of Wales Island. At 12,830 square miles (33,230 square kilometres) in area, Prince of Wales Island is Canada's tenth-largest island (and the 40th largest in the world). It was first sighted by Parry in 1819, but the earliest landing there was by sledge parties of a Franklin search expedition commanded by Captain Horatio Austin in 1851. During that voyage, members of his crew published the *Illustrated Arctic News*, the most northerly newspaper ever produced – at least until the *Svalbardposten* began publication at Longbearbyen on Svalbard, Norway, in 1948 – and which bore the inspirational motto *Tuto et sine metu* ('safely and without fear'). The island was named for Queen Victoria's son, Albert Edward, the future King Edward VII.

6 | Boothia Felix (anagram of 'aloof exhibit'). Just to the east of Prince of Wales Island, Boothia Felix (or the Boothia peninsula) was discovered by John Ross, during his voyage in search of the Northwest Passage. He named it in honour of his patron Felix Booth, a gin-distilling magnate (Booth's Gin was produced from the 1740s, and has recently been revived). The island was visited in 1859 by Francis McClintock during his voyage in search of Franklin and by Roald Amundsen in 1904 during the expedition in which he established the position of the magnetic north pole.

AFGHANISTAN

ALFRED CONCANEN

1 | Peshawur (anagram of 'washer up'), or Peshawar. Already ancient in the fourth century BC, Peshawar formed part of the Persian Achaemenid Empire, was conquered by Alexander the Great in 327 BC, and then became the capital of the Indo-Greek kingdom of Gandhara and a centre of Buddhist influence (when it was known as Purusapura). The giant Buddhist stupa built by the Kushan ruler Kanishka, who also chose Peshawar as his capital, was once possibly the tallest building in the world (at 394 feet/120 metres). The region was gradually Islamicised from the eighth century, a process which accelerated after its conquest by Mahmud of Ghazni in 1001, and it finally became a part of the Mughal Empire in 1530 under whom it acquired its present name (the words *pesh awar* mean 'frontier forts'). It was captured by the Sikhs under Ranjit Singh in 1818 and was then taken by the British after the Second Anglo-Sikh War in 1849. During the Soviet occupation of Afghanistan, the city and its surrounding region played host to many Afghan refugees and it has suffered an increase in insecurity since the resurgence of the Taleban in the 2010s.

2 | Gilgit, with a modern population of just 8,000, sits at the centre of a particularly turbulent area in an already troubled region. A remote outpost of the Maharajahs of Kashmir, its exposed position close to both Afghanistan and Russia troubled the British, who leased the area in 1935 for a period of 60 years. At the time of partition in 1947, Lord Mountbatten, the British viceroy, decided to terminate the lease and so Gilgit reverted to Kashmir, whose Maharajah Hari Singh, although initially deciding to exercise his right to remain aloof from both India and Pakistan, finally signed an Instrument of Accession, joining his territories to India. Advances by the Pakistan army and a mutiny in Gilgit, led to the western part of Kashmir, including Gilgit, remaining in Pakistan except for the very northern tip, which Pakistan ceded to China in

1963 in exchange for its support over Kashmir. The area received limited self-government status in 2009 as Gilgit-Baltistan and contains part of the route of the Karakoram Highway, the highest paved road in the region, which runs between China and Pakistan and offers the region enhanced prosperity if security can be assured.

3 | Moultan ('moult'-an), now called Multan. Known in ancient times as Kashep Puri, Multan was visited in 641 by the Chinese Buddhist pilgrim Xuanzang, who was on his way to India to collect Buddhist texts. He visited the renowned sun temple there, whose cult image he described as 'cast in gold and ornamented with rare gems'. A man of notable religious stamina, Xuanzang only finally returned to China in 645, 18 years after his original departure, but bringing with him over 600 sacred texts. The city passed through a series of Islamic dynasties from the seventh century, including the Mughals, and finally fell to the expanding Sikh Empire in 1772. In 1848–49 it was the subject of an eight-month siege by forces of the British East India Company because two of its envoys were killed after attending the inauguration of the city's new governor. It was the birthplace in 1722 of Ahmad Shah Durrani, who served as a senior army officer under Nadir Shah; after his master's assassination in 1747, he seized the throne and established a dynasty that laid the foundations of modern Afghanistan. Multan is also the hometown of the cricketer Inzamam-ul-Haq, the only Pakistani batsman to score 20,000 runs in international cricket.

4 | Quettah (at the beginning, 'quet' turns to 'quit'). A district capital in Pakistan's Balochistan province, Quettah (now spelled Quetta) sits at 5,495 feet (1,675 metres) above sea level. Its name is derived from the Pashto word *kwatkot*, meaning 'fort', reflecting the town's strategic position on the North-West Frontier, commanding the Khojak Pass. Captured by Mahmud of Ghazni in the early eleventh century, it was also the spot where the Mughal emperor Humayun left his one-year-old son Akbar after he retreated from an expedition in Sindh in 1543 (only finally managing to return to Delhi 12 years later to reclaim his throne). The city was occupied by the British in 1876 as they inched towards Afghanistan in a bid to head off the threat of Russian expansion southwards from Central Asia. It was the subject of a poem by Rudyard Kipling about a soldier named Jack Barrett who was transferred there and soon died in the unhealthy conditions. As Kipling muses: 'And, when the Last Great Bugle Call/Adown the Hurnai throbs/And the last grim joke is entered/In the big black Book of Jobs/ And Quetta graveyards give again/Their victims to the air,/I shouldn't like to be the man/Who sent Jack Barrett there.'

5 | Jellalabad (also spelled Jalalabad), with three 'l's. The first accounts of Jalalabad came from the Chinese Buddhist pilgrims Faxian (around 400) and Xuanzang (in 630) who both visited the city, which was then called Adnipur. It was refounded by Babur, the first Mughal emperor in 1560. Located on a strategic crossing point into Afghanistan, it was occupied by the British during both the First and Second Anglo-Afghan wars (in 1839–42 and 1878–80). The first war in particular was a disaster for the British. Having invaded Afghanistan to place their candidate, the former ruler Shah Shujah Durrani, on the throne, the British occupied Kabul, but were then forced to abandon it and make a protracted and bloody retreat during which almost the entire force was slaughtered. At Gandamak, around 25 miles (40 kilometres) north of Jalalabad, the 60 or so survivors made a last stand, forming a makeshift square in the frozen ground and using their dozen working muskets to drive off a series of Afghan charges. In the end they ran out of ammunition and all were killed, save nine who were taken prisoner and Assistant Surgeon William Brydon who escaped and made it to Jalalabad, the sole survivor of the 4,500 soldiers who had begun the trek from Kabul 12 days earlier. Jalalabad was a major Soviet base during the occupation of the country from 1978 to 1989, when anti-communist Mujahideen guerrillas controlled the surrounding mountains, and from 1996 became a stronghold of the Taleban.

6 | Kandahar (anagram of 'aha, drank'). Situated at the foot of the Qaitul Ridge, Kandahar provided an oasis in an otherwise semi-arid region, and was settled as early as the Iron Age. Already a provincial capital under the Persian Achaemenids in the fifth century BC, it was conquered by Alexander the Great, in 329 BC, who refounded it as Alexandria in Arachosia. It fell to the Mauryan Indian ruler Chandragupta in 305 BC and then, at a strategic crossroads, was subject to a dizzying succession of rulers – Greco-Bactrians, Parthians, Shakas, Kushans, Sasanians, Saffarids, Ghaznavids, Mongols and Mughals – all the while falling further and further into decay. In 1738 the site of the old city was sacked by Nadir Shah and the city transferred to its current site, some three miles away. It then underwent something of a renaissance, becoming the capital of a unified Afghanistan in 1747. From 1994 it was the main stronghold of the Islamist Taleban movement before their removal from power by a US-backed coalition, and recently has become the focus of attempts by a revived Taleban movement to re-establish themselves. Nur Jahan, the wife of the Mughal emperor Jahangir and aunt of Mumtaz Mahal for whom the Taj Mahal was built as a mausoleum, was born in Kandahar in 1577.

7 | Bamian Pass (anagram of 'sampan bias'). The Bamian (or Bamiyan) Pass offers the main route into the Bamian Valley, a 15.5-mile-long (25-kilometre) stretch bordered by cliffs that are pocked with hundreds of caves hosting Buddhist shrines. The grandest Buddhist monuments of all, however, were two monumental Buddhas, one 125 feet (38 metres) high and one 174 feet (53 metres) high, which dated from the fifth to the sixth centuries AD and were described by the Chinese pilgrim Xuanzang in 630. After around 1,500 years in place, the statues were destroyed on the orders of the Taleban leader Mullah Omar in March 2001, because he regarded them as idolatrous. Anti-tank mines, artillery and dynamite were all used in the demolition, which caused a massive international outcry. During later stabilisation and recovery work carried out at the site following the fall of the Taleban, the remains of a third Buddha (62 feet/19 metres long) were found, a reclining statue that had also been described by Xuanzang, but of which all trace had vanished over the succeeding centuries. A sampan is a type of flat-bottomed Chinese boat.

POVERTY IN LONDON'S EAST END

CHARLES BOOTH

1 | Nelson Street, named like so many roads in the nineteenth century after Horatio Nelson, the great British admiral and victor of the Battle of Trafalgar, has no discernible maritime heritage. It is the site of the East London Central Synagogue, established in 1923, and now the East End's last fully functioning purpose-built synagogue.

2 | Hanbury Street (anagram of 'hunts betrayer') was the scene of one of the brutal killings perpetrated by the murderer known as 'Jack the Ripper', who terrorised the East End for months in 1888–89. Annie Chapman was the second of the Ripper's victims, one of five women living at the edge of society who were almost certainly killed by him (with half a dozen more murders possibly attributed to his hand). Chapman had fallen on hard times after the death of her eldest daughter and was working as a prostitute. On the night of her death (8 September 1888), she found herself without enough money to pay for her lodging house and went out in search of a customer to earn her rent. She was seen on Hanbury Street at 5.30 a.m. talking to a man, but then her body, horribly mutilated was discovered just half an hour later. The murder was soon linked to that of Mary Ann Nichols who had been killed the previous week, her body showing signs of similar wounds. Despite a huge manhunt, three further murders and even a taunting postcard sent to the police from 'Saucy Jack', claiming to be the killer, Jack the Ripper was never identified. The case has generated a huge lore and a long list of suspects, both at the time and subsequently, which expanded to include outlandish accusations against men such as the Duke of Clarence, the author Lewis Carroll and the artist Walter Sickert.

3 | Whitechapel Road or Whitechapel High Street, leading from Aldgate out of the City to the east, was paved as early as the reign of Henry VIII. It was named for the 'White chapel' of St Mary, built in the thirteenth century, which gave its name to the whole district. Long one of London's most-impoverished quarters, it already had a reputation for overcrowding and poverty in the seventeenth century. It has also been the reception ground for generations of immigrants seeking affordable housing in order to establish themselves. Its reputation as a centre of Jewish life in London was reinforced by the influx of tens of thousands of Jewish refugees from pogroms in eastern Europe in the 1880s.

4 | Sidney Street (anagram of 'eery dentists') was the scene of a notorious siege in January 1911. Five weeks earlier, members of the City of London police force had stumbled upon an attempted burglary on nearby Houndsditch. In the ensuing shoot-out, three policemen were killed and the criminal gang fled into the maze of alleys around Stepney. One of the gang, though, had been fatally wounded and when his body was found, it allowed the authorities to focus their suspicions on a small group of Latvian anarchists. On the night of 3 January, they ran two of them to ground at 100 Sidney Street. The cornered anarchists opened fire at the police and a brief siege ensued. Reinforcements were summoned in the shape of 20 marksmen from the Scots Guards and even Winston Churchill, then Home Secretary, came to take a look. After five hours fire took hold of the house where the Latvians were holed up and one was shot as he poked his head out of a window for air, while the corpse of the other was later found in the building's ruins. The siege was filmed by Pathé News for its newsreels, making it one of the earliest such crime-scenes to hit the cinemas.

5 | Fashion Street. The street's name has nothing to do with the fashion industry or modelling, but is a corruption of Fasson, the name it took from Thomas and Lewis Fasson, two brothers who owned the land on which the street was built in the 1650s. The confusion is understandable because Whitechapel became known for the garment industry, with hosts of small textile workshops and tailoring businesses clustering in the streets around the Commercial Road by late Victorian times.

6 | Fieldgate Street ('field' and 'gate') was the site of the Fieldgate Street Great Synagogue, established in 1899 and opened by the banker Nathaniel Charles Rothschild. As well as working in the family banking business, Charles was an eminent entomologist who built up an enormous collection of over one-quarter

of a million fleas. He went as far as the Sudan in search of new specimens and – perhaps alarmingly for the rest of his family – was sent examples of plague-bearing fleas by the Indian Plague Commission, which was seeking his opinion after bubonic plague broke out there in 1896. In all, he described 500 new species of flea, and seven species are named after him.

7 | Angel Alley took its name from the Angel Inn, which once sat on its southwest corner. In later Victorian times it was part of an area of low-grade lodging houses. It was in next-door George Yard that Martha Tabram, sometimes considered as Jack the Ripper's first victim, was murdered on 6 August 1888.

MAP OF THE TUBE
LONDON UNDERGROUND RAILWAYS

1 | West Kensington (between Barons Court and Earls Court). Barons Court does not have any particularly aristocratic provenance: its name was simply given to it by the owner of the land, Sir William Palliser, who developed it in the late nineteenth century and gave it a name alluding to next-door Earl's Court. That derives its name from the feudal court of the Earls of Warwick and Holland, who were formerly lords of the manor. West Kensington was developed in the 1870s, and was originally called North End. A dip in the housing market in the 1880s led to many properties left unsold, and the developers rechristened the area West Kensington in the hope that some of the cachet of upmarket South Kensington would rub off on it. The ruse failed and they went bankrupt. The tube station on the District Railway opened in 1874, when it was called North End, and was – in keeping with the rest of the district – rechristened West Kensington in 1877.

2 | Westminster Bridge Road. London had long had a shortage of river crossings, historically being confined to the bridge that led to Southwark, the city's first suburb. There had been many proposals for a bridge at Westminster, but even support from politicians (who would have a much shorter journey to cross from the Houses of Parliament to south of the Thames) was not enough to overcome opposition from the powerful Thames boatmen and the Corporation of London. Finally, in 1721 the project was revived, but even then it took until 1738 before Charles Labelye began construction work, and the bridge was only opened in 1750. An early regulation, curiously, forbade dogs from crossing, while defacing or damaging the bridge was punishable by death without 'benefit of clergy' (which in essence meant actual clergymen, or those who could pay a bribe to become one, could not claim immunity). The current bridge was built in 1854–62 by Thomas Page. Westminster Bridge Road tube station

was opened in 1906, and was renamed Lambeth North in 1917.

3 | Dover Street was named for Henry Jermyn, the 1st Baron Dover, a courtier at the time of Charles II and James II with a highly colourful personal life that led to several duels (in one of which, over the rights to the affections of Lady Shrewsbury, he was left for dead). A Roman Catholic, he rose to further prominence after the accession in 1685 of James II (who was believed to have converted to Catholicism in secret). On James's deposition by William of Orange in the Glorious Revolution in 1688, Jermyn initially supported the deposed king, but submitted to the new order and lived a quiet life in London thereafter. Dover Street is part of a development off Piccadilly that Jermyn funded as part of a consortium in 1684. Among the notable residents of the street were the poet Alexander Pope, the architect John Nash and the composer Frederic Chopin, who gave piano lessons from his lodgings there. The first successful telephone call in Britain is said to have been made from Brown's Hotel on Dover Street by Alexander Graham Bell, the telephone's inventor, who had brought the required apparatus with him on a visit from Boston in 1877. Dover Street underground station was opened in December 1906, but was renamed Green Park in 1933.

4 | Mornington Crescent (anagram of 'concerning torments'), built in 1821, was originally part of the Fitzroy estate belonging to the aristocratic descendants of Henry FitzRoy (1663–90), the illegitimate son of Charles II and Barbara Villiers, the Countess of Castlemaine. It was home for a time to the artist Walter Sickert, a member of the Camden Town School of painters, among whose masterpieces was *Ennui*, a fine encapsulation of a moribund marriage. The tube station was opened in 1907 as part of the Charing Cross, Euston and Hampstead Railway, but was long underused. In 1992 it was closed, supposedly temporarily, but remained shut for six years. The campaign to reopen it featured prominently on the BBC radio quiz programme *I'm Sorry I Haven't a Clue*, which ran a game called 'Mornington Crescent', a satirical take on other panel games with a fiendishly complex and rapidly metamorphosing set of rules (which in truth were largely made up on the spot), which ended when one of the participants announced he had reached Mornington Crescent.

5 | Paddington. An ancient parish just some way to the north of the historic City of London, Paddington sparked to life in the era of the canal (the Grand Junction Canal section running through it was opened in 1801) and the railway, which first opened in 1838. Paddington underground station formed part of the very first line, the Metropolitan, opened in 1863. The mainline station was the key location in *A Bear Called Paddington* by Michael Bond, published in 1957, in which a bear named Paddington has stowed away on a boat from 'darkest Peru' and is now lost with only a note asking for someone to 'Please look after this bear'. Adopted by the Brown family, Paddington enjoys a series of adventures around London, enlivened by his love for marmalade.

6 | Elephant & Castle. The suburb which grew up around the junction of the roads to Kennington, Walworth and Lambeth took its name from a tavern built there in 1760. That name, in turn, is said to have been a corruption of the 'Infanta of Castile', the Princess Maria Anna, daughter of Philip II of Spain, who was the object of a marriage proposal by Charles I and negotiations which dragged out from 1614 to 1623. Although a marriage contract was actually signed, the mooted match stirred up anti-Catholic sentiment in England and no wedding took place. The whole affair only served to increase parliamentary resistance to

the Crown, which would ultimately explode in the English Civil War in 1639. The area was extensively bombed during the Blitz in 1940–41 and experienced an extensive – and little-loved – reconstruction after it. The underground station was opened in 1890 as part of the City and South London railway. The station is two stops on the Bakerloo line south of Waterloo, whose mainline railway station was opened in 1848 and named after the location of the Duke of Wellington's victory against Napoleon in 1815.

7 | King's Cross – was originally a tiny village called Battle Bridge, which began to grow once the Euston Road was cut through around 1756 as a bypass just to the north of the then edge of urban London. In 1836 an octagonal monument was erected to King George IV, adorned with Doric columns and statues of saints George, David, Andrew and Patrick, the patrons of the constituent kingdoms of Britain. The monument was so loathed that in 1845 it was dismantled and in 1851–52 King's Cross Station was built near the site. King's Cross underground station was opened in 1863 as part of the Metropolitan Railway.

8 | Blackfriars. The Dominican monks – known as 'Black Friars' because of the black cloak they wore over their white habits – established a community in London in 1221, and in 1278 were given land by the river to establish a monastery, which became known as Blackfriars. It was sufficiently important that Parliament met there several times and in 1529 the divorce case against Henry VIII's wife Catherine of Aragon was held there. After the Dissolution of the Monasteries in 1538, it fell into decay, although parts were demolished for fashionable housing – William Shakespeare bought one of them – and the rest was destroyed in the Great Fire of 1666. Blackfriars underground station opened in 1870 (16 years before the nearby mainline railway station).

GALLIPOLI

GENERAL HEADQUARTERS, MIDDLE EAST FORCES

1 | The Sphinx. The 330-feet-high (100-metre) jutting stone gravel cliff known as the Sphinx was just one of the obstacles which the ANZACs had to face when they landed on the Gallipoli peninsula on 25 April 1915. Luckily, the almost unclimbable slope was only lightly defended that day and the Turkish troops along this sector soon melted away when they saw the strength of the Allied force, meaning that it did not have to be scaled under heavy fire. The feature was so-called because the ANZACs had been on training near Cairo just before deployment to Gallipoli and would have seen the massive stone monolith just beside the pyramids. Legend had it that the statue (which is actually of a pharaoh, probably Khafre, who reigned c.2603–2578 BC) was originally a monstrous woman who would kill and eat any passers-by who failed to answer the riddle: 'What creature walks on four legs in the morning, two legs at mid-day and three in the evening?' The Greek hero Oedipus was the first to give the correct answer: a person (because he/she crawls on all fours as a baby, walks upright on two legs as an adult, and uses a stick as a third leg for support in old age). Distraught that the riddle had been solved, the Sphinx killed herself and the grateful locals gave Oedipus the throne of Thebes and the hand of their widowed queen, Jocasta, in marriage. Oedipus may, in hindsight, have wished that he had failed to solve the riddle, for it later turned out that Jocasta was his mother, and that he had earlier killed his father in a family riddle worthy of the Sphinx herself.

2 | Monash Gully (anagram of 'manly ghouls'), or Monash Valley, was a steep-sided continuation of Shrapnel Valley (whose name suggests the kind of torment the troops stationed there had to endure), which led deeper into Gallipoli. It was the type of terrain in which the initial offensive foundered as Kemal Ataturk, the future founder of the Turkish Republic, and one of the few officers to keep their

nerve when the Allies landed, rallied his troops and threw the invaders back. The gully was named for John Monash, commander of the Australian 4th Infantry Brigade, who had his headquarters at the head of the valley and who took part in many of the successive attempts to advance further into Gallipoli. Transferred to the Western Front in June 1916, he ended the war as commander of the Australian Corps.

3 | Walker's Ridge is named for Brigadier General Harold Walker, who devised the plan for the initial landings on Gallipoli. When the commander of the New Zealand Brigade became ill, Walker took command of the unit, which was positioned along a ridge on the left flank of the Allied beachhead and this then took his name. He later took command of the Australian 1st Division when its commander was killed – the casualty rate for senior officers at Gallipoli was high – and he took part in the August Offensive, which tried, in vain, to drive the Turks from the peninsula. It is the site of a small Commonwealth War Graves Commission cemetery containing the remains of 92 casualties of the campaign.

4 | Lonesome Pine. A strategically important plateau towards the south of the Gallipoli peninsula, Lonesome Pine was along the edge of the high-point of the Allied advance on 25 April, the day of the landings. It then became a Turkish strongpoint, which they called Kanli Sirt (or Bloody Ridge). The ANZACs' August offensive successfully took it amid fierce fighting, and the position remained in Allied hands until the final evacuation in December. It took its name from a single tree that survived the Turks' use of the rest of a copse as firewood, but eventually succumbed during the fighting that followed. A single Turkish pine was later planted as a memorial in the cemetery on the site that holds 1,167 Commonwealth casualties.

5 | Hell Spit formed a southern continuation of ANZAC Cove, at the southern edge of the initial landings. It was among the many topographical features that derived their name from the appalling conditions faced by the Allied forces.

6 | ANZAC Cove (the letter 'z') was the site of the first Allied landings on 25 April and became the main beachhead and supply point for the Gallipoli campaign. The failure of the Allies to advance beyond their initial objectives meant that it remained within shelling range of the Turkish army throughout the campaign, but was held by the ANZACs right up until the final evacuation on 20 December 1915. The Allied lines had gradually been thinned out throughout the preceding weeks, but on the final night itself the Turks were fooled by self-firing rifles (triggered by dripping water), which made it seem as though the Allied trenches were still manned. Twenty thousand men were evacuated from ANZAC Cove and nearby Suvla beach without the Turkish army realising what was happening. The only casualties were mules, which could not be embarked and had to be slaughtered.

7 | Johnstone's Jolly was named for the commander of the 2nd Australian Division's artillery, Brigadier General George Johnston. Just north of Lonesome, it was reached by the ANZACs on the morning of the landing, and Johnson ordered his artillery to 'jolly up' the Turks entrenched opposite. It did not work, and the Allies never made any further substantial gains in the area.

8 | Nek ('neck'). The narrow ridgeline of the Nek saw one of the bloodiest actions of the whole Gallipoli campaign on 7 August 1915, when 600 men of the Australian 3rd Light Horse Brigade were ordered to attack it as a diversion from a larger New Zealand-led offensive against the height of Chunuk Bair. Advancing in four waves, the Australians were scythed down by hails of Turkish machine-gun fire before they got anywhere near the ridge. Around 370 Australians were killed, while the Turks suffered almost no losses and remained firmly ensconced on the Nek. The charge was described by a senior officer of the Australian Light Horse as 'nothing but bloody murder'.

THE SYKES-PICOT AGREEMENT

MARK SYKES AND FRANÇOIS-GEORGES PICOT

1 | Haleb ('hale', or healthy, and 'b' as the second letter of the alphabet), more commonly spelled in English as Aleppo, is the second city of Syria after Damascus, and vies with its rival for antiquity, having been the capital of the Amorite Kingdom of Yamkhad as long ago as the early second millennium BC. The city is said to have derived its name from a tradition that the biblical patriarch Abraham milked his cows there and then distributed the milk to the poor (with *halab* meaning 'he has milked'). It was held by a succession of ancient Middle Eastern empires – the Hittites, Assyrians, Neo-Babylonian, Persians, Greeks and Romans – before it fell to the advancing Arab armies in 637. It fought off concerted attempts by the crusaders to capture it, but was virtually razed to the ground by the Mongols during their rampage through the Middle East in 1260 (in which Baghdad was also destroyed). From the sixteenth century Haleb/Aleppo spent four centuries as the centre of a rich province of the Ottoman Empire, during which time it acquired a number of beautiful mosques and a labyrinthine *suq*, which stretches for over four miles (seven kilometres). Much of the historic centre, including the citadel, whose current form dates to the thirteenth century, was damaged or destroyed during the Syrian Civil War from 2011, when pro-government and rebel forces fought a prolonged battle over the city centre.

2 | Alexandretta (anagram of 'an exalted rat'). At the time the Sykes-Picot map was drawn up, Alexandretta was in Syria, but the city is now Iskenderun in Turkey. It was originally founded by Alexander the Great ('Iskender' being the Turkish form of his name) as Alexandria ad Issum to commemorate his victory over the Persian king Darius III at the Battle of Issus in 333 BC. France administered the area as part of its League of Nations mandate over Syria, but in 1939 handed the

sanjak (province) of Alexandretta over to Turkey, and it has been the subject of a dispute between the two countries ever since

3 | Deir-ez-Zor (two 'z's). Far down the Euphrates, Deir-ez-Zor is the largest city in southeastern Syria, the first part of its name (Deir) indicating that it was once the site of a Christian monastery. Although not itself richly provided with ancient sites, it sits in a region with more than its fair share, including Dura Europos to the east, a citadel that served as a bulwark against Persian advances into the Roman Empire, and Mari, a mud-brick metropolis that first flourished in the Bronze Age around 2900 BC. In another region decimated by the Mongols, Deir-ez-Zor flourished under Ottoman rule, only to be badly damaged (along with the nearby archaeological sites) during the Syrian Civil War.

4 | Kalaat Saman (five 'a's), or St Simeon's monastery, was one of the great pilgrimage centres of early medieval Syria. Aged around 20, Simeon joined a monastic community at nearby Telanissos in 410, but his excessive asceticism – he locked himself up in a hut for 18 months, refusing to take anything but the barest level of sustenance, and took to standing for extended periods without rest – so annoyed his monastic companions (who presumably did not want to have to prove their holiness by competing with him) that they expelled him. Simeon took up residence on the site of the present monastery, but became so aggravated at the crowds of wonder-seekers attracted by reports that he was performing miracles that he retired to the top of a pillar, from which he refused to come down for any reason. Even food had to be hauled up to him on the basket. Needless to say, this only had the effect of reinforcing his saintly aura, and even larger crowds of pilgrims came, causing Simeon to order that his pillar be built up yet higher to get away from their rowdiness. After he finally died in 459, a great cruciform basilica was built, along with guesthouses for the pilgrim throngs, from whom local hawkers made a handy income selling mementoes of Simeon, who had by now acquired the nickname Stylites (or 'pillar dweller') and had inspired a curious rash of copycat hermits each atop their own vertiginous column. Simeon's edifice came tumbling down in an earthquake in 528 and was not fully restored. Even so, the faithful continued to come, though in fewer numbers after the Muslim conquest of the seventh century. Many of them took to chipping off a piece of the pillar to take home as a relic, and by modern times all that was left of Simeon's lofty home was an oversized egg-shaped lump, just higher than a grown man and with hardly a hint of the saintly about it.

5 | Hama ('ha ma') is a town that became famous in the Middle Ages for its enormous *nouria* or waterwheels used to scoop up water from the Orontes River, which may date back to AD 469 (if a mosaic from Apamea, further south in Syria, is accurate). Now largely unused, the characteristic creak of the wheels as they supped up the flow of the river was once one of the town's major draws, although the 1876 *Baedeker Guide* grumpily complains that it is 'excessive'. Now only 17 of the many dozens of *nouria* remain.

6 | Antioch (anagram of 'to China'). Now Antakya in Turkey, Antioch sits in a region which has been occupied by humans since very ancient times, although the current city was only established in 300 BC by Seleucus I Nicator, one of the generals of Alexander the Great who carved up his empire after the great conqueror's death. In fact, he had intended to found a settlement elsewhere, but at the ceremony to mark its inauguration an eagle carried off the meat from the animals which had been sacrificed to bring the city good luck and then deposited them some distance to the south where Seleucus, to avoid the wrath of the gods, felt he had to transfer his new city. He was not wholly successful in staving off bad luck, as Antioch has suffered devastating earthquakes throughout its history, including one in AD 115 in which the emperor Trajan, who was on a visit to the eastern provinces, barely escaped with his life by sheltering in Antioch's circus – he was lucky, as around 200,000 people are said to have perished. Another devastating tremor in 526 destroyed one-quarter of the city and killed another 250,000 of its inhabitants. The last major earthquake took place as recently as 1872 and Antioch's seismic history means it lacks some of the more ancient monuments of other Syrian cities, although it does possess what may be one of Christianity's oldest places of worship: a rock-cave in

the hills on the outskirts of the city at which (St) Peter is said to have prayed before embarking on his first missionary journey.

7 | Rakka ('Ra' and 'k', the 11th letter of the alphabet, and 'ka'). Ra was the most important god in the ancient Egyptian pantheon, a god of the sun, who was believed to be swallowed up each night by the sky goddess Nut, only to be reborn in the morning. His name formed part of that of 11 Egyptian pharaohs, all called Ramesses (meaning 'born of Ra'). The *ka* was believed by the ancient Egyptians to be a component of a person's soul, the life force which persisted after death, but needed to be fed and protected until it took its rightful place in the afterlife. The grave goods and paintings of food contained in many Egyptian tombs were intended to sustain the *ka*. Rakka was another foundation of Alexander the Great, but was for a long time named Callinicos after Seleucus II Callinicos, the great-grandson of Seleucus I, under whom the Seleucid Empire lost a great deal of territory, leaving it more or less on the frontier with the Persians, a border position it retained into Roman and Byzantine times. It rose to glory under the Abbasid caliph Haroun al-Rashid who made it his capital, a position it retained for 13 years until the court decamped back to Damascus. This brief phase in its history had unfortunate echoes, as it led to the city being chosen by Islamic State (IS) as its capital and the headquarters of its self-proclaimed caliphate in 2014, and then to the destruction of much of the city during its recapture by the Syrian Democratic Forces (a largely Kurdish-led group) in 2017.

8 | Harran (Arran with an 'h' at the start), 24 miles (38 kilometres) southeast of Urfa in southeastern Turkey, began life as a strategic trading settlement in the third millennium BC. Its position astride the road that led from Antioch to Nineveh, the capital of the Assyrian Empire, and beyond to even further east into Persia guaranteed it both wealth and trouble, as successive empires fought over it. It was alleged to be the place where Abraham and his family had settled for a while on their way from Ur of the Chaldees to Canaan, and a sense of this biblical time can be gained from the many traditional beehive-shaped homes which remain in the town, looking every bit as though a patriarch might step out at any moment and continue his long-delayed journey to the promised land. Harran, known to the Romans as Carrhae, was also the site of one of their most disastrous defeats when, in 53 BC, an army led by Marcus Licinius Crassus, the rich Roman financier who was one of Julius Caesar's partners in the first triumvirate, was cut to pieces by a Parthian army, whose mounted archers befuddled the Roman legionaries by riding to bowshot range, letting off a volley from horseback, and then retreating before their opponents could react.

THE TRENCHES NEAR ARRAS
BRITISH MILITARY INTELLIGENCE

1 | Hindenburg Trench. Paul von Hindenburg was the commander of the German land army from 1916, after the offensive against Verdun and the Battle of the Somme had incurred enormous casualties for very little gain. He was a proponent of the submarine warfare against Allied shipping in the Atlantic, which in the end brought the United States into the war. His Spring Offensive in 1918 drove the Allies back to the Marne and very nearly won the war, but the arrival of fresh American troops allowed the Allies to reverse German gains and force an exhausted Germany to sue for an armistice in November 1918. Hindenburg successfully avoided blame for the debacle and became Germany's second elected president in 1925. In January 1933 he acceded to Hitler's demands that he become Chancellor of Germany, paving the way for the complete seizure of power by the Nazis.

2 | Fontaine Trench ('*fontaine*', French for fountain, and Joan Fontaine). Joan Fontaine was an English-American actress (and sister to Olivia de Havilland). She won an Oscar for her role in Alfred Hitchcock's *Suspicion* in 1941, having been nominated for an adaption of Daphne du Maurier's *Rebecca* the previous year.

3 | Two (Brown Trench and Grey Street). Trenches were often named for colours which had represented objectives for various offensives. The plans for the First Battle of Arras in April 1917 had included a Black Line (the German frontline trenches and first objectives) and subsequent objectives were marked by a Blue and a Brown Line.

4 | Rotten Row. The troops who manned this sector named this stretch of road 'Rotten Row', a punning reference to a bridle path in London's Hyde Park. It was a fashionable place for the aristocracy to ride and be seen in the seventeenth and eighteenth century,

laid out by William III in the 1690s as a shortcut from Whitehall to his palace at Kensington. One theory has it that the name is a corruption of the French *route du roi* ('route of the king'), although it may equally refer to the rather boggy sand of the path's surface. The latter would fit more appropriately with the marshy trench landscapes common on the Western Front, where soldiers who could not pronounce (or could not be bothered to learn) the local names of topographic features, simply dreamed up their own. At the time this map was compiled, this sector of the line was garrisoned by the Princess of Wales's Own Yorkshire Regiment, which on 6 September lost two officers and 23 other ranks to a German gas attack on Rotten Row and Wood Trench.

5 | Ten (Robin Trench, The Nest, The Rookery, Pelican Lane, Eagle Trench, Bullfinch Trench, Crow Trench, Starling Trench, Thrush Lane and Sparrow Lane). Outside the area shown in detail, there are also Albatross, Gannet, Falcon and Jackdaw trenches. The commanders in this section clearly had a penchant for the avian. Their men were more likely to have a fondness for canaries. Tunnelling beneath the lines to set explosives was a hazardous business and the miners risked being overcome by carbon monoxide gas that built up underground. The mine rescue station in each sector of the line was supposed to have two or three canaries, which the miners would take with them when digging. The birds are particularly sensitive to carbon monoxide and would show distress when it was present. Some veteran canaries became heroes, and were even promoted to serve at base headquarters, well away from the fighting.

6 | Curtain Trench. The nearest a soldier in the trenches would get to an actual curtain was the anti-gas curtains, which were draped at the entrance to dugouts to stop the poison cloud penetrating to the inner area where troops sheltered, ate and sometimes slept. Unfortunately, if a soldier entered the dugout already contaminated with gas, the vapour would be unable to escape, killing everyone inside.

7 | Bootham Trench is named for the Bootham district in York, close by the Bootham Bar, one of the medieval gateways to the city, and home to the Bootham School, an independent Quaker boarding school founded in 1823. It was also the name given to a war cemetery around four miles (six kilometres) southeast of Arras, and a little to the west of this map, in which 186 Allied soldiers are buried.

8 | York and Durham (York Trench and Durham Lane). Trenches were often named as a reminder of home and regiments from the north and northeast

of England formed a significant contingent in the 'Pals' battalions for which friends and work colleagues signed up en masse in 1914, eager to fight for their country and little realising the long years of fighting, appalling conditions and terrible toll in casualties which lay in store for them. The Durham Light Infantry, formed in 1881, had already seen service in India, Sudan and in South Africa during the Boer War before its ranks were boosted by an influx of young men from County Durham's pit villages. Several battalions from the regiment fought just south of Guémappe in the sectors shown in the map in April 1917, and the Durhams were involved in most of the major offensives in the region until the Hundred Days' Offensive that drove the Germans back out of France in August to November 1918. In all, the regiment lost around 12,500 men during World War One.

LONDON

STANFORD'S LIMITED

1 | Falcon Square – has today disappeared, replaced after World War Two (when it was bombed extensively) by an extension to London Wall. It took its name from the Castle and Falcon inn, which stood opposite. It is the base of John Jasper when he visits London in Charles Dickens's final novel *The Mystery of Edwin Drood*, described approvingly as a place that 'bashfully almost apologetically, gives the traveller to understand that it does not expect him, on the good old constitutional plan, to order a pint of sweet blacking for his drinking, and throw it away; but insinuates that he may have his boots blacked instead of his stomach, and may also have bed, breakfast, attendance, and a porter up all night, for a certain fixed charge.'

2 | Royal Exchange. As commerce became more sophisticated in the sixteenth century, prominent Londoners were painfully aware that their city, unlike continental rivals such as Antwerp, lacked an exchange where shares in trading ventures could be bought and sold. Sir Thomas Gresham, a fabulously wealthy cloth merchant who acted as a kind of private banker to successive Tudor monarchs, offered to fund the building of an exchange himself. After several delays, the first Royal Exchange was opened by Queen Elizabeth I in January 1571, complete with stone grasshoppers set at each corner (the insect was an emblem of the Gresham family and a great copper grasshopper still sits on a weathervane above the modern building). The Royal Exchange has burned down twice: in 1666 during the Great Fire, and again in 1838 when a blaze took hold of the rooms occupied by the insurance market Lloyd's. A new building was opened in 1844 by Queen Victoria, who did so with words which directly echoed those of her ancestor Elizabeth I, more than 250 years previously: 'It is my royal will and pleasure that this building be hereafter called the Royal Exchange.'

3 | Mansion House (anagram of 'moonshine USA') is the official residence of the Lord Mayors of London. Prior to its completion in 1752 they either lived in their own houses or used the Guildhall for official functions. It shared in eighteenth-century London's sometime turbulent political life: in 1768 every window in the building was broken by rioters celebrating the election of the radical John Wilkes as a Member of Parliament. A man who found it impossible not to attract trouble, he had been expelled from Parliament in 1763 for criticising George III's speech in favour of the Treaty of Paris, which ended the Seven Years' War. Restored by the Lord Chief Justice on grounds of parliamentary privilege, he was then definitively expelled for obscenity in a scurrilous poem he wrote about the Earl of Sandwich's mistress, Fanny Murray. As a result, when he was elected MP for Middlesex in 1768, he was not allowed to take up his seat, being technically an outlaw, which led to the riot that wrecked the Mansion House. Wilkes managed to take up his seat in Parliament the next year and achieved a measure of respectability when he was appointed a sheriff of London in 1770. In 1936 Britain's millionth telephone to be manufactured, was cast in gold and presented to Mansion House.

4 | Paternoster Row. 'Paternoster' forms the first two words of the Lord's Prayer in Latin (*Pater Noster, qui es in caelis* – 'Our Father, who art in Heaven'). The street acquired its name, according to the antiquarian John Stow, because of the host of stationers and religious trinket vendors who gathered there in a convenient position just north of St Paul's Cathedral, including 'turners of beads ... called Pater Noster makers'. After the Great Fire, it became particularly noted for publishers, including William Taylor who published one of the eighteenth century's bestsellers *Robinson Crusoe*, there. Charlotte Brontë and her sister Ann stayed above the Chapter House coffee house when they came to London in 1848 to meet their publisher. It was a momentous meeting, for the sisters had written their books under the pseudonyms Acton (for Anne) and Currer (for Charlotte) Bell. Anne's American publisher was exploiting Charlotte's (or Currer's) fame to make out that she was the author of what was actually Anne's *The Tenant of Wildfell Hall*. Charlotte's British publisher George Smith was amazed when the two women came to see him, and even more so when Charlotte proved who she was by perfectly reproducing the signature of Currer Bell, which had appeared on all the publishing contracts.

5 | Aldermanbury ('bury' and 'alderman'). The aldermen, one elected from each ward of the City of London, formed the government of the City of London. They were originally chosen annually, but from 1377 they served for life once selected (although a retirement age of 70 was introduced in the 1970s). Aldermanbury may in fact have gained its name from an earlier species of aldermen, who were high officials to the Anglo-Saxon kings. St Mary's Church, which stood here, was badly damaged during the Blitz in 1940, so that only the shell survived. In 1965–69, the surviving stones were transported to Fulton, Missouri, where they were used to build a replica of St Mary's as a memorial to Winston Churchill, who in 1946 had made a speech there warning of the 'Iron Curtain' which was descending to cut off western Europe from the Soviet-controlled bloc to the East.

6 | Threadneedle ('thread'-'needle') Street may have gained its name from the emblem of the Needlemaker's Guild, which included three needles in its arms. The street once included four churches, all of which (St Christopher Le Stocks, named for the stocks which once stood nearby; St Christopher by the Exchange; St Martin Outwich; and St Benet Fink) have been demolished. Its most famous resident by far is the Bank of England, popularly known as the 'Old Lady of Threadneedle Street' after a cartoon by James Gillray in 1797 in which a banknote-festooned old lady is being ravished by a figure representing William Pitt, the Younger, who was the prime minister and intent on getting his hands on the Bank's reserves of gold to help prosecute the war against France.

7 | St Bride Street (and St Bride Church), named for the Irish saint Bridget, is best known for the church of the same name. There was a church already in Saxon times, and it was sufficiently important for King John to hold a parliament there in 1210. Among its parishioners were Ananias Dare and Eleanor White, the parents of Virginia Dare, the first child of English origin to be born in the Americas. Her birth in 1587 at the colony of Roanoke in Virginia (from which she derived her name) should have been a moment of celebration and the beginning of great things, but when her grandfather, John White, came back to Roanoke in 1590, having returned to England for provisions, he found the colonists had vanished, including little Virginia. Their houses had collapsed and the only trace of them was the word 'Croatoan' carved on a tree. The mystery of their disappearance was never solved. St Bride has been associated with journalists and printers ever since Wynkyn de Worde, apprentice to William Caxton Britain's first printer, set up a press in nearby Fleet Street in 1500. When the church was destroyed in the Blitz in 1940, it was restored with funds contributed by newspaper-owners and journalists.

8 | Snow Hill once had the dubious reputation in Georgian times as the haunt of a street-gang known as the Mohocks, who, as well as more conventional violence such as gouging out the eyes of their victims or poking swords towards their legs and making them 'dance', were given to capturing old ladies, stuffing them into barrels and rolling them down Snow Hill. So notorious was the practice that it was immortalised by the poet John Gay in his poem 'Trivia; or, The art of Walking the Streets of London':

'...*Where from Snow-hill black steepy torrents run;*
How matrons, hooped within the hogshead's womb,
Were tumbled furious thence; the rolling tomb...'

The poet John Bunyan, the author of *Pilgrim's Progress* and a much more sober character who would heartily have disapproved of the Mohocks, died in 1688 at the house of a friend who owned a grocer's shop on the street.

NEW ZEALAND

MACDONALD GILL

1 | Nelson (anagram of 'no lens'), or Whakatu in Maori, is the second-oldest city in New Zealand. The area was the subject of early exploration by Europeans: Tasman Bay on which it lies was discovered by the Dutch explorer Abel Tasman in 1642 and Captain Cook visited the area in 1770, which he named Blind Bay. When the town authorities subsequently renamed it for the great British admiral Horatio, Lord Nelson, they probably did not have in mind the incident during the Battle of Copenhagen in 1801 when, ignoring orders to retreat, Nelson placed a telescope to his blind eye – which he had lost eight years before at the siege of Calvi in Corsica – and claimed not to have seen the signal. Nelson was identified by the New Zealand Company – which had begun attempts to found a colony as early as 1825 – as a good place for a settlement and on 9 October 1841 the *Whitby*, *Will Watch* and *Arrow* arrived to establish a town which has since grown into South Island's third-largest city.

2 | Christchurch ('Christ' and 'church'), or Otautahi in Maori, was founded in 1850 and received its name because many of the leaders of the original settlers, most notably John Robert Godley, had attended Christchurch College, Oxford. Land had already been purchased by European whalers from the Maori (who had been present in the area for around 600 years) and this formed the nucleus of the settlement established by the Canterbury Association. The largest city on South Island, Christchurch was hit by two tragic events in the twenty-first century: first, the massive magnitude 6.3 earthquake which shook it on 4 September 2010, killing 185 people and damaging thousands of buildings; and then the attack in March 2019 on a mosque in which a white supremacist killed 51 people.

3 | Wanganui ('wan'-ganui), officially spelled also as Whanganui since 2009, was originally founded as

Petre in 1840, but negotiations over a land purchase with local Maori groups had been mishandled and hostilities broke out, with two battles fought in 1847 between Te Mamaku, a local chief, and British troops. The greatest scandal in Wanganui's history broke out in 1920 when its mayor Charles Mackay shot the poet Walter d'Arcy Creswell, who had been blackmailing him and threatening to reveal his homosexuality. Convicted of the shooting, Mackay served seven years hard labour in Mount Eden prison. Disgraced, he went to England on his release, where he became a journalist. Ironically, he died in 1929 when he was accidentally shot by a German policeman while covering a riot in Berlin.

4 | Wellington (Te Whanganui-a-Tara in Maori) at the southwest tip of North Island is New Zealand's capital and the southernmost national capital in the world. It was originally named Britannia by the New Zealand Company, which founded it as New Zealand's first colonial settlement in January 1840. After the original site chosen by the settlers aboard the *Aurora* proved unpromising, they moved and christened the new town after the Duke of Wellington, who was a war hero for his victory against Napoleon at Waterloo in 1815, a still-influential politician (he was prime minister from 1828 to 1830, and would serve as Leader of the House of Lords from 1841 to 1846), and a supporter of the New Zealand Company's colonisation project. The city replaced Auckland, New Zealand's first capital, as the colony's seat of government in 1865. There had been complaints for some years that Auckland was too remote and inconvenient for most of New Zealand's parliamentarians, but the issue was so heated that the decision about where to move it to was handed to three Australian commissioners. After visiting Wellington, Wanganui/Whanganui, Picton, Port Underwood, Havelock and Nelson, they finally opted for Wellington. The Wellington boot was designed by 'the Iron Duke' himself to provide footwear better adapted for riding in battle. Calf-length and with low heels, the boots were originally made of leather and only changed to rubber after the process for vulcanising rubber was developed in the 1850s.

5 | Dannevirke (sounds like 'Dane' and 'work'), in Maori Tamaki-nui-a-Rua, was named by the 13 Danish families who settled in 1872 after the system of fortifications built along the neck of the Jutland peninsula from the 730s to protect Denmark from attacks by Saxons and Franks. It was a pun, as it means 'the work of the Danes', and so refers both to the medieval defensive work back home and their own handiwork. It soon grew modestly prosperous from the lumber industry, hosting dozens of sawmills by the late nineteenth century. It was the birthplace of Joh Bjelke-Petersen, premier of the Australian state of Queensland from 1968 to 1987 (his family had moved to Australia in 1913). He had a reputation for extreme conservatism, and shaped his adopted state in his image, before finally falling because of his involvement in a police corruption scandal.

6 | Palmerston North (15 letters) received its geographical suffix because there was already a Palmerston on South Island, northeast of Dunedin. The area, long settled by Maoris, was first visited by Europeans in 1830 when the trader Jack Duff went there, but the town was only established after a survey in 1866. It developed slowly, reliant on sawmills and agriculture, before the arrival of the railway in 1886 accelerated its growth. Lord Palmerston, after whom the city was named, had died a year before the city's foundation. Twice prime minister (from 1855 to 1858 and 1859 to 1865) he was also Foreign Secretary and acquired a reputation for muscular diplomacy (such as the incident in 1850 when he sent the British fleet to blockade the Greek port of Piraeus, on the grounds that the Greek police had failed to protect a Gibraltarian merchant with British citizenship from being roughed up by a mob which contained relatives of Greek ministers).

7 | Greymouth (anagram of 'rogue myth'). Situated at the mouth of the river of the same name, Greymouth is indirectly named for Sir George Grey, who had been twice governor of New Zealand (from 1845 to 1853 and 1861 to 1868). Both tenures saw conflict with the Maori – the Flagstaff War and the first Taranaki War, respectively – over what was seen as European faithlessness in implementing the Treaty of Waitangi with Maori chiefs that in 1840 had facilitated the establishment of the colony. Greymouth – or Mawhera in Maori – had been the largest Maori settlement in the area, and an important source of the coveted greenstone. The town site was laid out in 1865, not long after viable lodes of gold had been discovered and begun to attract miners. It later also became an important coalmining district.

THE GERMAN AUTOBAHN

HEINZ BÜTTGENBACH

1 | Glückstadt (meaning 'lucky town' in German). As German towns go, Glückstadt is a comparative infant, having been founded in 1617 by Christian IV of Denmark, in whose lands this area of Schleswig-Holstein then lay. It was a wild, swampy, trackless tract and the king decided to have it drained to provide a stronghold at the extreme end of his domains to tame possible German expansion north (and to provide a bridgehead if the opportunity arose to acquire further land to the south). He also wanted a greater slice of the Baltic and North Sea trade dominated by the great German entrepôt of Hamburg. At the town's official foundation celebrations, Christian bestowed on it a coat of arms that featured a personification of Fortuna, the goddess of luck, and announced: '*Dat schall glücken und dat mutt glücken, un dann schall se ok Glückstadt heten*' ('We shall have luck and we need to have luck and therefore I name the town Glückstadt'). Glückstadt indeed prospered and remained in Danish hands until 1864, when the Danes were defeated by an Austrian-Prussian coalition in the Second Schleswig War. The conflict was the violent resolution of a tangled dispute between Denmark and the German states over who should have the rights to the border territories of Schleswig-Holstein, an issue so complex that the British Prime Minister Gladstone is reported to have joked that there were only three people who had ever fully understood it: the Prince Consort, Albert, who was dead; a German professor who had gone mad; and Gladstone himself, who had forgotten. In the end, the southern part of Schleswig, and Holstein, in which Glückstadt lies, were awarded to Germany and have remained there.

2 | Lüneburg (anagram of 'ruble gun' – the ruble, or rouble, being the currency of Russia). Lüneburg is a town whose fortune was built – literally – on salt, pools of the stuff, which local legend says were first discovered when a hunter shot a boar which had

been bathing in a pool and when he hung the carcass up to dry, found it encrusted with salt crystals. First mentioned in a charter of 956, Lüneburg supplied its salt throughout northern Germany and to Scandinavia, where it was needed to pickle and preserve the herring catches. The town prospered mightily, and the business provided substantial fortunes for its aristocracy of salt, the Sülzbegüterte, and a coveted position as a member of the Hanseatic League of north European trading cities. In the sixteenth century, however, the herring trade subsided and Lüneburg's importance declined. During World War Two, Lüneburg formed part of the last enclave controlled by the Nazi government in northwestern Germany, based around Flensburg. It was at Lüneburg Heath, to the west of the town, that the surrender of German forces in Holland and Schleswig-Holstein to General Bernard Montgomery was signed. Salt continued to be mined in Lüneburg as late as 1980, when the salt mine was finally closed down.

3 | Soltau ('sol' and 'tau'), whose name actually means 'salt town' was already in existence in 936, when the Holy Roman Emperor Otto I granted it to the great convent at Quedlinburg. Soltau was eclipsed by nearby trading rivals during the Middle Ages and largely destroyed during the Thirty Years' War (1618–48), which devastated Germany, and its recovery to modest prosperity by the nineteenth century was long and slow. The largest German prisoner-of-war-camp in World War One lay near the town. 'Sol', the Latin for 'sun', became the focus of a religious cult under the later Roman Empire, when Sol Invictus, the 'unconquered sun' became the personification of the supreme deity. Emperor Aurelian added the god to the official pantheon in 274, and Constantine the Great was a devotee before his conversion to the Christian cause after the Battle of the Milvian Bridge in 312 (although the fact that he claimed to have seen a flaming cross in the sky encouraging him to victory and that he was persuaded that this was a sign from the Christian God, rather than the equally fiery sun, suggests that he was not strong on theological nuances). The tau, named for the nineteenth letter of the Greek alphabet, is a sub-atomic particle, resembling an electron, in that it is negatively charged, but is 3,500 times heavier. It is highly unstable, with a half-life of approximately one three-trillionth of a second.

4 | Itzehoe (sounds like 'it's a hoe') is the oldest town in Schleswig-Holstein, originating as Esefelth, founded in 809 by Egbert, a count despatched by Charlemagne to consolidate the Frankish hold against encroachment by the Danes. The Danish king Godfrid had ambitions to expand in the area against the Slavic Obodrite tribe, designs which were thwarted by his assassination in 810 – some said on the orders of Charlemagne himself. Itzehoe was the home for nearly 30 years of Wenzel Hablik, a German Expressionist artist active in the 1920s, whose paintings create an absorbing world of jagged crystalline structures.

5 | Lübeck ('be' – to exist – between the letters for 'luck'). Originally the Obodrite Slavic settlement of Liubice (meaning 'beautiful'), a new German town was established in 1143 by Count Adolf II of Holstein. Strategically sited on the main east–west trade axis across northern Germany, it became the chief city of the Hanseatic League, a loose trading confederation that dominated the mercantile life of northern Europe from the thirteenth to the fifteenth centuries. Its trading rules, the 'Laws of Lübeck', were adopted by more than 100 members and associate towns, and by the early fifteenth century Lübeck was the second-largest town in Germany after Cologne. The novelist Thomas Mann, author of *The Magic Mountain* and *Death in Venice*, was born in Lübeck in 1875. Together with his brother, Heinrich, also a novelist, he was a prominent anti-Nazi and forced to flee Germany in 1933, eventually dying in Switzerland in 1955.

6 | Cuxhaven (sounds like 'cook's haven'). The historic fishing port of Cuxhaven was captured by Hamburg in 1394, allowing it to dominate the lower part of the River Elbe and protect its access to the sea. Nordholz, some eight miles (13 kilometres) to the southwest, was the main base during World War One for the Imperial German Navy's fleet of Zeppelin airships. On Christmas Day 1914, Cuxhaven was attacked by Short seaplanes of the British Royal Naval Air Service, which were carried by a naval taskforce positioned offshore. It was the first ever ship-launched air raid, although it did not stop Germany's own air offensive, as zeppelins began raiding the British coastline just weeks later, beginning with an attack on Great Yarmouth and Kings Lynn on 19–20 January 1915.

7 | Neumünster (anagram of 'menu unrest') took its name from the Novum Monasterium ('new monastery') founded there in 1127. Among its notable residents was the nineteenth-century classicist Ernst Eduard Hudemann, who wrote a history of the Roman postal system.

8 | Ochsenzoll (sounds like 'oxen') was a district on the borders of the territories of Hamburg and Norderstedt. It marked the point at which tolls had to be paid on cattle being driven up the *Ochsenweg* ('cattle path'), which led all the way up to Viborg in Denmark. This *Ochsenzoll* or 'cattle toll' was one of many customs borders which divided the German states and hindered their unification. Efforts at pan-German customs unions were instrumental in the political consolidation of Germany, beginning with the Zollverein customs union, established in 1834 and revived in 1867. The *Ochsenzoll*, however, was very resistant to absorption in the new system and Hamburg and nearby Bremen only joined the Zollverein in 1888, finally abolishing the cattle tax a full 17 years after Germany unification.

YORKSHIRE RAILWAYS

ESTRA CLARKE

1 | Whitby (Whitby jet, Captain Cook, Dracula), or the 'White settlement', is one of Yorkshire's most venerable towns, which began in 657 when King Oswy of Northumbria founded a monastery at nearby Streonshalh in thanksgiving for his defeat and killing of the pagan warlord Penda of Mercia. The abbey was the venue for the Synod of Whitby in 664, an ecclesiastical gathering that ruled on the question of whether the date of Easter should be calculated and celebrated in accordance with Roman custom or that of the local Celtic Christian church. The seemingly esoteric point had caused the embarrassing situation that the king might be celebrating Easter while his queen was still observing her Lenten fast. Whitby became famous for Whitby jet, the prized black stone – whose sombre tones made it a favourite for Victorian mourning jewellery – which could be found washed up along it shores, but it found its true destiny as a maritime town; it was from Whitby that the first English whaling vessel set out for Greenland in 1753, bringing the town further wealth from the trade in blubber. It is no surprise, therefore, that Whitby's most famous son was a mariner. James Cook was not actually born in Whitby (but in Marton, near Middlesbrough), but he moved to the town when he was 18 and gained his sea legs there aboard colliers plying the coastal trade. In a sense he never moved away, as it was in command of a former collier – the *Endeavour* – that in 1770 he became the first European explorer to reach the east coast of Australia. Over 1,200 years after its hosting of the Synod of Whitby, the novelist Bram Stoker chose the abbey as the setting for several scenes in his seminal 1897 vampire novel, *Dracula*.

2 | Market Weighton (14 letters). A market town at the junction of two Roman roads, Market Weighton (or 'Wicstun') was granted a charter to hold a market by Henry III in 1251, but remained of modest size until the excavation of the Market Weighton Canal in 1772–82 and the building of a turnpike road to York in 1765. The town's most famous resident was William Bradley, the 'Yorkshire Giant', who by the time he reached the age of 20 in 1787, stood a massive seven feet nine inches (236 centimetres) tall. He travelled with a circus for many years before going freelance and charging would-be gawpers a shilling a time to see him.

3 | York (four letters) began life as the Roman legionary fortress of Eboracum, founded in AD 71 during the conquest of the north. From around AD 122 it served as the garrison headquarters of the Sixth Legion, one of the units responsible for the construction of Hadrian's Wall. One of the few places in England to make a transition to Anglo-Saxon rule with its urban centre partially intact, Roman Eboracum had become Saxon Eoforwic by the seventh century, and an important centre of the Kingdom of Northumbria. Its wealth attracted the Vikings, raiders from Scandinavia who had been engaged in opportunistic plundering along the north coast of England since the 790s and whose operations increased vastly in magnitude in the 860s. In 866 they took York and made it the capital of a Viking kingdom, which held sway over much of the North for the next 88 years until its last ruler, with the suitably sanguinary nickname Erik Bloodaxe, fled and was killed somewhere in the Pennines. The Vikings also changed its name to Jorvik, Eoforwic proving too much for their Norse tongues to get around. It was only in the Middle Ages that the city settled down to its current, abbreviated, form of York (which it reached around 1300, though the archbishop continues to sign himself 'Eboracum').

4 | Northallerton (anagram of 'northern atoll'). The Romans established a signal station to the west of Northallerton, but today's town grew from a church established by Paulinus, a Christian missionary despatched by Pope Gregory the Great to England in 601, when it looked like its predecessor mission established by Augustine was about to fail. Nearby in 1138 was fought the Battle of the Standard, so-called because the English formed up around a battle wagon bearing banners consecrated to an array of northern saints, including Peter of York, Wilfred of Ripon and Cuthbert of Durham. The divine trio did their work and by the end of the day the Scots were in full flight back to the border.

5 | Pickering (sounds like 'pick a ring'). Local legend has it that Pickering was founded by a British prince, Peredurus, around 270 BC and that the town's name is a corruption of his; or, more picturesquely, that Peredurus lost a ring and accused a young woman of its theft – the ring was later found inside a pike caught in a local stream and Peredurus, repenting of his accusation, married the woman, while the local area acquired the nickname 'pike-ring'. The town's parish church, of Sts Peter and Paul, contains a memorial to the father and son Robert and Nicholas King who were the surveyors of Washington, DC. Robert's wharfing plans of the city, at a scale of 200 feet to the inch, were the finest early representation of Washington, DC, an irony considering his eyesight was believed poor and he had originally been sent there by his father who thought the climate would improve his vision.

6 | Scarborough ('scar' and 'borough') is said to have been founded by the Vikings in the tenth century, but there is no trace of this settlement and the town is not mentioned in the Domesday Book. It grew instead in the shadow of the castle, constructed in the 1130s and became most famous for the fair held annually from 1253, which gave rise to the traditional song 'Are you going to Scarborough Fair?' It became a fashionable spa resort from the seventeenth century, its popularity vastly enhanced by the arrival of the railway in 1845. The novelist Anne Brontë, author of *Agnes Grey* and *The Tenant of Wildfell Hall*, died in Scarborough in aged 29 and is buried at St Mary's Church. Terminally ill with tuberculosis, she had decided on one last trip with her sister Charlotte to see the sea. Frederic Leighton, one of Victorian England's most fashionable artists (and president of the Royal Academy for 18 years) was born in Scarborough. His fame finally brought him the distinction of being made a hereditary peer in the New Years' Honours list of 1896. Leighton died just a day after with no heir, making his the shortest-lived hereditary peerage on record.

7 | Helmsley ('helms' and 'ley') was founded in Anglo-Saxon times, but the growth in the wool trade enabled it to grow prosperous after the Norman Conquest and on into the central Middle Ages. It possessed a fine castle built by Walter Espec, who also founded nearby

Rievaulx Abbey and, as an old man and High Sherriff of Yorkshire, led the English forces at the Battle of the Standard against the Scots in 1138.

8 | Richmond ('rich' and 'mond', or mound/hill) owes its beginnings to the grant by William the Conqueror of extensive lands to his supporters who had followed him from Normandy. He gave a great swathe of North Yorkshire to the Breton nobleman Alan Rufus, one of whose French titles was the Count of Richemont, a name he bestowed on his new English fiefdom. Its great Norman castle generated a series of legends, including that of a drummer boy who was lowered down a well, walked down a passage he found at the bottom and continued drumming on underground, never to be seen again. A certain Potter Thompson was also said to have entered passages beneath the castle, where he found King Arthur, slumbering with his knights. It was clearly not England's moment of crisis, because the hero king slept on.

9 | Bridlington (anagram of 'bring dolt in') got off to a slow start in life. It was probably originally settled by invading Angles in the sixth or seventh century, but by the time of the Domesday Book in 1086, it still had only four burgesses, hardly the sign of a great metropolis. In the fourteenth century it was still outshone by nearby Hunmanby and Kilham, but had outstripped its neighbours by the seventeenth century. A small market town, it still had a substantial priory (founded in 1113 by the Augustinians). Its last prior, William Wood, was executed for treason in 1537 after he took part in the Pilgrimage of Grace, an uprising that represented the last spasm of traditionalist Catholic reaction against the Reformation. In 1643 the town was the landing place for Charles I's queen, Henrietta Maria, when she arrived with reinforcements and arms for the Royalist cause (although in the end, in vain). In 1779 it once again entered the historical annals, when the American revolutionary naval commander John Paul Jones attacked the port, before heading off to intercept a British merchant convoy off Flamborough Head. He found more than he bargained for, because it had a naval escort, including the 44-gun HMS *Serapis*. A hard-fought duel ensued, in the early stages of which Jones was asked by the British commander Captain Richard Pearson whether he would strike his colours (and surrender), and retorted: 'I have not yet begun to fight'. Later, when his vessel the *Bonhomme Richard* was reduced to a floating wreck of shattered timbers, he still refused to give in, proclaiming, 'I may sink, but I'll be damned if I strike'. Astonishingly, Jones turned the tables, causing Pearson, aboard the *Serapis*, to surrender. This exploit made Jones the toast of the American Revolution and even won the grudging admiration of the Royal Navy for his exploits.

THE MOON

UNITED STATES GEOLOGICAL SURVEY

1 | Buys-Ballot ('ballot'), named for the Dutch meteorologist Christophorus Buys-Ballot whose Buys-Ballot law states that in the northern hemisphere if you stand with your back to the wind, the atmospheric pressure will be lower to your left, and higher to your right. In 1854, he founded the Royal Netherlands Meteorological Institute, and in 1873 he became the first chairman of the International Meteorological Organisation, established to exchange information between nations regarding weather observations and to aid in weather forecasting.

2 | Spencer Jones – Spencer Perceval, British prime minister from 1809 to 1812, became the only holder of the office to be assassinated, when he was shot dead in the lobby of the House of Commons. His assassin, John Bellingham, believed the British government had done nothing to help him claim redress for his five years of imprisonment in Russia for failure to pay a debt. At his trial, Bellingham complained that in Russia he had been 'being banded from prison to prison, and from dungeon to dungeon, fed on bread and water, treated with the utmost cruelty, and frequently marched through the streets under a military guard with felons and criminals of the most atrocious description', and that Perceval had failed to answer his petition asking for redress. He was found guilty and hanged three days later at Newgate Prison. John Paul Jones became known as the 'Father of the American Navy'. He joined the Continental Navy in 1775 and conducted several raids on Britain during the American Revolutionary War.

3 | Safarik ('safari'-k) was named for Vojtěch Šafařík (1829–1902), a Czech biochemist. He worked on the chemical composition of platinum and helped prove that the *Queen's Court* and *Green Mountain* manuscripts, which purported to be medieval Czech texts, were forgeries, because the ink used to

write them contained Prussian Blue, a substance not developed until the eighteenth century.

4 | Hayford ('hay' and 'ford') was named for John Fillmore Hayford, (1868–1925), an American astronomer best known for his work on isostasy, the study of the equilibrium between the Earth's crust and its mantle, based on the theory that the distribution of rocks within the crust must be such as to exert a constant pressure on the deeper layers that constitute the Earth.

5 | Stein (in German 'one' is *ein*, so Stein is what is left when *ein* is taken away from Einstein). The crater was named for Johan Stein, a Dutch astronomer and Jesuit who was director of the Vatican Observatory in the 1930s.

6 | Zernike (Zer-'nike') – Nike is both the Greek goddess of victory and the name of a brand of sports shoe. Frits Zernike (1888–1966) was a Dutch physicist who won the Nobel Prize for Physics in 1953 for his work on the phase-contrast microscope, which permitted the examination of the internal structure of cells without having to damage them through staining.

7 | St John and Dante. In fact, the first crater is not named for the saint and disciple John (who might be found in heaven), but for Charles E. St. John (1857–1935) the American astronomer who did work on sun spots and established that Venus did not have enough oxygen in its atmosphere to support life. The second crater is named after the Italian poet Dante Alighieri, whose *La Divina Commedia* (*The Divine Comedy*) was one of the works which established Italian as a literary language. Two of the epic poem's three parts were the *Paradiso* ('Heaven') and the *Inferno* ('Hell'), which detailed the sufferings inflicted on sinners (some of them quite creative, such as the excrement which the flatterers are forced to stand in Dante's Eighth Circle of Hell, in an ironic reference to the sweet-smelling words with which they seduced their victims in life).

8 | Morse – the crater is named for Samuel F.B. Morse (1791–1872), the inventor of the single wire telegraph and of Morse Code, which enabled messages to be passed through it and as a result travel significant distances almost instantaneously. The first telegraph message using the code was transmitted by Morse between the US Supreme Court and the Capitol building in Washington, DC, in May 1844 – it consisted of the biblical phrase 'What God hath wrought!'

9 | Two – Trumpler (Donald Trump) and Fitzgerald (John Fitzgerald Kennedy). Trumpler was named for Robert Julius Trumpler, the Swiss-American astronomer who designed a system for the classification of open star clusters. Fitzgerald crater takes its name from George Francis FitzGerald, (1851–1901) a professor of physics at Trinity College, Dublin, most famous for his part in the Lorentz-FitzGerald contraction, the hypothesis that objects travelling at speed become foreshortened in the direction of their motion, which in turn later informed Albert Einstein's Special Theory of Relativity.

LIST OF MAPS

ACKNOWLEDGEMENTS

In an illustrated title such as this, the author is but the tip of the iceberg of the many people who have helped bring it to fruition. I would like to thank in particular John Lee at the British Library, who commissioned the title and has been a great source of support and advice, and Sally Nicholls for all her wonderful work in helping identify maps within the library's collection for use in the book. Grateful thanks, also, to Christopher Westhorp (www.westhorp.co.uk) for his sage and diligent editing of the text and to Allan Somerville at Blok Graphic for the beautiful and sympathetic design.

BIBLIOGRAPHY

The following British Library publications have provided the source for many of the maps included in this puzzle book and include further information for those wanting to find out more about them. They also all provide a wonderful starting point for readers wishing to explore the library's amazing cartographic collections further.

Bryars, Tim and Harper, Tom, *A History of the 20th Century in 100 Maps*, 2014.

Harper, Tom (edited by), *Maps and the 20th Century: Drawing the Line*, 2016.

Harper, Tom, *Atlas: A World of Maps From the British Library*, 2018.

Hatfield, Philip J., *Lines in the Ice: Exploring the Roof of the World*, 2016.

Schulten, Susan, *A History of America in 100 Maps*, 2018.

Whitfield, Peter, *London: A Life in Maps*, 2017.

Whitfield, Peter, *Charting the Oceans*, 2017.